THE REAL GREAT ESCAPE

THE REAL GREAT ESCAPE

The story of the First World War's most daring mass breakout

JACQUELINE COOK

VINTAGE BOOKS
Australia

A Vintage book
Published by Random House Australia Pty Ltd
Level 3, 100 Pacific Highway, North Sydney NSW 2060
www.randomhouse.com.au

First published by Vintage in 2013

Copyright © Jacqueline Cook 2013

The moral right of the author has been asserted.

All rights reserved. No part of this book may be reproduced or transmitted by any person or entity, including internet search engines or retailers, in any form or by any means, electronic or mechanical, including photocopying (except under the statutory exceptions provisions of the Australian *Copyright Act 1968*), recording, scanning or by any information storage and retrieval system without the prior written permission of Random House Australia.

Addresses for companies within the Random House Group can be found at
www.randomhouse.com.au/offices

National Library of Australia
Cataloguing-in-Publication entry

Cook, Jacqueline, author.
The real great escape: the story of the first world war's most daring breakout/Jacqueline Cook.

ISBN 978 0 85798 114 1 (paperback)

Prisoners of war – Germany – Holzminden – Biography.
Prisoners of war – British – Biography.
World War, 1914-1918 – Prisoners and prisons, Germany.
World War, 1914-1918 – Prisoners and prisons, British.
Prisoner-of-war escapes – Germany – Holzminden.

940.4724321

Front cover image © Otto Liebert; back cover image courtesy Oliver Harris
(Norman Birks Collection)
Cover design by Natalie Winter
Map courtesy Tom Vaughan
Typeset in Garamond 13 by Midland Typesetters, Australia
Printed in Australia by Griffin Press, an accredited ISO AS/NZS 14001:2004
Environmental Management System printer

Random House Australia uses papers that are natural, renewable and recyclable products and made from wood grown in sustainable forests. The logging and manufacturing processes are expected to conform to the environmental regulations of the country of origin.

Contents

Map	*vii*
Introduction	*1*
Author's Note	*7*
PART I: HOLZMINDEN, SEPTEMBER 1917 TO DECEMBER 1918	**9**
Chapter 1: Welcome to Hellminden	11
Chapter 2: A Kingdom of Tyranny	24
Chapter 3: Survival	34
Chapter 4: Air, Sea and Land	59
Chapter 5: Home and Hearth	84
Chapter 6: Art and Entertainment	98
Chapter 7: Barbed Wire Disease	105
Chapter 8: Crime and Punishment	124
Chapter 9: Unbreakable Spirit	146
PART II: THE REAL GREAT ESCAPE	**161**
Chapter 10: The Tunnel	163
Chapter 11: Flight Plan	182
Chapter 12: The Big Stunt	193
Chapter 13: Flight to Freedom	204
Chapter 14: Back in Enemy Hands	216
PART III: BEYOND HOLZMINDEN	**229**
Chapter 15: Life After the War, an A to Z	231
Chapter 16: Friendships Forged	276
About the Author	287
Acknowledgements	289
Image Credits	293
Notes	295
Bibliography	299
Index of Names	303

Introduction

Many a man and woman has been forged by fire in the unholy pressure cooker that is war. It is an environment in which the best and worst of humanity is illuminated in equal measure.

Of the courageous stories to emerge, many serve to spark the collective imagination. One true tale of note is *The Great Escape*, by Paul Brickhill, an account from the Second World War of the mass escape from the German POW camp Stalag Luft III in Sagan (now Żagań), Poland, by Allied prisoners of war (POWs). The 1963 film of the same name starred Steve McQueen, James Garner and Richard Attenborough and has become a well-loved classic.

But few people know that the Sagan escape was not the first of its kind. A band of determined First World War prisoners had claimed that honour twenty-five years earlier.

It has been suggested that the real-life prisoners who took part in *The Great Escape* may have been inspired by the extraordinary feat achieved by their First World War counterparts. Most escapees from Stalag Luft III would have been boys or teenagers during the last days of the First World War and perhaps they devoured the true tales of derring-do from the books and articles that started to appear shortly after the successful mass breakout of 1918. As grown men incarcerated behind barbed wire, they might have recalled that the seemingly impossible had been made possible.

Over the course of the First World War, up to 8.5 million military personnel were taken prisoner on both sides. By the end of the war, Germany alone had incarcerated 2.5 million individuals on home soil, which included 191,652 military personnel from Britain and her dominions. As the war dragged on, Germany struggled to find a place to keep them all. Structures from castles to convents were hastily turned into prison facilities.

Captured British troops faced the stark reality of an interminable incarceration behind the patrolled walls and barbed wire boundaries of prison camps. But as soon as the doors slammed shut and the key turned in the lock, determined inmates set their minds to the business of escape. All across Germany and occupied territories, POWs plotted their way out via every manner of scheme, ranging from the ludicrous to the ingenious. Many managed to escape their confines, only to be recaptured days later.

In Lower Saxony, Germany, a camp designed for officers who had made repeated escape attempts quickly earned itself a reputation as the country's most inescapable camp – a reputation the egomaniacal Kommandant, Karl Niemeyer, was determined to maintain. Escape attempts had been made, but all failed, and he took a cocky delight in his unblemished record.

That is, until the early hours of 24 July 1918. During the mass tunnel breakout that came to be known as 'the big stunt', twenty-nine prisoners made a bid for freedom.

The story of the big stunt was begging to be brought to a wider audience. With the passing of time and ex-servicemen came the risk that people might forget aspects of the First World War.

But Ross J. Thomas, an Australian mining entrepreneur, hadn't forgotten.

Passionate about telling First World War stories, Ross – who was Executive Producer of the Australian First World War drama feature film *Beneath Hill 60* – approached me and it didn't take us long to settle on a concept that illuminated the lives of the men at the heart of the Holzminden story.

The Holzminden escape had appeared in books before and we had no desire to recreate the wheel. The breakout of 1918 was the chessboard but, we wondered, who were the players who took their positions in the game? Where did these men come from? What were their hopes, dreams and talents? Did they suffer behind the barbed wire or did they emerge victorious despite their hardships? How did they come to be there? What happened to them after the war?

Who were behind the faces of Holzminden?

We were not to know that the seed of our 'little project' would take root so deeply and, well tended by the burgeoning team, would grow into a mighty oak tree. After gathering research material and accounts, we realised that for the men of Holzminden to be truly honoured, we needed to make contact with the descendant families and cultivate the stories first hand – and with family consent.

While our researchers were busy researching, we put out a call via a website designed to attract Holzminden descendants and followed it up with a Facebook page.

At first it was a trickle, but I found myself receiving emails from all corners of the globe from Holzminden descendants who had found our page and were eager to contribute. Those contacts then tipped off other descendants, and quite a few more were tracked down by our team through sheer persistence. Some of the individuals we 'cold-called' had no idea their father, grandfather, uncle or great-uncle had been a POW in Holzminden, but many became fascinated by the revelation. Detective hats were donned as they made their way around the family to find out more about their Holzminden internee relative in order to flesh out the stories.

Online military forums and websites across the world agreed to post articles and 'shout-outs' to Holzminden descendants.

The most astonishing thing began to happen. Unpublished wartime diaries, artwork and poetry from Holzminden began to arrive in my email box. Ross and I exchanged many an excited email, marvelling over the latest shining gem that had dropped in unannounced. We lost count of the number of times we uttered the words: 'Does it get any better than this?'

This is when we knew we were truly onto something.

Our intrepid researchers, Jenelle McCarrick and Sue Baker Wilson, found scores of POWs through military documentation and other official sources, and I began to build an internee list, which was regularly expanded as information came to hand. Eventually it was uploaded to our website, where visitors could check it for familiar names, inform me of ones that were missing and correct errors.

By the time the information-gathering phase for the book was closed off – and between the relentless digging and exposure on the internet – I found myself with a collection of firsthand accounts from the families of an astonishing fifty-six POWs who had gladly opened their treasure chests to assist our project. At last count, there were more than 540 POWs on our internee list, which remains a living document.

To my further amazement, the emails kept coming, but they were different now: messages of gratitude from descendants whose involvement in this book had opened the door to family reunions. Time and again I was informed that this project had brought people together – reuniting far-flung family members and forging introductions to new ones, often relatives whose existence had been previously unknown.

In September 2013 – as a result of this project – a large group

Introduction

of descendants from all over the world made the pilgrimage to the current Holzminden barracks to visit the place where their relatives had been incarcerated a century ago.

Lest we forget.

– Jacqueline Cook

Author's Note

One of the greater challenges in writing a book of this nature is untangling clashing eyewitness versions of the same event.

A handful of books have been written on the subject of the Holzminden tunnel escape; the very first, published in 1920, is *The Tunnellers of Holzminden* by the Camp Adjutant, Captain Hugh George Edmund Durnford of the Royal Field Artillery, who was there at the time of the outbreak. Among these books, many of the facts are undisputed, but distortion and rumour still surround the escape in small measure. The discrepancies appear to have resulted from a combination of confusion and panic after the tunnel collapse and media misreporting at the time – with maybe just a smattering of embellishment thrown in for good measure.

The slight discrepancies do not in any way diminish the stunning feat achieved by this band of intrepid captives who were equipped with little more than determination, ingenuity and a fistful of kitchen cutlery.

PART I

Holzminden, September 1917 to December 1918

ONE

Welcome to 'Hellminden'

Until the outbreak of the First World War in August 1914, John Richard 'Dick' Cash and his wife, Cissy, had led unassuming lives with their five small children in the rural community of Thirlmere, New South Wales, Australia.

Over the years, they had earned a well-deserved reputation as hard-working pillars of the 400-strong community. Their cosy town lay 55 miles (86km) south-west of Sydney in a region that had grown on the back of the early railway and timber industries.

Dick, who had emigrated from England at the age of twenty-four and married Cecelia Lobb at thirty-one, made a moderate living from the photographic studio connected to a small grocery store he ran with his elder brother, Arthur. A keen sportsman, the community-minded Dick organised the local Gala Sports Days, staging competitions in woodchopping, throwing, races and relays, hosting the events on 8 acres (3.25ha) of family land, which had originally been purchased for £1200 and lay only a short distance from the business premises. The property supported a modest four-roomed brick house with a galvanised iron roof plus a nearby hall, which was hired out to friends and neighbours for dances and meetings.

The Cashes owned neither a horse-and-sulky nor a motor car, but the lack of transport was no barrier to the athletic photographer. To reach locations, he cheerfully loaded up his camera on his bicycle and pedalled furiously to his destination, irrespective of the distance. One of Dick's finest achievements – and one that possibly left him saddle-sore for many days thereafter – was the Great Ride from Thirlmere to the nation's infant capital, Canberra, to capture an historic moment in Australia's history: Declaration Day, 5 May 1913.

These days, on the Hume Highway in an air-conditioned car, the drive is around two and a half hours. No-one knows how long it took Dick to cover that distance on a bicycle loaded with a turn-of-the-twentieth-century camera and tripod, but he reached his destination in time to photograph Lady Denman, the wife of the Governor-General, declaring Australia's capital 'Canberra'. Happily, the efforts of the intrepid photographer were repaid: Dick's historic Declaration Day image was published in the newspaper.

As he snapped away at the dignitaries and guests, no-one would have predicted the life-and-death wartime role his photography skills would play only five years later.

In 1914, the storm clouds of the First World War began to brew in Europe. When Australia was drawn into the conflict, Dick received official permission from the Provost Marshal of the Department of Military Forces in September 1914 to photograph troop movements and spent much of the next year and a half at the Sydney docks.

The relatively new nation of Australia was electric with anticipation – the cream of the nation's youth flocked to recruiting stations, declaring loyalty to the mother country, England. Despite the lack of conscription, the Australian military forces were inundated with volunteers – to such an extent that many were turned away, disappointed.

Dick snapped countless young faces eagerly leaving for the

Welcome to 'Hellminden'

European theatres of war. He also wistfully watched two of his younger brothers enlist: twenty-year-old Ernie in August 1914, with Service Number 8; in January 1916, twenty-four-year-old Wally was assigned Service Number 10222. From this systematic numbering, it is clear that just over 10,000 men had enlisted in less than eighteen months.

Even though the much older Dick must have struggled with the decision to leave his wife, young family and businesses, by February 1916 – not long after the height restriction was lifted – the call to adventure was all too much for him and, just shy of forty, the 5'2" (1.6m) father of five enlisted as a private in the Australian Imperial Force (AIF) to 'do his bit'.

After completing the military training, and with the rank of acting corporal, he sailed with his battalion aboard the *Ascanius*. Just after Christmas 1916, following a journey of two months, he disembarked in Folkestone, England, with the 1817 troops who had sailed with him – no doubt all anticipating the adventure of a lifetime.

The year 1917 was to hold considerable personal loss for Dick. In January, while he was awaiting orders, one of his twin nineteen-month-old daughters, Myrtle, died of illness. His mother passed away in March after a battle with cancer. Then in June his brother Albert, a long-time tuberculosis sufferer, finally succumbed to the disease. The Public Trustee Office 'handed the whole of the business assets of the partnership to the wife of the surviving partner on her undertaking to settle all debts' on 20 September 1917, meaning that Cissy became the business owner and was liable for any monies owing.

Having received no mail from home, Dick was unaware of Cissy's mounting pressures; indeed he was to remain oblivious to all three deaths for quite some time. In February he received orders to board SS *Golden Eagle* for the English Channel crossing. Destination: the Western Front.

When Dick reached France on 1 March 1917, the Germans had created a 100-mile (160km) line of defence, stretching from Lille in the north to Metz in the east, which came to be known as the Hindenburg Line. Fortified with vicious barbed wire in order to split up, slow down and pick off advancing British troops, and strategically located by the Germans to place themselves on higher ground, it was formidable. It dominated the crater-filled, desolate landscape to which Dick, now reverted to the field rank of private, was sent.

His 19th Battalion was to relieve the decimated 28th Battalion, whose fatigued troops had been fighting in torrential rain, snow and sucking mud. The order was to take the strategic town of Bullecourt, 12 miles (19km) south-west of Vimy Ridge. Nothing seemed to go to plan for the operation; among a series of disasters to befall the British, support tanks failed to show. When the cumbersome beasts finally did make an appearance, they quickly became bogged in the slush.

The subsequent death toll on British troops was costly, with wave after wave of advancing soldiers mowed down by the Germans in a barrage of machine-gun fire. For the British, it was soul-destroying.

Yet, in the midst of battle, an extraordinary thing happened to Dick that no doubt saved him from likely battlefield slaughter.

A mortar shell exploded nearby, catapulting him upwards, then cart-wheeled him through the air – incredibly, landing him feet-first in a shell-hole. The blast knocked Dick out; dislodged earth rained down on him, burying him up to his neck and effectively entombing him in a soil prison. The weight of the soil and his internal injuries made it impossible for him to free himself.

Weakened, he watched the battle rage around him for a full day and night from his ant's-eye position.

The trapped soldier could only watch helplessly when the boots of German troops advanced towards him. Dick would have posed a curious sight to the enemy, with his head protruding from the ground, but he was dug out and, on 3 May 1917, Private Dick Cash was taken as a prisoner of war.

The journey of more than 300 miles (482km) from France was an agonising one. Every bump and shudder exacerbated his substantial internal injuries – a bullet lodged in his left lung, wounds to his breast, back and left shoulder, and all his teeth had been blown out in the mortar blast – but eventually he found himself in the care of nursing staff in a hospital outside Hameln in the region of Lower Saxony, north-west Germany.

It was here that he learned of the British–Australian Red Cross, based in London, and twelve days after capture, he sent his first postcard – his style polite, calm and self-effacing:

> 15-5-17 – Gentlemen, I am writing to ask if you would send to an old L[iver]pool boy a box of comforts, foods, tobacco etc. I lived at 12 Roscommon St from 87-97, then left to go to Australia. Have lost the run of all English friends. Had your add[ress] given so am asking this favour. I was taken prisoner on 3-5-17, wounded and buried in a shell hole. My Australian add[ress] is Thirlmere, NSW. If I presume too much please forward this card to the proper quarter and oblige me. Yours, JR Cash

Evidently, Dick was determined not to slip through the cracks behind enemy lines. He fired off requests every few days, repeating the same information in the hope that at least one of them would reach the Red Cross. What he didn't know was that it was taking a full two months for his postcards to find their way to London, and it would take that amount of time again for mail from there to reach Australia.

In the typical turmoil and confusion of war, the authorities in London had received word that Private Cash had been killed on the battlefield – supposedly observed by an eyewitness – but when his recently dated postcards started turning up, it was clear that not only was he alive, but also that he was not going to be the least bit quiet about it.

Meanwhile, he cast his letter-writing net wider and started sending missives to the Care Committee for Australian Prisoners and the Australian YMCA. Months after hospitalisation, Private John Richard Cash of the Australian Imperial Force finally registered on the radar of the Red Cross and military authorities.

By then, Dick had recovered sufficiently from his injuries to be discharged. In October 1917, he had written to military authorities in England and reported his impending relocation to a newly opened POW camp, located 31 miles (50km) south of Hameln in the same province of Lower Saxony: Holzminden.

Having been hospitalised for four long months, he had not yet experienced firsthand a life of confinement behind barbed wire and, as such, had no idea what to expect.

Throughout the war, one of Germany's major headaches was how to accommodate the steadily mounting flow of military and civilian prisoners: over two million POWs by the end of the war; the Allies – Russia, Britain, France, United States and Turkey – held six million.

The Hague Convention, the international rules of war governing the care of prisoners – the fourth iteration of which came into force on 26 January 1910 – stipulated that an enemy government was required to provide a reasonable level of humane care for POWs. Consequently any building that could hold several hundred individuals at one time was converted to a prison facility – hotels, monasteries, castles, fortresses and military establishments across Germany and German-held territories.

Situated on the River Weser, the town of Holzminden – with a population of around 11,000 – had been a provincial farming community for centuries until it was pressed into service at the outbreak of the First World War as a garrison town. The compound at Holzminden had served for a year as a preparatory institute for young military volunteers before its refurbishment for troop accommodation. But with floods of prisoners to be housed, the barracks was converted to a POW camp for British officers.[1]

In September 1917, after the barbed wire had been hastily raised, gates and walls secured, panelling nailed shut and every corner of the camp rendered escape-proof, the first intake of British officers was driven through the gates of the camp; it would become known to the inmates as 'Hellminden'.

Thirty-two-year-old 2nd Lieutenant Hugh George Edmund Durnford of the Royal Field Artillery was one such prisoner. In his 1920 book, *The Tunnellers of Holzminden*, he described his impressions of the countryside surrounding the prison in deceptively lyrical terms:

> . . . a broad level, methodically cultivated plain; a horizon of wooded slopes with, every few degrees or so, the suggestion of winding valleys and watercourses; to the northward, the river Weser, nature's barrier beyond the wire, flowing between us and freedom, and visible from our upper windows is an occasional gleam of silver against the shadows of the steep further bank; to

the west, the town, red roofed and picturesque with adjoining allotments . . .

The layout inside the camp, which could accommodate up to 700 POWs at a crush, included twin whitewashed barracks at the north and south ends of the compound. Both sets of barracks were divided down the middle internally by a concrete wall. The southern half of Kaserne A housed the *Kommandantur*, closest to the front gates. In the other half, officer inmates were accommodated over the four floors. The windows on the ground floor of Kaserne A had been whitewashed over to prevent prisoners from reading the identity cards pinned to the chests of visitors.

Lieutenant Charles Edward Burton Bernard of the 10th West Yorkshire Regiment was twenty-eight years old when he was first sent to Holzminden. The talented Yokohama-born artist noted the cramped living conditions in his diary:

> We were crammed ten to eleven in a room and space was so limited that we had to 'double-deck' our beds, that is, place one above the other, the beds being so constructed as to enable us to do this, in order to relieve the awful congestion. As we were not allowed to have our boxes in our rooms – indeed, lack of room made it impossible for us to have them in any case – and only a small locker was provided for each, the rooms became a medley of clothes and household goods immediately, causing great discomfort and inconvenience. We were simply sitting on each other's laps, almost.

A handful of smaller rooms, allocated to the higher ranks, accommodated three or four men each and were prized for their improved privacy.

At the northern end of the compound, Kaserne B overlooked a rye and bean field; it housed the orderlies on the ground floor and officers on the three floors above. Kaserne B also boasted a potato patch, wood shed, canteen, parcel room for the distribution of Red Cross parcels and letters from home, the bath-house, cookhouses, married guards' quarters, a gym and storage shed. The *Spielplatz*, or parade ground, located between the two barracks, doubled as the exercise area and an *Appel* (roll-call) assembly point.

A wire fence running the circumference of the compound designated the territory called no man's land, into which no POW could venture or else risk being shot, and was backed by a wall reinforced with barbed wire. Sentries were stationed at regular intervals, patrolling the perimeter with their guard dogs. The entire compound was illuminated by powerful arc lights.

There had been insufficient time to prepare the place for the first intake of prisoners and many of the facilities were still incomplete. Consequently, the guard dogs were housed in the bath-house, which meant that the officers were required to bathe at the horse troughs – even through their first freezing European winter – until the bath-house became functional. The toilet facilities were grossly inadequate; there were only two per floor, each expected to service dozens of POWs.

The first Holzminden POWs bore the brunt of the deficiencies. Hugh Durnford noted, with some measure of disgust, the state of the camp upon arrival:

> The buildings were there, and that was about all. The crockery had not arrived; there were three large boilers in the German cook-house to cater for the bodily wants of 500 English officers and 100 Germans; there were two or three wretched cooking-stoves for our private use; there were about half a dozen British

orderlies – the rest, we were told, were on their way; the bathroom had not even been begun; the parcel room was not yet open, nor was the canteen; the German staff were incomplete, new to the ropes, and totally inefficient . . .

Initially, mealtimes presented problems of epic proportions. Between the number of prisoners and the lack of kitchen facilities, food preparation was a logistical nightmare. The officers, who considered this barbaric, were outraged by the lack of amenities.

Charles Bernard recalled:

We were not permitted to deface the parade ground with homemade stoves, and the Huns only provided us with two very small domestic stoves with a twelve by fourteen inch hot-plate – it can be imagined that cooking for five hundred hungry souls was an impossibility. The crush in the 'cook-house' – merely an open shed – at meal times, can only be left to the imagination. Later on, large well-built stoves were made for us, which were a great boon, though cooking out of doors in the winter was anything but pleasant.

In the fifteen months of the camp's operation, long-term prisoners experienced two long, harsh winters. For heating, they were more or less left to fend for themselves, and in the absence of warm clothes, blankets or fuel, the men resorted to desperate means to stay warm.

In his post-Holzminden diary, Charles noted:

We suffered intensely from cold during the first half of the winter at Holzminden, owing to the entire absence of fuel for heating our rooms. There were stoves in the rooms, but no coal

Welcome to 'Hellminden'

was supplied by the Germans. The weather was bitterly cold, with snow and heavy frost. At first we managed to get some warmth by burning anything combustible that we could lay our hands on – and our rooms were stripped bare of every vestige of woodwork – skirtings, locker doors, bed-boards and surplus furniture being broken up and put into the stoves. There was a cinder path running round the barrack square, and we were treated to the amusing spectacle of dignified British officers of the higher branches of the services – peers and baronets and other respected sons of the aristocracy – crawling round on their hands and knees with sacks, denuding the path of whatever they could pick up that was likely to burn . . .

Captain Roland Corbett of the Royal Flying Corps (RFC) had arrived at Holzminden in September 1917 as one of the first intake. Transferred from Schwarmstedt POW camp, he and some of his fellow prisoners had been promised exchange to Switzerland or Holland but had instead found themselves in Holzminden with a Kommandant who professed to know nothing about their guarantee of freedom.

Roland observed wryly:

A canteen was opened which sold necessary articles such as toothpaste, paper and pencils at a colossal price, also poisonous liquid called wine at 12 Marks per bottle and many drowned their sorrows in it, which certainly helped the German exchequer, but ruined their own innards.

The POWs were locked inside the barracks buildings from 6 pm until seven the next morning, with not much to look forward to in between other than a twice-daily rollcall. The men were under threat of being shot at if they opened the windows to give themselves relief from the summer heat or if they were caught gazing out of the windows at night-time.

Twenty-five-year-old Lieutenant Arthur Stanley Bourinot of No. 70 Squadron Royal Flying Corps, a budding Canadian poet, composed verse throughout his internments, many from his barracks in Holzminden. 'Night in Holzminden' is filled with Stanley's characteristic quiet observations:

> The drummer sounds the summons to our room,
> The light-encircled Spielplatz soon lies bare
> And desolate, except where buildings loom
> Limning their shadows on the vacant square.
> A gramophone grinds out a raucous song
> And boisterous laughs resound along the halls
> Now comes the muffling silence, slowly throng
> The multitude of stars where darkness falls.
> Inside the room stentorian breathings sound
> Or preparations made for nightly rest
> Without the windows silence sleeps profound
> Now comes the moon above the far hill's crest.
> Asleep the buildings seem in pallid light
> Adream, we prisoners pass the peaceful night.

Despite Stanley's romanticised prose, sleep did not come easily to many of the inmates: their mattresses and pillows were uncomfortably stuffed with wood shavings or parcel room packaging. The sheet – one per inmate – was changed once a month, sometimes less frequently; the dirty blankets were never washed; and a washstand in each room ran only cold water.

Welcome to 'Hellminden'

The dreary, repetitive routine of camp life began from the moment the gates shut behind the internees.

Lieutenant David Edmund Atree Horne of the Royal Engineers, a forty-three-year-old architect in civilian life, recounted a typical Sunday behind the barbed wire:

> Rose 7.30. Bkfst 8.00. Appel 9.00. Reading and walking until 11.00. Service 11.00. Lunch 12.00 (today hard biscuits and tea without sugar and milk, larder being almost like Old Mother Hubbard's). Quantities Surveying 1–2.30. Tea and biscuits again at 3.00. Bible class 3.30 (subject: the spikenard[2] anointings). Appel 5.00. Dinner 5.30. reading and writing until 8.15. Got room ready for Evening Service at 8.30. Appel 9.30. To bed 10.00pm.

Inmates were permitted an allocation of letters and postcards so they could write home or to the Red Cross. These passed through the German camp censor, who obliterated *verboten* (forbidden) words or sentences to render them unreadable. It was pointless for the prisoners to complain of their treatment in writing to authorities, as they knew that such a potentially volatile letter would never reach its intended destination.

Holzminden was a world away from the life of elevated status enjoyed by the officers before their capture and incarceration. Deprivation of food, clothing and the liberties they had always taken for granted was a new and profoundly startling experience. They were accustomed to a system in which rank afforded them privilege; in its stead they found abuse and a disregard for the officer honour system they treasured above life itself.

Two

A Kingdom of Tyranny

Holzminden had been allocated the status of a *strafe* (punishment) camp.

Strafe camps held the worst of the serial offenders – mostly those who had attempted escapes from previous prisons. Although many had tried to escape from Holzminden by going over or through the perimeter barriers, no-one had successfully done so.

This iron-clad reputation was a point of pride with its Kommandant, Captain Karl Niemeyer, a veteran of the Franco-Prussian war. In his sixties, he had just been transferred after a wildly successful despotic stint at Ströhen POW camp, so impressing his superiors with his cruelty that he was assigned the command of Holzminden.

Niemeyer, who initially had been second-in-command at Holzminden, took over the running of the camp after the geriatric Colonel Habrecht was transferred out, most likely because his kindly nature was deemed too soft for such a role. Eager to prove himself in the top position, the egomaniacal Niemeyer set about shaping the camp into the punitive kingdom of his dreams.

Roland Corbett commented:

> Niemeyer had become omnipotent in his own imagination. He strutted around the camp with his cap on one side, his hands in his pockets, a huge cigar in his mouth and spurs on upside down,

saying 'I am the Commandant, you know. I guess you must salute me.'

The Kommandant was fond of wearing his German greatcoat as a mark of authority. He was a large man, prone to a paunch and was rarely seen without a cigar jammed between his lips. He carried a walking cane and he had a retriever puppy that seemed to dislike his master as much as did everyone else in the camp.

Charles Bernard described the bellicose Kommandant as 'an arrogant and loud-voiced individual with a portly figure, fleshy face, and a pair of bulbous, fish-like eyes'. Niemeyer also boasted a bushy Kaiser-like moustache in an expression of hero-worship of Germany's leader.

New arrivals were treated to a welcome speech by Niemeyer intended to convey spirit-crushing hopelessness.

Charles recalled:

> ... he made it quite clear to us that, although we had had an easy time in past camps, he was there to treat us as prisoners of war and that we were not to expect any decency from him. He would see to it that we would be treated with the contempt we deserved. He flourished a revolver with the words: 'I have the pistol, you know! I am the top dog, you know! And I will shoot you, you know! I guess you know!' We came to know that revolver pretty well later on ...

Niemeyer and his twin brother, Heinrich, who commanded the nearby POW camp of Clausthal, had spent seventeen years living in the USA before the war. There they had picked up a strange bar-room style of American English that earned Karl Niemeyer the nickname 'Milwaukee Bill'.

In a place devoid of laughter, the prisoners took any opportunity to create their own fun. Niemeyer's take on the English language became the butt of gleeful jokes around the camp. The men never wasted an opportunity to taunt their gaoler with cries of 'I guess you know!' as the Kommandant, almost inarticulate with rage, fought for control. Niemeyer could not fathom the POWs' hoots of laughter when he bellowed at them: 'You think I do not understand the English, but I do! I know damn all about you!'

Niemeyer had friends in high places. Holzminden officers' camp was one of four camps in the district – along with Clausthal, Ströhen and Schwarmstedt – that fell under the command of the brutish General von Hanisch, the supreme commander of the Xth Army Corps. Nicknamed 'the Pig of Hanover', von Hanisch was also the head of the Pan-German Party, a political group dedicated to annihilating the British. He harboured a deep-seated hatred for the enemy and he was out to make the lives of the POWs in his camps as miserable as humanly possible. Von Hanisch gave Niemeyer free rein to run the camp as he wished.

The General made spasmodic visits to the camp, which often entailed forcing the prisoners to stand to attention on the parade ground while he spat contemptuous insults such as *die Schweinhund Engländer* (English pig-dog) in their faces. Any prisoner slow to obey an order or to display insolence – real or imagined – was marched off to solitary confinement. The barracks rooms were inspected while the POWs stood at attention, and once again the General's insults would fly.

During von Hanisch's visits, a deferential Niemeyer – who both idolised and feared him – trailed his raging superior in a state of nervous anticipation, poised to fulfil every order or whim like a lapdog eager to please its master. After the General took his leave, Niemeyer would be edgy for the next several days, plastering all the notice boards with lengthy lists of newly *verboten* activities and behaviour, which the inmates dutifully ignored.

Even though Niemeyer's behaviour was abhorrent, he seemed genuinely perplexed that the POWs held him in such low esteem. Once he approached a senior British officer and, within earshot of several milling POWs, asked, 'Tell me, major, as man to man, what do your officers think of me?'

'As man to man, captain,' the British officer replied, 'they think you are a damned scoundrel.' If this scene had taken place in an environment where one man did not have supreme power over the other, the officer's retort may have been a great deal more colourful.

The camp ran a canteen where POWs could use their ration cards to obtain basic necessities as well as wine. Purchases were made with specially printed camp currency that held no value outside the camp. Prices on items were grossly inflated to support Niemeyer's habit of skimming off the top and pocketing the profits. It was estimated that by the end of the war, he had amassed a small fortune at the expense of those in his care.

The senior British officer (SBO), a position that was held by many over the duration, was responsible for presenting grievances to the camp authorities on behalf of the POWs. He often attempted to approach von Hanisch with a list of the men's complaints, but on each occasion was dismissed with a barrage of insults. In the absence of recourse, the SBO began a secret diary of the Kommandant's tyrannical command in the hope of bringing him to justice after the war.

Many officers were not accustomed to such disrespectful conduct from their counterparts – even by the enemy. For those who had passed through camps where gaoler and prisoner afforded a respect to one another – and they did exist – it was indeed a shock to witness the Kommandant striding around the camp, shrieking at his sentries to shoot indiscriminately at the POWs standing at the barracks windows, forbidding this, punishing for that, indulging in screaming fits, taunting the prisoners and firing at them with his revolver during drunken rampages.

Unlike the many conflicts that followed, the First World War was considered a 'gentlemen's war'. Honour among officers was held in the highest regard, even between opposing sides. It was commonplace for a German to shoot down a British aviator, only for the two enemy officers to salute one another on the ground, share a smoke and engage in a spot of banter before the captured combatant was either sent to hospital for treatment or interned in a POW facility.

At the time of his death in combat on 21 April 1918, ace German fighter Manfred Albrecht Freiherr von Richthofen, the *Luftstreitkräfte's* (German Air Force's) highly decorated First World War flying ace, was credited with the highest number of air victories of any pilot in the conflict. A brilliant tactician, Richthofen – best known as the Red Baron – had risen to command the *Jagdgeschwader* 1 (Fighter Unit 1), the notorious 'Flying Circus', so named for the brightly coloured aircraft and the unit's superior mobility capacity.

Richthofen's eighty official air victories included the disabling of several RFC aircraft piloted by men who were later incarcerated in Holzminden officers' camp. Richthofen was known to either send his compliments to his surviving adversaries or insist on meeting them and shaking their hands in deference to the era's fascination with and respect for a worthy opponent.

One officer imprisoned in Holzminden courtesy of the Red

Baron was twenty-one-year-old Lieutenant Algernon 'Algie' Bird. The young pilot, who came from a family of Norfolk millers, was flying his first mission with No. 46 Squadron RFC when his squadron was intercepted by the Red Baron and his Flying Circus. At the same time, Dutch aircraft designer Anthony Fokker happened to be on the ground below; a German camera crew had been trailing him, capturing footage of his visit to the Front to see his designs in action.

Peppered with relentless machine-gun fire, Algie's aircraft all but disintegrated under him and he was forced to land. After he was joined on the ground by Richthofen, the young British pilot found himself in the position of shaking hands with both the infamous Red Baron and Anthony Fokker as the surreal event was captured on film by the German camera crew. Inevitably, the jolly exchange was not to last long – when the camera stopped rolling, Algie – Richthofen's sixty-first conquest – was taken prisoner and interned.

For much of the war, a chivalrous 'no hard feelings' policy existed between officers on both sides, whether it be in the air, on land or at sea.

Twenty-year-old Canadian pilot Lieutenant Ian Donald Cameron had been underage when he had enlisted. On one of his first missions behind enemy lines, Ian was allocated an older aircraft; the cumbersome beast had lagged behind the rest of No. 65 Squadron RFC, making Ian easy prey. When the inevitable occurred, the Ontario-born pilot brought his plane down, only to find himself shaking hands with his foe and exchanging contact details. Years later, in the 1930s, the German pilot who shot him out of the sky became Ian's house guest during a visit to Canada.

When von Haebler of *Jasta* 36 shot down Canadian pilot 2nd Lieutenant Robert 'Bob' Cowan, also of No. 65 Squadron RFC, the two met amicably on the ground, with Bob presenting his nemesis with his own flying cap. Although von Haebler was killed later in the war, Bob – who spent some time in Holzminden – made contact with his former foe's father in the 1930s and the two maintained a warm correspondence for a while. In fact, Herr von Haebler grew to consider the British pilot his surrogate son.

Eighteen-year-old Lieutenant Frederick Norman Insoll was not exactly shot down by the enemy. In 1916, out on one of his first bombing missions, his opponent persuaded him to land with a hand signal. Norman managed to bring his plane down on a tethered cow. It was the German fighter pilots who intervened to protect him from the angry mob of French villagers who insisted on milking the unfortunate creature before they shot it to put it out of its misery. The Germans later treated Norman to a Boxing Day lunch in their officers' mess before they sent him off to prison in a barouche – a stylish horse-drawn carriage.

The respected twenty-six-year-old Lieutenant Norman Birks of No. 29 Squadron RFC, a Yorkshireman born and bred, noted in his memoirs that by 1917:

> . . . it was considered not 'quite the thing' [by both sides] to continue firing on a machine which was already incapacitated, but this sense of chivalry was rapidly disappearing [in the later part of the war].

This extraordinary sense of chivalry and honour was also expected to extend to life behind the barbed wire. This is never so clear as in the case of officer parole cards.

Upon admittance to a camp, officers received a parole card that stated the terms and conditions extended to them in exchange for being permitted to take an accompanied stroll outside the wire.

The card, bearing the conditions in both English and German, read:

> I, herewith, give my word of honour that I shall not, in case of my taking part in a walk, ie from the time of leaving the camp until having returned to it, at the same time strictly obeying any orders given to me by the accompanying officer and not to commit any acts that are directed against the safety of the German Empire. I know that according to 159 of the M. St. G.B., a prisoner of war who escapes in spite of the word of honour given is liable to death.

Once he had signed his card, the officer had solemnly pledged not to attempt escape during one of these walks. The faith in this word-of-honour system was so implacable that the German guards accompanying strolling POWs did not even bother to take their weapons.

Many officers crossed out unacceptable terms in the parole card, then signed it – but unless the officer agreed to all the terms in full, they were not permitted to leave the compound.

Second Lieutenant Reginald Gough of the 4th Oxfordshire and Buckinghamshire Light Infantry, a dedicated and gentle teacher of the blind and deaf back home in England, said:

> It was possible to get some idea of the surrounding district and must have proved quite useful to intending escapers. On returning we were handed our parole card again and were then perfectly justified in endeavouring to escape.

David Horne, a devoted Christian, was devoid of the animosity towards the enemy felt by most other POWs, and took long parole walks. He often went as far as the neighbouring towns of Bevern

3 miles (4.8km) away and Höxter, a very substantial 5 miles (8km) from the camp. David carried his notebook, and took great delight in stopping to sketch rural buildings along the way.

In exchange for a change of scenery, the German officers fully expected the British officers to adhere to the 'no escape' policy. And the British officers wouldn't dream of signing the card then attempting to escape outside the wire, even though they had every opportunity. It just wasn't done. An officer who did so would undoubtedly find only wrathful contempt among his own if captured and returned – not for being captured, but for dishonouring the officer system.

Accordingly, although von Hanisch's loathing of the British was legendary and he took any opportunity to belittle and humiliate the prisoners in the camps under his jurisdiction, the day he accused the prisoners of breaking parole was the day they perceived that the belligerent general had stepped over the line. Outraged by this untrue accusation – it was unthinkable to question the honour of a single officer, let alone several hundred of them – unanimously they agreed to force an apology from von Hanisch by refusing to go on parole walks.

Roland Corbett recalled:

> Needless to say this meant remaining in camp and we were confined to the tiny patch of ground on which Appels were held and our only exercise was to prowl round and round this patch, which was a regular treadmill and most congested as new officers kept arriving and the buildings were soon filled up with 600 officers.

After the POWs had trudged the *Spielplatz* circuit for what seemed like an eternity, they were forced to admit they were not dealing with a gentlemanly officer; it would be a cold day in hell when von Hanisch apologised to the English pig-dogs, and their gaolers didn't care one way or the other if officers took parole walks or not. So eventually walks were resumed, with the collective POW pride a little dented.

This officer-and-a-gentleman ideology applied not only to parole walks but also to all manner of officer conduct.

Twenty-seven-year-old Kent-born Lieutenant Colin Laurance of the Royal Navy Air Service had been a steeplejack on the construction of tall buildings in Australia before the war. He sustained a serious head injury after being shot down over Zeebrugge and found close confinement unbearable. His head injury affected his behaviour and he more than likely obtained alcohol from the canteen in order to take the edge off his discomfort. He was often reprimanded by his superior officers for being intoxicated in the presence of enlisted men, a serious military infraction. Intoxication was acceptable, but only among officer peers, and to appear drunk in the presence of lower ranks – including Germans – was considered 'ungentlemanly'.

To the modern-day observer, this is almost laughable. Why should it matter how Laurance conducted himself in front of the enemy? Why shouldn't an officer attempt escape if given half the chance? Why didn't they sign the parole cards then melt into the German countryside during a stroll?

Almost a century ago, a different set of rules applied. An officer's word of honour was trusted implicitly by both sides and mutual respect of superior ranks was paramount.

But shortly after Niemeyer set about converting the camp into his own personal penal colony, this extraordinary honour system was reduced to a pile of ashes. No longer protected, the prisoners found themselves exposed to the mercy of a despotic, vengeful gaoler.

Three

Survival

It was into Niemeyer's thuggish world that Australian Private Dick Cash arrived in October 1917 after his lengthy hospital confinement. The moment the imposing iron gates of Holzminden POW camp closed with a clang behind him, his life of servitude began.

As an other ranks[1] soldier in an officers' prison camp, his duty was clear. He was now an orderly[2] assigned to serve the officers under prison conditions – a role that amounted to domestic drudgery. In a camp of 500–600 officers, more than a hundred orderlies had been sent to Holzminden to make the lives of the privileged officers more bearable.

While the officers continued to wear their service uniforms throughout their imprisonment, orderlies were required to wear a shapeless, humiliating yellow and brown uniform with a shellcut jacket, which marked them as military servants. To add insult to injury, the back of the tunic bore the large red letters 'KG' *Kriegsgefangener* (prisoner of war) and the front displayed the orderly's POW number.

In his 1978 book, *Black Bread and Barbed Wire*, Irish author Michael Moynihan refers to orderlies as 'Jeeves in khaki'. Of their servant status he comments:

> Taken for granted by officer prisoners of war were the other rank orderlies who waited on them hand and foot, from making their

beds and polishing their boots to preparing and serving their meals. Private Norman Dykes was at Crefeld and Schwarmstedt at the same time as Capt. Lyall Grant, but from their two accounts of life there, they could have been in separate worlds . . .

Both Norman and Douglas were also imprisoned at Holzminden, where the yawning gap between the privileged officers and other ranks was no different from anywhere else. Orderlies' daily duties included preparing tea service at appointed times of the day, cleaning the officers' quarters, sweeping floors, dusting, emptying ashtrays and straightening the British officers' barracks.

Norman recalled of his 'chamber-maid' duties:

We had come to accept rank and privilege as a central factor of army life, but I suppose there was more to it than that. In civilian life, we had taken for granted the bridge between the classes in a way that would not be tolerated now . . . Upstairs/downstairs was a reality then, remember. Being an orderly meant that you were comfortably housed and well fed, and most officers were generous with 'perks', both in payment and kind. So far as I was concerned, if an officer treated me as a human being, I responded to him; if he treated me like dirt, there were ways of getting back at him . . .

Disgruntled orderlies could not afford to display open hostility towards superior officers. While nothing could be done to punish insubordination as long as they were all under prison conditions, recalcitrant orderlies could fully expect their names to be recorded in a little black book, and to face a court-martial after the hostilities had ceased.

Subtle reprisals, however, were the order of the day – measures designed to irritate the targeted officer, but not obvious enough to draw accusations of deliberate insolence from the officers. Favoured methods of orderly payback included running late with the tea or dinner service; food intended to be served hot was delivered cold, burned or undercooked; crockery was 'accidentally' dropped and a host of other trivial but satisfying tricks were employed to undermine the superior officer who dared to mistreat his orderly.

Not every officer looked down his nose at other ranks. As Norman had noted, an officer who treated an orderly with respect as a human being could generally expect loyal service in return.

In between his orderly duties, the unassuming Dick Cash kept up his campaign of letter-writing from behind the barbed wire, fully utilising the allowance of four postcards and two letters per month. As he had arrived at Holzminden still minus his teeth, which had been blown out on the battlefield, he was keen to rectify this.

Several months into his incarceration in Holzminden, he was triumphant in his efforts and was supplied with new dentures at a cost of 170 Marks. Judging by his correspondence to the Red Cross, he was satisfied with his new chompers, somewhat cheerfully writing in one letter dated June 1918 that he was:

> . . . still alive and as well as can be expected. Have my new set of teeth in. They will do me until I get home and get a good set.

★

Like every other POW, Dick was entirely reliant on the extraordinary work of the Red Cross for survival.

At the onset of the war, the British Red Cross joined forces with fellow humanitarian organisation the Order of St John to form the Joint War Committee to pool their resources to assist the war effort. As the foremost provider of POW services, the Red Cross was critical to the survival of the men detained in prison camps. The organisation was staffed by dedicated volunteers who put in long hours to ensure that written requests from POWs were met and parcels containing food staples and clothing were distributed on a regular basis. Although the quality of the German food supplies varied from camp to camp, it was deemed virtually inedible in most of them.

The Red Cross in Britain and her dominions didn't hesitate to leverage the star power of the era's celebrities, gratefully welcoming influential politicians, sports personalities, movie stars and British royals to their ranks to raise awareness. Australian opera sensation Dame Nellie Melba became the face of the Red Cross in Australia when she conducted concerts to raise funds for the humanitarian cause. American silent film stars Frances Starr and Bijou Fernandez lent a hand at Red Cross fundraising drives. Princess Mary of England was only seventeen when she became the high-profile poster girl for the war effort, raising £100,000 to send cigarette and candy boxes to every serviceman for Christmas in 1914. She joined the British Red Cross as a nurse, personally nursing injured servicemen, and later became the Commandant-in-Chief of British Red Cross detachments. As with many owners of grand estates, socialites Waldorf and Nancy Astor offered the grounds of their palatial Buckinghamshire mansion, Cliveden, to the Canadian Red Cross for the purpose of building the HRH Duchess of Connaught Hospital[3] for injured servicemen.

Back home, in whatever pocket of the globe that might be, communities, families and loved ones were doing what they could to support the troops at the front line and in POW camps. Those left at home – mostly women – flocked to community halls and other locations in cities and towns where packing stations were set up to collect, pack and distribute comfort parcels on behalf of the Red Cross for shipping to the battlefields and POW camps of Europe.

In *A Woman's War*, an account of women's roles on the home front during the First World War, the hustle and bustle of a Red Cross packing station located in Collingwood, Melbourne, Australia, is vividly described – this was a familiar scene taking place in packing stations across the British Empire:

> The Town Hall is a hive of activity. I've never seen the like of it. About two hundred women, busily packing comforts parcels for the troops 'somewhere in France.' Women are criss-crossing the hall on a hundred different tasks, boot heels scraping the floor. Noise and chatter like you wouldn't believe.
>
> Agnes and I are in a group shuffling along a line of trestle tables. We're each holding a cardboard box with a pair of thick woollen socks lining it. As we inch forward, women across the tables hand us different 'comforts,' which we pack into the box. A bottle of Bovril or cod-liver oil, a cake of sand soap, a tin of condensed milk or a tin of boiled sweets, a little Christmas cake wrapped in calico, and an old copy of either the *Weekly Times* or the *Argus* or the *Winner*. Then we get handed a small tin of tobacco or biscuits, a cloth bandage and a chocolate bar.
>
> At the end of the line there's an empty trestle where we spend a minute packing the items in, wrapping the perishables up in the newspaper, wedging in the tins and padding the top with another knitted item – maybe a vest or a balaclava.
>
> With any luck the boys'll get their parcels before the European winter sets in, or at least in time for Christmas. Agnes nudges me as she slips a contraband bottle of brandy under the tins in her parcel, a small note attached by a bit of string. 'What does it say?'

Survival

I ask. 'Medicinal use only,' she laughs. 'Enjoy – and share.' I'm standing right beside her, but with all the noise and voices echoing high up in the ceiling I can hardly hear her. And with Agnes, that's saying something.

We hand our parcels to the ladies at the next trestle. Sleeves rolled, they shear off lengths of brown paper and wrap the boxes methodically, binding them up with string. Lastly, they paste on a bright label – '22nd Battalion AIF, from the Collingwood District Red Cross Comforts Fund.' I reckon the men will get a kick out of that. The 22nd's mostly made up of men and boys from Collingwood or Richmond. I watch the parcels get stacked on a growing mountain at the end of the hall.

Those 'growing mountains' of comfort parcels from the Collingwood District Red Cross – and from the many other Red Cross packing stations across Australia – were destined for a central point in London.

They were then to be distributed under the watchful eye of Australian-born Miss Mary Elizabeth Chomley, who, as the Secretary of the POW Branch of the Australian–British Red Cross Society, became known as the prisoners' divine angel of mercy.

How had an Australian woman, and an unmarried one at that, come to hold such a position so far from home?

By the time Mary entered the world in 1871, the woman whom the little girl was to grow up idolising – Florence Nightingale – was already fifty-one and was well on her way to becoming a living legend. Florence had defied the wishes of her outraged family by following what she believed to be her God-given call to nursing – a much-maligned profession at the time – most famously tending to Crimean War soldiers in both wound and spirit throughout the 1853–56 conflict. She was also undeterred by the resistance she encountered with her subsequent advocacy for sanitary living conditions to avoid infection. Florence had been blessed with a breathtaking persistence and her outspokenness eventually sparked improvements to the prevailing unhygienic nursing and medical practices.

The Times was to romantically portray the Lady of the Lamp, as she came to be known, as:

> . . . a 'ministering angel' without any exaggeration in these hospitals, and as her slender form glides quietly along each corridor, every poor fellow's face softens with gratitude at the sight of her. When all the medical officers have retired for the night and silence and darkness have settled down upon those miles of prostrate sick, she may be observed alone, with a little lamp in her hand, making her solitary rounds . . .

Both women had been born into wealthy upper-class families and shared an undeniable inner drive to help the helpless. Mary was inspired by Florence's dedication to her calling but unlike her idol, she was not hampered by familial resistance to her choices. The Chomleys, who, among many things had a family-owned street in Prahran, Victoria, named after them, were unconcerned by the restrictive conventions of the day and took the unusual position of encouraging progressive thinking and action in all their children, including their daughters.

Mary's face bore no-nonsense, almost masculine features. Opinionated and unafraid of authority – qualities considered unladylike in the Victorian era into which she was born – she must have appeared intimidating to those around her if her nickname in adulthood, 'the Grenadier', is any indication. This attribute developed into an ability to fearlessly tackle bureaucracy in the later war years in support of the POWs she championed, earning her a legion of devoted fans.

Mary's mother, Juliana Charlotte née Hogg – the daughter of a well-known grazier – had given birth to her third child and eldest daughter in Malvern, Victoria, Australia, at the age of twenty-two.

Mary's father was the eminent Supreme Court judge Arthur Wolfe Chomley. Twelve years his wife's senior and originally hailing from Wicklow, Ireland, Justice Chomley was an upstanding and honourable member of the Australian Victorian community; his sense of judicial fair play and serene decisions in the face of the heated debates of the courtroom earned him great respect in legal circles. He was remembered not only for his ability to elicit the truth from witnesses on the stand but also for his copious note-taking and sketching on trial documents during session. Of note was his appointment in 1880 as Assistant Crown Prosecutor in the trial of infamous Irish–Australian bushranger Ned Kelly. One of Arthur's six brothers, Hussey Malone Chomley, was by all accounts an exemplary police officer: he was superintendent of three districts in the colony of Victoria during the Kelly Gang skirmish and later appointed Chief Commissioner of Police.

The teenaged Mary's first claim to fame within family legend was to dive into a creek at the Chomley home, Glenmore – fully clothed in voluminous Victorian layers – to rescue a drowning swimmer, a feat that illuminated a fledgling but deep-seated need to save others, as Florence had done in her role as a Crimean nurse.

In 1889, when Mary was eighteen, her father built Dromkeen[4] at Riddells Creek in Victoria, named for his mother's ancestral home in Tipperary, Ireland. By then Mary had five surviving brothers and sisters – Frederick, Edith, William, Eileen and Aubrey (brothers Arthur and Stawell had died in infancy). Fourteen years separated the eldest from the youngest.

When Mary turned twenty-one, her father financed a trip for her to Burma and India, where she stayed with her uncle, Brigadier General J.H. Barnard, who had commanded Mandalay from 1896. Somehow she persuaded the brigadier to allow her to travel up to the Chinese frontier on elephant-back, accompanied by a *naik* (corporal) and six *sepoys* (soldiers); there she stayed in Buddhist pagodas – unheard of at the time. Admiring a white stone Buddha, she attempted to persuade the abbot to sell it to her, but was refused. However, on departure the next morning, she was already astride her elephant when she was presented with the stone Buddha as a gift by one of the monks.

While staying with another prominent uncle in India who commanded a regiment at Nowshera, near Peshawar, Mary was invited to meet the *Wali* (leader) of the princely State of Swat.[5] Access to and from the State of Swat was typified by narrow roads along sheer cliff-faces, indicating that Mary must have possessed an unusually adventurous spirit for a young upper-class woman of her era.

It was only three or four years later that Mary's mother, Juliana, died at the relatively early age of forty-seven and was buried at Riddells Creek. As was customary, Mary, then twenty-five years of age, as the eldest unmarried daughter, stepped into the role of her father's society hostess.

As she grew older, Mary's connection to the sisterhood burgeoned. She was surrounded by independent, high-achieving women and men within her own family and sought the same within her social circle. It seems inevitable that her exposure to what is now known as feminist ideology would contribute to and shape her own fearless attitudes.

Mary's cousin, Violet Ida Chomley, an outstanding mathematics scholar, was one of the first female graduates of Melbourne

University. She belonged to the Princess Ida Club, a group formed by female students of the university to foster the cause of women by social interaction, debates and literary discussions. Violet defied the conventions of the day by travelling with a female companion from Australia to England via the Philippines, Japan and Russia. Although the trip had been intended as a holiday, she remained in England for the rest of her life, taking up various postings – as a teacher, school principal and a county councillor.

Another cousin, Charles Henry Chomley, a law graduate and later a journalist, edited a gossipy, illustrated weekly magazine called *The Arena*, devoted to the arts, politics and fashionable society. Artist brothers Lionel and Norman Lindsay, who in later years were to become synonymous with the Australian art and literary world, contributed illustrations and cartoons, mainly of a political nature. Charles also went on to write the book *The True Story of the Kelly Gang of Bushrangers* (1900) after his family's involvement in the trial.

It is unknown whether Mary influenced Charles or perhaps it was the other way around but, despite polite Victorian society's resistance to allowing women a voice, *The Arena* took up the suffragette cause, supporting the movement in its articles.

Mary's social circle included yet another woman who thumbed her nose at the era's conventions – prominent feminist artist Violet Teague, who painted thirty-eight-year-old Mary's portrait in 1909. In it Mary appears regal and self-assured.

What with highly educated suffragettes, judges, lawyers, high-ranking military officers, outspoken writers and police officials making up Mary's family and social circle, clearly the Chomleys' orbit was not for the faint-hearted.

Given Mary's influences, it comes as no surprise that in 1907, at the age of thirty-five, she became the Secretary to the Art Section of the Australian Exhibition of Women's Work, which was held in Melbourne over a five-week period. The exhibition was the brainchild of Lady Northcote, wife of the Governor-General, and showcased arts and crafts from needlework to photography by women from all over the world. This led to Mary's involvement in founding the Arts and Crafts Society of Victoria, of which she became Secretary.

Although the exact motivation for Mary's relocation to England at the age of forty-two has been lost in the mists of time, she travelled to London in 1914. Was she bored with her life? Was she seeking a deeper sense of purpose? Perhaps cousin Violet's travels and relocation to England influenced Mary to consider an adventure across the seas. Whatever her motivation, Mary set sail on the *Maloja* in June 1914 with the intention of travelling around Europe for twelve months. Mary wasn't to know she was sailing straight into the gathering storm clouds of the First World War.

Within a month of her arrival, war was declared and Mary found herself caught up in the maelstrom. Like many others, she was galvanised into action to assist the war effort; she took up a posting at the Princess Christian Military Hospital for Officers. By 1917, there were just under 2500 hospitals in the United Kingdom caring for military personnel. Although Mary was not a trained nurse, it's likely she was appointed to a role in which she could flex her sharp administrative skills.

Now forty-three, Mary had flouted the conventions of the day by remaining unmarried; however, she was not alone. Two sisters – Eileen (thirty-five) and Aubrey (thirty-one) – followed Mary to England, the three of them settling together in a shared residence at Victoria Water, Surrey.

A scant four months later, the sisters learned with much sadness that their father had passed away back home in Australia at the age of seventy-seven. Only one of Arthur's brothers, George, now survived.

The *Euroa Advertiser* reported Judge Chomley's death in the 27 November 1914 edition, making special note of his composed courtroom sessions:

> The retirement of Judge Chomley was the occasion for a very cordial expression of goodwill by his colleagues on the bench and by members of the bar. The principal speech was delivered by the late Mr. Purves, K.C., who referred to the conspicuous ability, the untiring industry, and the unfailing courtesy which Judge Chomley displayed. These remarks were supplemented by Mr. (now Judge) Wasley. One of the finest characteristics of the late judge was that nothing disturbed his judicial serenity. In his court displays of ill-temper rarely occurred, as counsel and the parties took their tone from the presiding judge, with the result that trials were always conducted with the greatest decorum.

In October 1915, the news of the execution of British nurse Edith Cavell by the Germans shocked and outraged citizens of the British Empire. Edith and a comrade, who were working in German-occupied Belgium, had been caught assisting British airmen to escape and were subsequently tried, found guilty and sentenced to death before a firing squad. Although Edith had admitted to her crime (though, some say, by coercion) and accepted her fate with dignity, the British government protested their inability to intervene; the English propaganda machine went into overdrive, whipping up a frenzy of aggression against the Germans, with Edith as their martyred poster girl.

The burning embers of anti-German sentiment did not take much to fan into a red-hot furnace. A dramatic and emotive story began to circulate that the commandant attending the execution, outraged by his squad's refusal to shoot the unconscious nurse – who had supposedly fainted at the execution post – had personally dispatched her with a bullet to the head at point blank range. Propaganda postcards depicting this version of events began to circulate, with the intention of inciting fresh anger against the enemy.

The British government's propaganda campaign was highly effective. Young men caught up in the whirl of patriotic, anti-German fervour joined up to take on the 'beastly Hun' and outraged women handed out white feathers – the symbol of cowardice – to any man not in uniform.

Despite the rumours concerning the manner of Edith's death, the fact remains that the British nurse was indeed executed by the Germans.

British women were being urged to respond in ways never before seen. The Pankhurst women, a family of British suffragettes who rallied women to the cause of gender equality, often with aggression and violence, had helped form in Britain the most active feminist movement in Europe. When war was declared, influential matriarch Emmeline Pankhurst saw the Germans as a threat to all humanity. She dropped her suffragette activism and urged women everywhere to get to work while men engaged in combat. It is estimated that more than a million women were formally added to the British workforce between 1914 and 1918.[6]

Mary took up the post of Secretary of the POW Branch of the Australian Branch of the British Red Cross Society (ARC) in 1916. The Australian arm had been formed in August 1914, at the outbreak of war, by the wife of the Australian Governor-General, Lady Munro Ferguson.

In the beginning, most of the staff were female. They worked from 9.30 am to 6 pm, with an hour for lunch between 1 and

Survival

2 pm. The office was in Grosvenor Place, London, and Mary would have been commuting back and forth to Surrey by steam train – even today the trip takes a good 50 minutes one way by car. However, Mary had found her calling, and fell upon her hectic role with gusto.

As an increasing number of servicemen were captured and incarcerated, staff were bombarded with administrative paperwork, but they refused to allow any man to slip forgotten through the cracks if they could avoid it. The ARC were meticulous in keeping track of POWs as they were moved from camp to camp, diligently noting their transfers on index cards as the information came to hand – an enormous undertaking given the ARC alone were coordinating the care of 3853 incarcerated personnel in German camps and 217 in Turkish camps.

Mary took it all in her stride. Her talent for administration, capacity for hard work and sheer dedication to the cause eventually saw Miss Chomley, as she was always respectfully known, wholly responsible for all sections of the Prisoners of War Department.

Mary's duties were wide and varied. In her no-nonsense style, she fielded enquiries from the ARC back in Australia and reported to the Comfort Funds Committees via cablegram as to how their fundraising monies were spent – usually on such items as fruit, eggs and honey. She replied to mounting piles of correspondence in letter and postcard form from POWs, facilitating their requests with due haste, lifting their flagging spirits and answering the call to locate missing relatives back home.

No matter how weary or overworked, Mary wrote to the POWs with compassion and kindness, instinctively understanding the heartache at the separation from their families, and the humiliation of POW life. She encouraged them to keep their spirits up, extending the hand of friendship and providing a voice of comfort as they faced the uncertainty of what might lie ahead through bleak winters and stifling summers, never knowing when or if the war was going to end – or if they'd survive.

When Australian pilot Lieutenant Alec Couston was shot through the jaw attempting to go over the wire at Holzminden with fellow Australian 2nd Lieutenant Cyril Fenton, Mary wrote on 6 November 1918:

Dear Mr Couston,
I have just received some news of you and am dreadfully sorry to hear you have been hurt. I think it is so plucky of you to make these attempts and it seems so hard that they so seldom succeed. I hope your wounds have been well looked after and that you will soon be better, as the time is coming very soon for you all to come home. We will send you some special parcels of invalid food, as they may be better for you than the ordinary kind, but I am afraid they will be so long in reaching you that I hope you will be on the way to recovery before you get them . . .

★

When Holzminden received its first guests in September 1917, the German populace was suffering the ill effects of three long years of the British naval blockade of Germany. The blockade, which had been put in place by Britain and the Allied powers immediately upon Germany's declaration of war, as planned, had completely shut down the flow of food and agricultural supplies to Germany from the USA. Not only had Germans been forced to tighten their belts but also, as the years wore on and nutritious food became scarce, food prices skyrocketed and the population – including the Holzminden guards – was forced to substitute their diets with poor alternatives, resulting in many deaths from malnutrition.

Survival

When Reg Gough arrived in the camp, he recalled:

We went up to see what kind of lunch the Germans were going give us. The menu consisted of 5 courses, though not knowing the language we were unable to decide what was to come. Anyhow soup was there in a large pot and we went to help ourselves. Then we found we had to buy our crockery and cutlery from the canteen at fairly fancy prices. When we came back the soup was still there, but decidedly cooler. We managed to get some of it down though it was not too tasty, and waited for the next course. The older prisoners, expecting this, had come in to lunch for a change, but merely sat and talked at their tables. Then one asked why we were waiting and of course we said, for the next ration to come along. Then it was explained to us in a very nice way that the menu card ran something like this: soup, meat, potatoes, butter (I query this last commodity) and prunes.

AND THE WHOLE LOT HAD BEEN IN THE SOUP.

The food shortage naturally flowed down to British and Allied prisoners held in Germany's camps. Reg further recalled the German bread with a mix of disgust and typical POW humour:

German bread was most unpalatable, and usually kept for fire wood as when hard it made excellent fuel. Once the Huns raided all the rooms and carted off the spare bread we had stored for our stoves and began to burn them in the cooking stoves . . . the [German] fellow who had the job of stoking had been shovelling a loaf at a time into the stove before he realised that an officer behind his back was just as quickly taking them out again, throwing them to his pals who went off to hide them more securely. It was only when he began to wonder how many more loaves the stove was going to take that he jumped to the ruse. Then he lost a few more out of the sack while he recovered from the shock.

The German authorities were obliged to keep the POWs fed but were struggling in the titanic wake of the blockade. The prisoners subsisted on the same food as the local population, only the internees had the benefit of receiving Red Cross food parcels. Then again, German pilfering was a common practice. Often, after the obligatory parcel inspection by the guards, a POW might receive a tin full of sawdust instead of biscuits or find cigarettes missing from a pack.

The queues were endless. Parcels from the Red Cross and home were delivered to the parcel room and the prisoners were required to line up for hours to receive them. But not before the German parcel room attendants had opened and decimated the contents of every package in the search for contraband. Tinned meat from the Red Cross was opened and sliced into tiny chunks, which meant that the prisoners had to eat it quickly or it would spoil.

Roland Corbett said:

> Of course our parcels were most essential and they were given out when the Boche felt inclined and consequently accumulated in their thousands, which awaited their sweet will to sort while we stood waiting in the endless queues for weary hours daily, often in piercing cold and wet. Every tiny thing received in our parcels was closely examined, soup squares even cut in pieces and almost eggs broken up. Officers were not even allowed to go into the tin office or touch their tins till they had been opened and cut up . . . Weeks went by and life was one long strafe. Snow and frost set in early and one was kept standing hours on Appel or in long queues for a parcel which often ended in a box of dog biscuits.

Survival

Reg remembered:

> Every parcel was opened by the Germans and all packets, such as tea, sugar etc, stabbed several times with a long skewer before being handed over to the prisoner. All tins were stored by them until they were demanded, when they would be opened by the Germans and the contents given to us on plates.

Often parcels were handed to inmates with items missing, and many believed the Germans had pocketed them. However, twenty-four-year-old Captain Maxwell Gore of the 50th Battalion, Australian Imperial Force, seemed to see it differently, saying:

> Another thing I would say on behalf of the Germans is that, although a lot of the parcels became lost in transit, few of us blamed the Germans but rather our own base wallah[7] heroes. Personally I found them honest as regards property, particularly if it was of Red Cross origin – a fact of which they prided themselves.

Twenty-three-year-old Lieutenant George William Mumford of No. 11 Squadron was a Port of London Authority clerk who had joined the RFC via the Mounted Military Police and British Army Service Corp. He developed a loathing of camp food after witnessing – along with many others – the stomach-churning sight of a horse's head floating in the stew cauldron. Red cabbage, a tasteless staple, fared no better in his estimation.

Charles Bernard also had vivid recollections of the food:

> There was a dining room on the top floor of each house, where meals were served once a day. Food consisted of stew, every day. This stew was merely a soap-suddy broth of potatoes in liquid form

interspersed with carrots at frequent intervals. A careful search sometimes revealed a piece of meat of doubtful character – probably horse-meat – but very few of us took advantage of the provender provided, and we relied entirely on our parcels from home. Occasionally, a longing for fresh vegetables made us poke about in the stew tub, but the taste was horrible and it was necessity rather than inclination that prompted us to act in this undignified way.

Captain Lyon Hatton of the Royal West Kent Regiment, whose sister married a fellow Holzminden POW after the war, attempted to grow his own nourishment when he received a packet of spinach seeds from home. Finding a spare patch of soil, the thirty-year-old planted the seeds, promising to share with his starving fellow officers. They eagerly awaited the spinach patch's maturity, their mouths watering at the thought of tucking into a plate of fresh greenery. But when the leaves were boiled, the spinach did what spinach does when it's cooked – it shrank to a tiny green pile: there was barely a teaspoon each to go around.

Of the canteen ritual, Reg remembered:

One day I went to the canteen to buy two articles which amounted to the equivalent of 7/6 and I handed over a note to the value of 10/-. The old chap in the canteen went away, muttering '7/6 . . . 2/6 . . . 7/6 . . . 2/6' and so on, but he got them mixed and came back with [change of] 7/6. I cleared off as soon as I could. There were 600 officers in the camp, and the chap had a poor memory for faces.

Reg went on to explain how the men restricted their purchase of over-priced goods from the Germans on principle, although this was relaxed for birthdays, which were embraced as an occasion for celebration. It was expected that the birthday boy would cough up for canteen wine to share around. Hence, a deceptive system developed:

> Ration cards were issued for wine. On festive occasions, the donor of the feast would ask some of his pals to sell their ration to him. Each owner of a card would go to the canteen to buy a bottle, taking a pal with him. The bottle would be handed to him, the card taken from him to be stamped, whereupon the pal hops off with the bottle. The canteen storekeeper returns the card, is asked for the wine and promptly hands over another bottle. This almost invariably occurred if the wine buyer was aware of this trick.

To compensate for the lack of adequate nutrition in the camps, three Red Cross comfort parcels per fortnight were sent to each POW, labelled X, Y and Z in order to keep track of consignments and what was sent to whom. The parcels were all funded by private donations made directly to the ARC and cost approximately 10/-[8] each. They typically contained tea, powdered milk, sugar, oatmeal, rice, barley, vegetables, tinned meat or fish, jam and butter, dripping or margarine, biscuits, cheese and concentrated soups. Every week, bread was sent directly from Berne, Switzerland, and tobacco and cigarettes – highly prized items – were diligently supplied in fortnightly shipments. Parcels were at first sent via American Express, then due to delivery delays, the ARC began utilising the parcel post system. With petty theft rife and a wartime mail system innately insecure, the ARC saw the wisdom in insuring the 11-pound (5kg) parcels 'against all risks', and quickly struck a deal with the Union Assurance Society Ltd, negotiating a per parcel rate, plus a brokerage stamp fee.

The Prisoners of War Department also received a landslide of requests for slightly more exotic foodstuffs than a POW would normally expect to find in his regular parcel – stewed kidneys, pilchards, Bovril (a thick salty meat extract), Slades toffee, Nestlé's milk, cured bacon, Ovaltine chocolate milk mix, licorice, split peas, soup cubes, Quaker oats, OXO cubes, spearmint chewing gum, orange marmalade . . . and, quite extraordinarily, *foie gras*. One incarcerated youngster, about to turn twenty-one, even poignantly requested a birthday cake.

Friends and family were permitted to send parcels, but were required to apply to do so. Parcel content was tightly controlled in order to avoid contraband items, which would ultimately be detected and confiscated by the German camp parcel inspectors. The ARC was keen to avoid offending the Germans, for fear of reprisals against the POWs. Consequently the men were only permitted to request items through the ARC, and were instructed not to appeal directly to family and friends in their letters and postcards home.

Upon capture, the ARC equipped the servicemen with a full uniform set, including a greatcoat and boots. Uniform suppliers such as Harry Hall, a company that promoted itself as *the* naval, military, mufti and sporting tailor in Oxford Street, were kept constantly busy with orders as the numbers of captured servicemen swelled. Mary and her team secured individual sizes from the Personal Records Office, placing orders on behalf of each POW – overcoats, boots, gloves, inner soles, balaclavas, underclothes, belts, braces and the Australian Imperial Force rising sun badge.

Mary instituted a subscription program whereby active units, battalions and squadrons could elect to pay a sum of money for the Red Cross to purchase books for Australian POWs. Some units were proactive in raising funds; others (who had no men in captivity) were not. However, the war ended before the scheme got up and running properly, and the funds raised were re-allocated for returning prisoner welfare.

The men, craving contact and the familiarity of Australia, bombarded Mary with queries about their favourite sporting teams back home, and were always impatient to know the winner of the Melbourne Cup, Australia's premier horse race, which ran in November each year. Mary would diligently investigate and reply with the answers.

There were some who wrote frequently, not saying anything in particular nor requesting special items – they simply desired contact from Mary. In the absence of traceable family, sometimes Mary was all a POW had on the outside.

One serviceman poignantly wrote:

> You ask if there is anything special which I need. There is one thing above all that I would like. If you have a piece of Ali Baba's magic carpet on hand, I would be pleased if you would send it per return . . .

Scratch not very far below the surface of this seemingly light-hearted request and one can sense the longing to be lifted above the misery of POW life and to be home with loved ones again.

Although some POWs were fortunate enough to be imprisoned in a camp where they were treated decently, those in the worst camps – including Holzminden – were unable to write to Mary openly of how they suffered at the hands of their German captors. It was pointless complaining as the German camp censors would simply black out or dissolve offending or revealing words.

Mary honed the skill of reading between the lines and she understood the conditions under which they were living. With the heart of a saviour, she was zealous in her care and attention of the POWs, and they in turn developed a dependency on her contact with them, often writing in code in order to convey information they didn't want the censors to catch.

Letters and postcards almost always began with the salutation, 'Dear Miss Chomley . . .'

In the absence of letters from home, Mary brought hope. The POWs took comfort in the knowledge that someone on the outside was relentless in her efforts to alleviate their suffering. She gained such a reputation as an angel of mercy that at camp mail time, not only did the Australian POWs rush to see if their dear Miss Chomley had written, but also prisoners from other countries joined the letter and parcel queue in the hope of receiving word from her.

What they didn't realise was that their angel of mercy had a pair of fangs which she wasn't afraid to bare in the direction of bureaucrats who got between her and her solicitous care of the men. In one letter to the Secretary of the Prisoners of War Committee in Thurlow Place, London, she wrote with feeling:

> . . . we have reason to believe our parcels are tampered with in transit – old worn out coats being substituted for new ones; old odd boots of different sizes being put in and other alterations made, which are not done at the German end . . .

Whoever was behind them – and suspicion must have fallen on the British postal service – the thefts were organised and heartless, their net effect demoralising. The emotional support from Mary was critical to the POWs' survival – almost more so than attending to their physical deprivation – for the human mind can cling to life tenaciously, even when the physical body is failing. She steadfastly wrote to the men, her words of comfort helping to alleviate the depression, humiliation, deprivation, boredom, shell shock, grief and anxiety experienced by the prisoners. No-one knew when the war would be over; in the meantime, their days at the hands of their German captors stretched into a distant horizon with no discernible end.

Not only did Mary write to the POWs to 'keep their chins up', but she also faithfully responded to correspondence from anxious family members seeking word of imprisoned loved ones. Over the duration of the war, Mary hand-wrote thousands of letters and typed just as many again in an official capacity on a rickety old typewriter.

The pressures of her role often exacted their toll on Mary, but she took it all in apparent good humour. In August 1918, she attempted to take a short holiday but, as she reported in a letter to Sister Connie Parish, fiancée of Australian Holzminden POW Captain George Guyatt 'Guy' Gardiner, with whom she was corresponding:

> . . . my attempt at an annual holiday was not a great success. I went to the other end of England on Friday and got a wire on Saturday morning to come back! I returned on Tuesday, much more tired with travelling than when I went away . . .

The ARC headquarters also became the post office and banking centre at which the POWs' correspondence and financial affairs were managed. Family members visiting London often dropped in to meet the dedicated team who were doing so much to keep their imprisoned loved one alive and spirits uplifted.

The words written by one POW indicate the effect that Mary had on the men, the gratitude they felt and how highly she was regarded. A POW's sister had called upon Mary at the ARC office and, after noting the wall papered with photographs of the POWs with whom Mary kept in contact, she wrote to her imprisoned brother of Mary's dedication.

In response, the POW wrote to Mary, saying:

My sister tells me she called upon you when in London. She is full of admiration for you all. I had hardly realised before how seriously you had made our welfare yours.

However, while English families could physically pay a visit to the London office of the Red Cross, those in the cities and towns across the expansive British territories were unable to do so.

With limited letters allowed out of camps and delivery slow, it was nothing short of an emotional rollercoaster ride for families back home as they anxiously waited for word from the military authorities, the Red Cross or their imprisoned relative as to the location and wellbeing of their loved one.

Four

Air, Sea and Land

Most of the Holzminden inmates were Royal Flying Corps (RFC) aviators, but the camp also held servicemen from the army and navy as well as merchant mariners. Prisoners hailed from Britain and her far-flung dominions, including Australia, New Zealand, Canada, India, Argentina and South Africa.

At the outbreak of the war, the Royal Navy immediately cut off Germany's access to the Atlantic Ocean for the duration of the conflict and eight months beyond to prevent the supply of food, a move that eventually brought Germany to its knees. Meanwhile, the Royal Navy, which had been in existence since the sixteenth century, shouldered the responsibility of transporting arms, food and raw materials to the United Kingdom as well providing sea-based defence throughout the conflict.

The RFC was the air arm of the British Army, providing support including aerial photography and bombing raids, and engaging the enemy in aerial combat. Many of the RFC pilots who entered prisoner-of-war camps exited as Royal Air Force (RAF) pilots – the service changed its name on 1 April 1918 as a result of the amalgamation of the RFC and Royal Naval Air Service (RNAS).

Despite the high mortality rate of wartime pilots, the RFC was considered the cream of the services. Many a soldier serving on the battlefield gazed wistfully skyward, imagining himself behind the controls of a fighter, soaring high above the mud and slush of the trenches. The skies offered adventure and glamour, but generally only those from the educated, privileged classes were accepted as trainee pilots.

New Zealander 2nd Lieutenant Edgar Henry Garland gained entry into that elite group at just twenty-one. The dashing Edgar had graduated from the New Zealand Flying School established in October 1915 in Auckland by aircraft designers and brothers Leo and Vivian Walsh. The brothers provided comprehensive, intensive training and turned out Royal Aero Club-qualified pilots ready for the RFC in Britain. Keith Caldwell, a local pilot trained earlier by the Walsh brothers, went on to distinguish himself with the RFC after becoming a highly decorated fighter ace in the First World War and rising to the rank of air commodore in the Second World War.

Edgar was one of four eager students training at the controls of Walsh brothers' flying boats – aircraft modelled on the Curtiss design by the aviator siblings, but modified with dual controls to accommodate instructor and student.

A Wellington College old boy, Edgar was an avid and vivid writer. He kept up a flow of letters to his proud parents, who then handed them over to the local newspaper for publication throughout his training.

In a Wellington *Evening Post* article of 4 October 1916, written by Edgar before he left for England, he observes that the North Island community 'show very little enthusiasm for aviation'. The Auckland flying school was getting by with just two machines, leaving little margin for trainee error: the school relied upon the pupils' safe handling of the aircraft. A second flying school, funded by local investors with deep pockets, was soon to be established in the South Island and stocked with several aircraft. In the article, Edgar exhorts his fellow North Islanders to share his enthusiasm for his own flying training *alma mater*, pointing out that with four aircraft, they could train twice as many pilots for the war effort.

Eloquent with the pen and charged with youthful passion, Edgar beseeched potential investors to:

> . . . consider the perfection of flying. Will not the happiness of the world be infinitely increased when every man can indeed vie with the birds for the mastery of the air? Does that not spell happiness and freedom?

It is not known if young Edgar's fervent pleading actually swayed anyone to prise open their wallets and give till it hurt, but he signed off by saying:

> And the day of at least a partial realisation of that dream is but a very short way off. If proof were needed of this, glance at the recent history of flying. Only four or five years have passed since the 'dark ages' of aviation, when flying was an uncertainty – when it was impossible to predict whether or not a man would even manage to coax his machine off the ground. What an extraordinary contrast we witness today!

Besides being quite the wordsmith, it seems that young Edgar had a magnificent physique, which someone in the art world had not failed to notice. Blond, bristling with biceps and with a chiselled face like Adonis, the charismatic Edgar posed nude for Wellington-based portrait photographer Stanley Polkinghorne Andrew in 1916, with little more than a far-off stare and a strategically placed rifle. He gazes upwards with a stoic expression – could he have been wishing he was at the controls of an airborne flying boat rather than standing naked in front of a camera? Or was he just as appreciative of his own physical charms as the art students who would use the photographs to render his likeness on paper in art class?

The same photographer took photos of Edgar, clothed this time in his military uniform, prior to his departure. He was also photographed with three other unidentified uniformed men, most probably his fellow flying-school cohorts.[1]

Now a qualified aviator, eldest son Edgar bid goodbye to his parents, Frank Le Manquais and Laura Garland (née Gibson), his sister, Eunice, and two brothers, Harold (John) and Frank, and boarded a ship bound for England. In early 1917, he was commissioned into the RFC and for the next three months threw himself into the business of pilot training in such aircraft as the Farman, a machine initially intended for reconnaissance but now used for instruction. The Farmans were a series of 8-cylinder biplanes with single pusher Renault engines designed by a pair of English brothers, Maurice and Henri, who later became French citizens.

Edgar was clearly unimpressed by the Farman's abilities, complaining in a letter home, dated 2 March 1917, that:

> . . . my machine was rocked about so much to-day with the air currents that if I had not been strapped in I could not have stayed in my seat. These machines [the Farmans] are the most dangerous of all to fly, as they have no natural stability, and you dare not leave the controls go for a second . . . the instability of the Farmans is shown by the fact that in this school alone, five men have been killed in nine weeks. The day before yesterday, one poor fellow 'nose-dived' about 600ft and was killed . . .

The young pilot's concerns about the stability of his aircraft were tempered by excitement about his own incredible flying achievements. In the same letter he writes:

. . . Thursday was the greatest day of my life. I went out for forty minutes with an instructor and made seven good landings. When I got back, I was congratulated and was told I would now have to go out by myself in a single-seater Maurice Farman. So, I went up and circled around the aerodrome and made a good landing without breaking anything . . . the Squadron Commander was very pleased . . . all the mechanics and other pupils wondered where I'd come from . . . passed my examination for machine gunnery, wireless and aerial observation and I am now going to be posted to an advanced position . . .

Trainee pilots were notorious for 'breaking things' – generally the aircraft's undercarriage. Edgar added in that letter that he was in the top five per cent of pupils – those who had landed the aircraft intact each time. His safety record soon drew the attention of the commanding officer, who recognised the young pilot's superior flying skills and nudged him towards even greater achievements.

The squadron boasted more than eighty training biplanes of varying models, a far cry from the tiny and underfunded two-beast stable back in Auckland. Edgar was like a child in a candy store, enthusing in his letters about the magnificent aircraft that came and went from the aerodrome, no doubt dreaming of the day he would earn a place behind the controls of a sleek thoroughbred rather than a broken-down old nag.

All the while, the Wellington *Evening Post* was following its home-grown hero's every move with devotion, publishing the letters Edgar sent to his family in the suburb of Oriental Bay. Even an English college football match in which he broke his leg was duly reported. Scout pilots (so named for the model of their aircraft, the Scout) of the day were considered dashing, brave and patriotic. No doubt local people clamoured to know as many details as possible, and the Garlands would have been proud to hand their golden-haired boy's letters to the press.

Edgar and his creative writing talents must have been every editor's dream; the newspaper frequently quoted his adventures verbatim, rarely needing to write a word themselves.

In his letters, Edgar presents as an adrenalin junkie who not only fearlessly obeyed any order by his flight instructors but also grasped the importance of performing with excellence to attract the attention of his superiors.

In a letter dated 8 April 1917, he wrote:

> Unless a pilot shows he has no fear in the air, especially when he has been told to do a certain thing by his flight commander, they will not have a very good opinion of you.

The *Evening Post* readers must have been spellbound by Edgar's descriptions of his life as a trainee pilot in England; indeed they provide a rare insight into what it was like to be a First World War pilot behind the controls of a biplane held together by . . . well, not much. In the same letter, Edgar recalls the sensations, the thrill and the heart-stopping danger of flight:

> Captain Beatty, our flight commander, is known as the 'human bird'. He told me to go up 3000ft and stall my engine, which is much more exciting to do than looping-the-loop. On my descent after my altitude test, when at the height of 5000ft I pushed the control forward, and dived my machine about 200ft, and then pulled it right back. The nose shot up vertically, and instead of going right over the loop, my machine stopped just before it got to the top. Every sound stopped during that moment and my speed indicator registered nothing. Then she slid back, tail first, but not

very far, and flattened out for a few seconds – and still there was no sound. Then suddenly the nose dropped absolutely vertical and I was looking straight down at the ground, and the faint sound of air whistling through the wires commenced, till in a few seconds it was a roar past my ears and a screaming noise was audible. I dived like this for about 500ft and then my controls began to act and she came out of the dive in a glorious upward swoop. The wonderful sensation is the sudden drop at the commencement of the dive, and the great feeling of the cushion of air on the plane . . .

And he hadn't even reached a combat zone.

Despite his excellent safety record, Edgar did manage to nose-dive his beast during a particularly rough landing, snapping the propeller and denting the airframe slightly. Although he thumped his head, he was grateful for the reinforcing steel frame that kept him from serious injury, fobbing off the accident as a 'mere trifle'.

The young pilot didn't devote his literary talents exclusively to death-defying airborne manoeuvres and hair-raising landing strip accidents. He also shared his poetic observations of the stunning English countryside:

One thing you notice when flying over England is the large number of hedges. All fields have hedges or trees around them, and the landscape looks like a quilt made up of scrap pieces of rag . . .

Between February and March 1917, Edgar served with the 8 Reserve Squadron (RS), 55 RS and 34 RS, graduating on 7 May as a flying officer. He undertook a two-week course at the School of Aerial Fighting and Gunnery before being assigned and sent to France with No. 66 Squadron RFC.

Edgar been there only a short time when the engine of his Sopwith Pup (more formally known as a Sopwith Scout) failed while his squadron was on a mission over Belgium, and he was forced to land near Ostend.

He recalled later in a letter:

> I made a bad landing on the beach in very shallow water in front of Middlekerke and felt that I was going to crash into stone breastwork. The most remarkable thing of all was that although there were hundreds of German soldiers and guns along the waterfront, not one of them fired a single shot and it was not until I loosened my belt and attempted to destroy my machine that they came charging down with fixed bayonets . . . I was brought before a naval officer and a German Major. They were politeness personified – saluted me first and said in English, 'Hard luck.'

Hard luck indeed, particularly since Edgar found himself standing at the business end of a cluster of fixed bayonets on that sparkling summer's day in August 1917.

Frank Garland was notified by cablegram that his son had been taken as a prisoner of war by the Germans. Frank suddenly found himself faced with an awkward, bureaucratic system which demanded that Edgar, as a New Zealand officer commissioned into the British forces, be 'adopted' by the New Zealand Prisoners of War Department. This then allowed the Garland family to despatch parcels and monetary support to him in the camp. Frank wrote to the authorities in October 1917, applying for permission to 'adopt' his own son via the system. Once approved, Frank was then required, on a weekly basis, to organise an international money order in the amount of 10 shillings, which was then forwarded to the High Commissioner for New Zealand in London to contribute towards Edgar's upkeep.

The young pilot was incarcerated in several POW camps in quick succession, including Ströhen, Saarbrucken, Kahlsruhe, Dulraen, Hesepe and Saarlouis, making determined escape attempts from most of them – all which inevitably ended in disappointing recapture.

A particularly bold effort – probably from Ströhen POW camp – involved Edgar and three accomplices disguising themselves as German Landsturmers, a common trick employed by POWs. They simply walked out past the guardroom and gate sentries, who mistook them for their own soldiers. The escapees' elation was short-lived, however. A German officer stopped them and quizzed Edgar as to their unit; the German-speaking pilot replied that they were from the 77th Landsturms. They might have got away with it but for the officer checking the contents of their sacks, which contained Red Cross tinned food. The officer surmised correctly that the tins belonged to English officers, and the four were promptly marched back to camp.

Edgar and his fellow escapees were thrown into solitary confinement with threats of courts-martial ringing in their ears. Undeterred, they formed a link with a willing new collaborator – a bribable guard who loathed the Kommandant – but before they could launch this second escape plan, the four were unexpectedly transferred to another camp.

Edgar kept up a steady stream of dedicated escape efforts. He and an accomplice managed to escape one camp, crawling across the terrain for nearly 3 miles (4.8km) to avoid German patrols, covering the distance in around four hours. During their eight nights on the run, they swam the River Ems at three o'clock one morning. The pair managed to cross into Dutch territory but, lost and disoriented, they wandered back into Germany again, where they were cornered by a German soldier as they climbed a stile while heading towards a farmhouse.

As Edgar's escape attempts continued, he became quite adept at impersonating members of the German military and locals – his blond Germanic appearance and linguistic abilities enabled him to blend in beautifully with his surroundings. With varying degrees of success, he managed to confound the enemy with his disguises as German officers, Landsturm soldiers and Dutch civilians.[2]

His relentless attempts to flee finally earned him a one-way ticket to Holzminden to join the ranks of other serial escapees.

★

At Holzminden Edgar met fellow New Zealander, the diminutive thirty-five-year-old Lieutenant William Henry Dean Gardner, who had been the navigator aboard a Royal Navy Q-ship (a heavily armed gunboat disguised as a merchant vessel) sunk by a German submarine.

Dean, as he was known, was born in Belfast, Northern Ireland, on 11 February 1883. The siren's call of the sea saw him take up a posting as a fourteen-year-old cadet. Among other duties, he was required to shimmy up the perilous rigging of late nineteenth-century tall ships. His salty travels brought him to New Zealand, where he settled ... to a degree.

When the First World War broke out, more than 14,000 New Zealand men volunteered in the first week. By the time of the proclamation of the National Registration Act of 1915, all men between the ages of seventeen and sixty were required to register their particulars. This was merely a civil register designed to ascertain resources, but penalties were stiff for non-registration or false statements – a NZ£100 fine or six months imprisonment. It was impressed upon the New Zealand population that civil registration was an obligation, and there was strenuous encouragement for men of an age to enlist, although this stopped short of actual conscription. This move attracted only a 30 per cent volunteer enlistment rate.

The sea was in Dean's blood. Prior to his capture, he had been travelling through England in civilian disguise under orders of the Royal Navy's Special Service and was not permitted to divulge his mission to anyone. While en route to the training facility, he had run the gauntlet of the White Feather Brigade – women who felt it their patriotic duty to bully men out of civvies and into uniform by presenting them with the white feather of cowardice. Getting about in civilian clothing in polite English society posed a problem for men of combatant age during the First World War. If he wasn't quick enough to dodge the disapproving onslaught, he could expect to be presented with a white feather.

By the time thirty-four-year-old Dean had reached his destination of Liverpool, England, in January 1917 he had silently amassed a collection of three white feathers.

In January 1915, several months after the outbreak of the war, Dean was appointed Chief Officer of the Union Steamship Company. Although the role placed him in a position to assist the war effort without joining up, something impelled him to voluntarily enlist in the New Zealand Army, which he did in January 1916. By then, the pro-conscription and the anti-conscription lobbies were at loggerheads, with the New Zealand government dithering between the factions. When conscription was up for serious discussion in the New Zealand corridors of power later in 1916, only four MPs opposed it. Later that year, conscription for Pakeha[3] was introduced to shore up reinforcements. This was subsequently opened up to include Maori.[4] The introduction of conscription saw thousands of the country's men fed to the war machine, with a total of 120,000 having served by war's end.

Unenlisted men of fighting age were made to feel like 'shirkers'[5] and perhaps this pressure goes some way to explaining Dean's decision to join up. Or maybe his inherently adventurous nature had simply got the better of him. It seems that one couldn't nail his boots to the boards for too long.

Upon acceptance into the army, Dean tendered his resignation to the Union Steamship Company and by February 1916, the seafaring man previously accustomed to giving orders as a ship's master was now a landlubber taking them.

He was promoted to lance corporal, then corporal, but as per New Zealand Expeditionary Force Regulations, these promotions were rescinded on transfer 'to the field'. Subsequently assigned to 1st Battalion, Wellington Regiment, Private Dean Gardner boarded the *Tofua* on 26 May 1916 under the command of Major Hickey and was finally en route to England.

After disembarking at Devonport on 27 July 1916, Dean marched 122 miles (196km) with fellow New Zealand troops to Sling Camp at Salisbury Plain to undertake further training.

But barely a week had gone by when Dean was charged with overstaying his leave on the night of 2 August 1916. Due back at midnight, he had not returned to Sling until the unforgiveable hour of 9.15 the following morning. It seems that the thirty-three-year-old Dean had fallen hard and very, very fast for a local sixteen-year-old girl, Doris Elizabeth Williams, the daughter of assurance agent Benjamin and his wife, Florence Williams. It's not known where they met exactly, as the port and training camp was in the south and the Williams's home in West Derby was in the north. Perhaps the family were visiting Devonport when Dean disembarked and the star-crossed lovers had briefly met before the Kiwi officer's transfer to Salisbury Plain.

Wherever or however they met, they were immediately smitten with one another, if their lightning-strike elopement was any indication. It's probable that Dean's disappearance coincided with his wedding night as the military charge levelled against him for overstaying his leave was dismissed.

It would have been an interesting physical pairing, as Dean clocked in at 5 foot 4 inches (1.63m) while Doris towered over him at 5 foot 9 inches (1.75m). Disproportionate heights notwithstanding, Doris's parents did not take too kindly to their schoolgirl daughter's elopement, and Mr Williams had the marriage annulled without delay.

By 29 August 1916, Dean had arrived in England for battle training, married in secret, had the marriage dissolved from under him by his bride's irate father and been transferred to Etaples military camp in France, leaving behind Doris – who was now no longer his wife – in England.

Training at Etaples involved assault courses designed to strengthen the offensive fighting abilities of the troops before they came face-to-mud with the real thing in the slush of the Western Front.

Resentment was a dish served piping hot at Etaples Camp. It was otherwise known as 'the bull ring', so named for the disciplinary 'bull' heaped on the trainees by the permanent personnel, who drew their subordinates' scorn for having landed themselves comfortable jobs well out of the way of actual danger. The animosity between recruits and trainers ran so thick and strong that the newly trained troops heading off to war typically vowed to shoot any instructor who should ever have the misfortune to be posted to their unit.

Dean eventually made it to the Western Front, catching the tail end of the Battle of the Somme in France, and when most of the troops had left the skirmish by 5 October 1916, Dean and the other men of his unit were sent as reinforcements to Armentières.

But he wasn't to tarry there long either. He received a commission into the Royal Naval Reserve, although exactly how this came about is unclear.

His grandson Ron Gardner muses:

Whilst the New Zealand Expeditionary Force did release soldiers for duty with other services, these transfers weren't common as the NZEF was having difficulty keeping their forces up to strength and preferred to keep their own people. It is possible that, as a merchant mariner, [my grandfather, Dean Gardner] was already a Royal Navy Reserve Officer and was called up for duty by the Royal Navy, in which case it would be unlikely that the NZEF would stop the transfer.

My view, however, is that he just didn't like being bombed, shot at and having no status. He therefore did everything he could to get back to the life he knew best and where he was comfortable. This just seems to fit with his personality . . .

After the silver-tongued Dean seemingly sweet-talked his way back to England via Etaples in November 1916, he embarked upon service as a lieutenant in the Royal Navy – back on the high seas to the life he knew well.

The Royal Navy had instigated a program that involved obtaining ordinary merchant vessels such as trawlers and colliers, outfitting them with hidden armaments and sending them out as enemy decoys. Guns were disguised among cargo and behind ports in the ship's superstructure; to complete the deception, they were manned by crews decked out in merchant marine uniforms. The purpose of these Q-ships was to attract German U-boat attention with their non-military appearance, and as the enemy got closer to the harmless-looking vessels, all hell broke loose as the weaponry sprang into action. The covert and dangerous program was to attain a certain measure of success, but was not quite the great triumph the Royal Navy intended.

After eight weeks' training at the navy gunnery school at Whale Island, near Portsmouth in Hampshire, Dean was assigned to HMS *Warner*, or Q27. The Q-ship program was naturally top secret and it was under this veil of secrecy that he travelled to Liverpool to take up his posting.

Commander Thomas Wyburn Biddlecombe, a distinguished Australian naval officer with a Royal Navy commission, was the master of the *Warner*, a 1273-ton former cargo ship that had been built in 1911. On 17 January 1917, the *Warner* steamed out of the port of Liverpool with Commander Biddlecombe at the helm and Lieutenant Gardner as navigating officer to commence duties as a decoy ship in the Atlantic Ocean.

The first eight weeks or so of the *Warner*'s operation were relatively uneventful, but early on the morning of 13 March 1917, as the ship was steaming through the Western Approaches to Ireland, a German U-boat (*U-61*) managed to approach the *Warner* unsighted.

Kapitänleutnant Victor Dieckmann, the U-boat's commander, had been observing the *Warner*'s erratic course with a keen eye. In his *Kriegstagebuch* (war diary), the captain wrote of his suspicions, which ultimately proved correct:

Superstructure like a small passenger steamer with no markings. About 1500t. She is making completely pointless changes of course

and strikes me as very small for this area. Therefore suspicious.
I believe she is a trap-ship . . .

The *Kapitänleutnant*'s reasoning proved to be sound. At 8.50 am, the U-boat closed in and fired torpedo rounds on the *Warner*. The vessel was no match and within four minutes, the *Warner* was sinking with all hands. Crew members Lieutenant F.J. Yuile and Chief Petty Officer Sims later reported their attempts to get as many as possible of the crew into the port and starboard lifeboats.

According to Dean's later account, he went down with the ship, but the vessel was blown back to the surface by a boiler explosion. In the story of his ordeal published on 8 January 1935 in the Wellington *Evening Post* back home, he wrote:

> . . . there was quite a sea running. I was clinging to a small bunker hatch with another man. The submarine came to the surface and headed straight for us and ran us down – went over the top of us . . . the next thing I remember was being in the submarine. I found later they had taken the other men – six of them. One was badly wounded – his jaw was shattered and his thigh fractured . . .

Eleven others are believed to have drowned. Yuile, aboard a lifeboat with the other survivors, was informed apologetically by the German U-boat captain that he was unable to take on any more due to the limitations of space in the submarine.

In his *Kriegstagebuch*, Kapitänleutnant Dieckmann's prisoner shopping list noted:

1 Lieutenant, the ship's Navigating Officer
1 Radio Telegraphist/Chief Petty Officer
1 Able Seaman

2 Stokers and
1 Officer's Steward

He again correctly presumed that these men were not merchant mariners who had come from Africa as they claimed, and described them as:

> . . . all men of strikingly good military appearance . . . dignified and composed bearing, unlike any steamer crew seen before in such circumstances . . .

Eventually the captured prisoners gave up clinging to their improbable story and admitted they were personnel of the Royal Navy.

With all torpedoes expended and no way to defend the U-boat if attacked, Kapitänleutnant Dieckmann set a course for home, leaving behind two lifeboats full of survivors.[6]

Dean told his son many years later that his treatment at the hands of Kapitänleutnant Dieckmann was 'very good'. The German commander offered his own cabin to the navigating officer in deference to his prisoner's officer status.

The U-boat first docked in the major German naval base of Heligoland, an island 44 miles (71km) off the coast of Germany. The prisoners were then relocated to Cuxhaven on the north coast, where they were processed before being transferred to permanent accommodation.

Dean was transferred to a series of POW camps – Karlsruhe, Crefeld and Schwarmstedt – before coming to rest in Holzminden.

★

While aviators were being shot from the sky and sailors plucked from torpedoed ships, tens of thousands of foot soldiers were being captured on the battlefield. In March or April 1918, a handsome, quiet British officer of regal bearing was transferred to Holzminden. The twenty-eight-year-old had not attempted a previous escape but as a relatively new camp, Holzminden was beginning to accept spill-over from other facilities already bursting at the seams with British prisoners.

Reginald George Henry Gough had entered the world on 7 November 1890, born to George Edghill Gough and Amy Hinton at the family home in Bullingdon Road, Cowley St John, a newly developing residential part of Oxford, England. He already had an elder sister, Winnifred Amy, who had made an appearance two and a half years earlier, and in 1893, his mother sadly gave birth to stillborn twins.

Young Reg's formative school years were spent at New College School, where his love of singing and music – which remained deeply ingrained for many years – led him to join the choir.

Reg was still a teenager in high school when his mother fell seriously ill with cancer. During her illness, he spent much time by her side, tending to her with immense love and care until she passed away in 1909 at the age of forty-four. His sister, Winnifred, was twenty-one and unmarried, but both the Gough siblings were no longer dependants.

After his mother's death, Reg enrolled in a teaching program at Culham College for Teachers in Abingdon, a few miles south of Oxford. He was eighteen years old and the first in his family to enrol in higher education, but certainly not the last. George's wages as a college servant would no doubt have been stretched by his son's tuition fees, but the elder Gough was determined for Reg to study hard, graduate and step out into the world an educated young man.

Culham College had been founded in 1852 by the outspoken Bishop of Oxford and passionate slavery abolitionist, Sam Wilberforce. Culham, a school for which Reg felt great pride, may be where he formed his fundamentalist religious views. He certainly agreed with Bishop Wilberforce's rejection of Darwin's theory of evolution. It's also more than likely he took the college founder's ideologies of social responsibility and reform to heart – Reg showed lifelong dedication to caring deeply for the disadvantaged.

After the successful completion of his teacher's training in 1911, he could have taken up a posting at one of the more prestigious schools in England, but instead opted for teaching special-needs children. At the age of twenty-one, he joined the staff of the Mount School for Blind and Deaf Children, established in 1897, in the heart of pottery country, Stoke-on-Trent. Deaf graduates often pursued a lifelong career in the art of pottery, one of the few occupations open to them at the time. Two years later, Reg transferred to Freeman's School, Wellingborough. This Church of England school had been established two centuries earlier by John Freeman as a gift to the children of the community's low socio-economic status families.

Still in his early twenties, Reg's eye fell on local Oxford girl Winifred Westwood. Two years younger, she was the daughter of Charles Westwood, the innkeeper of the Fox Inn in Bicester. Winnie had been a child when her father had left the family after an amicable separation to sail to America, where he took up a posting as a gentleman's valet. He regularly sent money home to the family, and toys for his daughter and son. Despite her father's absence, Winnie excelled at her private school, Oxford House. However, her education was cut short when her mother fell ill, and Winnie remained at home to nurse her.

Winnie's close school friend Mabel Meadows (known later to the family affectionately as Auntie Mabel), recalled in 1979 with amusement the 'courting' environment of her era:

> We were only about 17 and in those days we didn't have the freedom of the present day and had to do our lovemaking on the sly. So all one summer we all four used to get up at 6 o'clock and go swimming at the bathing place on the River and do a bit of cuddling on the way home. Winnie got married. I got jilted.

But long before the young teacher made it to the altar, Britain declared war on Germany, and Reg's life changed. Nine days later, his fifty-one-year-old father, George, remarried, taking as his wife a forty-seven-year-old widow by the name of Louisa Forty (née Soame), who had married her first husband, William Forty, in the year of Reg's birth of 1890 and brought three adult children to the marriage.

More dramatically, the twenty-four-year-old enlisted, along with thousands of other young men, and joined the 1st/4th Oxford and Buckinghamshire Light Infantry, a regiment whose lengthy name was inevitably shortened to the more manageable nickname 'Ox and Bucks'. The regiment raised many battalions that, throughout the Great War, were to serve on the Western Front, Italy, Macedonia and Mesopotamia. Reg's regiment saw action on the First Day of the Somme, 1 July 1916, a British–French offensive in which more than 57,000 Allied men were killed or injured when lines of advancing infantry were mercilessly mowed down by German machine guns. For the British Army, it was the bloodiest outcome in their history – the largest number of casualties sustained by their infantry service in a single day.

By then it had been many months since Winnie had seen Reg, but a bomb-inflicted wound to the shoulder – known in the ranks as a 'cushy Blighty' – sent her soldier suitor back to England for treatment and recuperation.

On recovery and determined to return to the fighting front,

Reg applied for a commission and was promoted to 2nd Lieutenant. A month later, he and Winnie were married, but not before he took the time for:

> ... duly considering how my wife would be placed as the wife of an officer if I was unlucky enough to get killed or badly smashed up.

The service was held at the Church of Saints Mary and John in Cowley St John, and one of those present was the bride's father – now returned from America and working as an asylum attendant. One of the witnesses, Winnie's cherished friend, Mabel, recalled:

> Being wartime it was quiet and I was her 'best girl'. She looked very nice in a cream suit and hat. There was a little reception at 7 Fairacres Road [Winnie's family home] and Reg and Winnie went to Henley for a short holiday.

It was another year before Reg was sent back to the Front. When he was gazetted back to the Ox and Bucks Regiment in July 1917, to his disappointment he was assigned to the 2nd/4th Battalion rather than his old 1st/4th. On his return to the war, Winnie was living with her parents, shopping for furniture and taking up a position at Lloyds Bank.

Eight months later, in March 1918, with Reg back on the bloody battlefields of France, word of an impending attack by the Germans on D-Company lines reached the British dugouts situated opposite the 100-yard (91m) high Mont Saint-Quentin, a strategic German stronghold. Reg was commanding half of the reserve company on the back lines when he received orders from Brigade HQ to take a small patrol into no man's land to investigate whether a particular copse was occupied by the enemy. It was clear to all and sundry that the copse in question was located in enemy territory and even the captain delivering the order snorted with amusement when Reg retorted, 'Any fool knows that!'

But orders were orders. Reg was instructed to take a sergeant and two men with him, and if the expected bombardment began before they reached no man's land, they were to return to the safety of the dugout. However, if they were caught by the attack, they were to maintain their position in no man's land rather than risk the perilous return journey.

The patrol set out in thick fog, but nevertheless made it to the front-line trenches. No sooner had they begun preparing for the reconnaissance mission than the Germans let loose with the predicted barrage, which drove Reg and his scouting party back via the network of fog-shrouded trenches to the safety of their dugout in the sunken road. Gas shells rained down around them and masks were hurriedly donned. A shell decimated the cookhouse, essentially a slab of corrugated iron propped up against the side of the road, but fortunately the cook had already fled, leaving the sizzling bacon in the pan to its explosive end.

As the Germans advanced, the patrol took evasive action, running from shell hole to shell hole for cover. Machine-gun bullets tore at the ground on either side of Reg's thundering boots. When he found himself staring down the barrels of a trio of German rifles 100 yards (91m) away, with a fourth enemy soldier beckoning ominously to him, he took off again, running 'like blazes', with bullets whizzing around him. He flung himself behind the only cover available, the remains of a wall only a few inches high. The Germans stopped firing, assuming they'd got him.

He was reported missing, believed killed, and for a fortnight his family grieved at the news. Reg was to say that it must have been a trying time for his family back home but, in his typical tongue-in-cheek fashion, admitted to feeling quite chuffed that the condolence letters to his father were full of 'nice things people said about me'.

After dodging and weaving around the enemy via the cover of shell holes, hedges and decimated stone walls for several hours, Reg's luck finally ran out: the fog descended again and he 'ran into four Huns on patrol', who disarmed him and marched him like a trophy back to their commanding officer, a German major.

Reg recalls that the German commanding officer:

> ... was one of the best – in fact, the best German I met. He spoke English quite well and asked me if I had had any food ... he apologised for not being able to give me any as the rations had not arrived, but produced a kind of coffee, made I believe from acorns, but it was warm and very welcome ... he gave me a packet of Goldflake cigarettes ...

Any expectation Reg might have harboured that all German officers were as respectful and solicitous was fleeting.

Now a prisoner of war, Reg was moved with eleven of the officers and other men from his battalion to a dark barn and fed what he believed to be horsemeat. He remembered that:

> ... some silly ass lit a candle and we saw the awful looking joint. It upset some, but I was too hungry to take much notice of it.

The following day, the barn-dwellers were added to a lengthy column of captured British soldiers which stretched for miles as they were marched through the German countryside. To Reg it looked as though the whole British Army had been captured, but they kept their spirits up by singing and attempting to cheer up the French civilians who watched glumly as the POWs passed by.

Eventually they were packed into steam-train cattle trucks for the final leg of the journey to Rastatt, a POW collection camp bursting with prisoners from all walks of life – British servicemen mingled with Belgian, French, Portuguese and Russian civilians.

Reg and five others were assigned a corner of a large hut, then made a frenzied dash for the canteen for a bite to eat, only to find the cupboard virtually bare. They were left to share a tin of sardines between the six of them.

Shortly after, they were transferred to Karlsruhe, the processing camp for military POWs. By comparison with Rastatt, Reg discovered with relief that the rooms were reasonably decent and small items of luxury such as razors were available for purchase. Even the poor-quality soap was a delight after the deprivations of the past weeks.

While Reg was at Karlsruhe, an Australian brigadier general managed to escape from the camp by dressing as the Kommandant and walking past the unsuspecting sentries. The Kommandant was absent from the camp at the time. It was thought that the British secret service had organised the breakout and had arranged a car to whisk away the high-ranking escapee.

Reg's stay in relative comfort was brief. Once processed, POWs were transferred to one of the many camps around Germany. He next found himself sharing a barracks room with thirteen other officers at Holzminden.

Reg recalled the daily dull routine:

> . . . for a few days, weeks even, after the strenuous life led in
> France, it came as a real rest. Eventually . . . when feeling fit again,

there was a terrible monotony about the daily programme and at the back of it all the fact that we were caged in, and lack of freedom can be very irksome.

Captured variously from the sky, sea and land, Edgar Garland, Dean Gardner and Reg Gough – along with every other prisoner with the misfortune to be sent to Holzminden – now faced a life of deadly monotony. And they were in the grip of the despicable Niemeyer, a man who had the means, and made it his mission, to visit hardship upon the British prisoners he so loathed.

Five

Home and Hearth

The Red Cross kept meticulous records of the prisoners' transfers through camps, but these were only as good as the information received from the British military authorities – or the men themselves, who, like Dick Cash, were anxious not to drop off the radar.

When Cash and Cissy began to exchange letters via the Red Cross, it was frustratingly slow – but at least it was something. Like many letters between the men and their loved ones, their poignant exchange reveals heartache at the separation and difficulties faced by Cissy as she struggled back home.

In one letter dated 6 November 1917, Cissy writes to Mary that although she'd like to write more frequently than each fortnight to her husband, she found that she couldn't because:

> . . . I am kept busy all day and at night and am too tired and my eyes are not too good. I have my four children and self to earn a living for as Mr Cash's pay (military) only pays the instalments on the property we're buying. I also have insurance, rates, taxes and licenses to pay. I have also had doctors and funeral expenses to pay for his baby and his brother . . .

Cissy was only one of hundreds of thousands of women struggling to keep the home fires burning. Although, in many ways, she was one of the fortunate ones – at least she knew her husband was alive, safe and not being shot at on the battlefield. Or worse – dead.

While prisoners and families were relieved to receive letters from each other, there were those who dreaded the possibility of receiving a letter such as the one written from the field by Captain Clement Briggs on 6 April 1917:

> Dear Mrs Birks, I regret to inform you that your son, Lieut N.A. Birks, is missing. He was on a piece of work yesterday and has failed to return to the S[quadron]. We offer you our most sincere sympathy in your moment of sorrow. We have not only lost an excellent officer, but a friend. The C.O. wishes me to convey to you his deep sympathy . . .

This was the chilling news received by Mercy Birks, the mother of twenty-four-year-old Norman. It was closely followed by other correspondence, notably a telegram from the War Office, dated 9 April, which hastened to add that this 'does not necessarily mean either wounded or killed'. On 20 April, Major de Crespigny, commanding officer of Norman's No. 29 Squadron RFC, also wrote to Mercy, attempting to reassure her, although the military authorities were unsure of the young lieutenant's fate themselves:

> . . . he probably landed in enemy country without being hurt . . .
> It may be of comfort to you to know that more than half our pilots who are shot down, land all right and become prisoners.

Despite the attempt at comfort, the notifications left the family in an agony of worry. Although Norman was engaged, his mother, Mercy, was listed as next of kin and as such received the flow of telegrams and letters from military officials.

Mercy Ann Wood, a Bradford lass, was a farmer's daughter when she married Walter Birks in August 1889. Walter also had a farming background; his family had cultivated their own land in Woodhouse, then a village just outside Sheffield, Yorkshire, since the seventeenth century. During the 1800s, the Birkses had developed a tannery, which had become the mainstay of the family business. It was run by Walter's father, William, and had grown impressively to employ fifty workers.

Walter was being groomed by his father to take over the business, but a dark cloud had begun to stalk the tortured young man. In 1893 – four years after they were married and a year after Norman was born – Mercy bravely removed the toddler and his elder brother, Douglas, after enduring several violent and abusive attacks by the alcoholic Walter. Mercy and her young sons settled in her birthplace of Bradford, West Yorkshire in northern England, near her own family.

Perhaps Walter resorted to the bottle to dull the intensity of the demons that plagued him, for many years later he would exhibit predatory homosexual behaviour.

Mercy obtained a judicial separation in November 1894 at which she was granted alimony from Walter, but as a single mother raising two young boys, they were by no means well off financially. As the boys grew older, they were keenly aware of their mother's struggles and both stepped into the role of protector, while cultivating their own strong spirit of self-reliance and brotherly affection.

Norman attended local Bradford schools and, as a sixteen-year-old, enrolled at Bradford Technical College, where he stayed until 1911. He found employment at Vickers Ltd, an engineering and armaments company, in the industrial city of Sheffield while studying part-time at the local university and serving a cadetship with the Sheffield University Officers Training Corps.

About the same time that Norman graduated with an Associateship in Mechanical Engineering, the First World War erupted and he found himself at an officers training camp at Ludgershall on Salisbury Plain. He was still unmarried, possessed technical qualifications and military training, and was therefore considered an asset to the army.

The York and Lancaster Regiment granted him a temporary commission in September 1914, which was promptly followed by a promotion to full lieutenant. He was attached to the newly established Motor Machine Gun Service (MMGS),[1] a unit formed to outfit motorcycle sidecars with machine guns to improve weapons mobility. The men of the MMGS were alarmingly dubbed 'the Suicide Corps', a startling but perceptive nickname bestowed upon them by the local newspapers.

In his 1972 memoirs, Norman recalled his training days under canvas at Frensham Ponds:

> Our ranks consisted mainly of miners from Barnsley [Yorkshire] area. They had no uniforms and, of course, no training; a formidable task before us young and inexperienced officers. They were a grand lot of men and proved gallant fighters in France.

In March 1915, Birks was posted to France with the MMGS, stationed near Armentières, but the gun-toting motorcycles proved useless in trench warfare, and the MMGS troops were redeployed into the trenches as combatants – minus their machines.

During a period of leave back home in February 1916, Norman proposed to Elizabeth 'Liza' Johnson, a distant cousin. On his return to training, an elated Liza wrote to him:

> For me the world is once more turning around – I've heard from you today at last . . . Well, old thing, it's lovely being engaged

and the loveliest thing on earth being engaged to <u>you</u> – my heart's desire!

Norman did a short stint in an armoured car battalion stationed at Aire-sur-la-Lys from 9 March 1916, but this was quickly abandoned in favour of attachment to the RFC. Throughout July and August 1916, he trained as a pilot in Oxford, Doncaster and Yorkshire, learning to fly Beatty Wrights, BE2Cs and his favoured machine, the de Havilland. The DH.2 – which Norman claimed could 'turn on a sixpence' and 'had a marvellous field of view' – also had the disconcerting habit of dropping into a vertical spin when making sharp turns, a design fault that saw many trainee pilots lose their lives.

Norman gained his certificate on 12 September 1916 with only four hours solo flying time under his belt. Before long he was posted back to France, where he joined No. 29 Squadron RFC, who were tasked with attack missions behind enemy lines at Izel-le-Hameau, near Arras, flying DH.2 single-seater fighters.

One mission saw Norman delayed on take-off due to engine trouble. Once in the air, the aircraft's faults proved to be nearly fatal: he was attacked from the rear, then his machine gun jammed. Unable to defend himself, he returned to base. On the ground he discovered that not only had the wings virtually collapsed as a result of the landing wires being severed by enemy fire but also the pewter bulldog mascot given to him by Liza, his fiancée, had taken a puncture from a machine-gun bullet, possibly saving his life.[2]

Fortunately, the Air Ministry were to see the folly of the inferior DH.2s flying against the might of the German fighters, and in March 1917 they were replaced with the more manoeuvrable Nieuport 17s.

Norman's last combat flight took place on 5 April 1917. During engagement with the enemy, his petrol tank was ruptured by anti-aircraft fire and he was doused in the burning chemical. Had tracer bullets ignited the fluid, he would have exploded in a fireball. He recalled:

I turned for home and my aggressor followed me down, firing continuously, causing me to twist and turn and lose height very rapidly. I saw my instruments in front of me disintegrate, but the only bullet hitting me was my right buttock, now known as my 'dishonourable wound'. I crash landed on the edge of a shell hole just behind the German front line trench, and turned turtle. I always like to think that if I had had my bulldog mascot fitted to my new machine, I would have got over to our own lines. Such is superstition.

He managed to release his safety belt and 'flopped into the mud and water' under heavy shelling of the Germans by the British. He surmised that the enemy must have taken cover from the bombardment as no-one seemed to have observed his crash-landing. Taking advantage of this, he crawled into an enemy trench, then into a sap – a particular style of trench used by both the British and Germans as night listening posts – which led to the British lines. He hatched a plot to crawl as close to his own side as possible, then lie low until the cover of darkness.

He'd hardly moved a few yards before a hand grenade exploded nearby, which knocked him flat on his back and wounded him badly in the hip. However, that was the least of his problems because a moment later he found himself staring down the barrels of two German rifles. Lying powerless on the ground, he raised his right foot to protect himself from the line of fire, shouting in his best schoolboy German, 'Nicht scheissen!' He may have wished that he'd concentrated a little harder in German classes because he had yelled 'Don't shit!' rather than 'Don't shoot!', the two words sounding as similar in German as they do in English.

However, the two young Germans seemed to get the idea, for they lowered their rifles and Norman was taken prisoner. He received basic medical treatment in an enemy dugout and then was transferred to a hospital in Douai on 8 April 1917, where he underwent surgery on his hip.

Hospital conditions were rudimentary, as Norman described many years later:

> My first visit to the operating theatre was a shock. It was complete bedlam resounding with the groans and screams of the patients. No anaesthetics were used. As far as I remember, the room was about 30 yards long and all operations appeared to be done on trestle tables. Amongst other things done to me was to put short rubber tubes in my wounds for draining purposes. I remember on one occasion there was a Scottish infantry man on the next table and two doctors were extracting shrapnel from his back with tweezers, and all they got from him was an occasional groan and then a good laugh . . .

Norman soon discovered that he had been the first casualty of thirty-four-year-old German fighter pilot Vizefeldwebel Carl Menckhoff, who, in the best tradition of First World War chivalry, paid his British victim a visit in hospital.

It was here that twenty-five-year-old Norman met fellow patient twenty-eight-year-old Lieutenant John G.H. Frew,[3] who occupied an adjoining bed, and the two men soon became fast friends.

Home and Hearth

Around this time his mother, Mercy, had received word of her son's missing-in-action status from Captain Briggs and several other military sources.

When Norman was well enough to be transferred – later in April 1917 – he and several of his fellow patients, including John Frew, were taken by train on a miserably wet day to a hospital at Mülheim an der Ruhr, Germany. He and John both underwent several surgical procedures – fortunately under anaesthetic – at the hands of a capable German doctor, Herr Dr Kohlhagen. Sadly, three of their comrades with whom they had been transferred from France died.

Food parcels had not yet caught up with Norman, and he was forced – as were many others, notably including the Germans – to subsist on meagre enemy rations: two small bread rolls, a lick of butter and a bit of sauerkraut. In June, a single food parcel for one of their dead comrades had arrived, which was given to Norman and John to share between them.

Both Mercy and Liza were elated to receive word of Norman's incarceration in a POW camp, as it meant he was most certainly alive. The family had suffered two months in limbo, awaiting news of Norman's fate, and on 4 June 1917, Mercy took delivery of a telegram from the Queen Victoria Jubilee Fund Association in Geneva, confirming her son's whereabouts, which perfunctorily read: 'Norman prisoner Muelheim on Ruhr.'

The following day, Liza received a postcard from Norman himself, sending her into an ecstasy of delight and relief. She wrote to him:

My very Belovedest of all the world,

Wot cheer?!! <u>Old thing</u>, I'm so intoxicated with joy that I can scarcely <u>bear</u> for joy! An hour ago I had a wire from [your] Mother just saying Norman a prisoner & my love – I live again. I'm hungering for more details . . . My darling I know we shall never know all you have suffered! Oh how my heart aches for you, dear . . . I do & have & shall pray God that you may be spared as much as possible dearest – I know how brave & splendid you will be my Hero of Heros! (Don't snigger! I'm sure this is nothing to what I shall do if some one doesn't chuck a bucket of cold water over me!) . . . Of course beloved, I <u>knew</u> every minute of the time that you were alive. Never for an <u>instant</u> did we give up hope – I could <u>always</u> hear you saying when ever I listened, 'Cheerio' & 'I shall come back to you alright little girl'.

The letter, which ran to fifteen double-sided pages, started when Liza first heard of Norman's incarceration. With no idea in which camp he was being held, she began the letter and kept adding to it as the days went on, until she was informed where to send it. Learning of correspondence restrictions, she sent two pages at a time, writing 'To be continued' at the end in pencil to let Norman know there was still plenty more to come.

His mother – just as overjoyed – also wrote to Norman immediately, filling her letter with underscored words for emphasis:

. . . I cannot tell you how <u>delighted</u> we are to have news of you at last! Liza got your P.C. [postcard] only y'day & it is 5 weeks since you wrote it, but oh, how <u>thankful</u> we are to see your dear old writing again! & it will be lovely to have letters from you, even if it is only <u>once</u> a <u>fortnight</u> (that seems <u>nothing</u> after waiting <u>2 months</u>!) & we will send you anything we can. Do you want money? if so, how can we send it? They have sent all your kit home about three weeks ago. I do hope dearest, you are not <u>badly</u> wounded, you say you are 'lying on your back', tell me what has happened & all about it, won't you? And keep smiling dear, <u>nothing matters</u>, now we shall see each other again. Liza & I have cheered each other . . . She is a brave little girl & we <u>knew</u> we should hear from you! Well dear tomorrow is <u>Douglas' wedding</u> day, the 7th of June, he is coming home today, <u>if only</u> you could have been with us! but we'll tell you all about it . . .

The extended family were equally relieved at the news. Later in the month, John Davidson, a family relative, wrote to Norman with the kind of fireside chatter that POWs were desperate to receive inside their barbed wire prisons:

We were all very greatly relieved to have visual evidence that, after so many weeks of anxiety, you were still alive, tho' what your injuries are we are still without any information. Wasn't it a funny coincidence that your p/card came the day before Douglas' wedding. You cannot imagine what a difference it made to your fiancee! & to Mother, of course . . . You will doubtless have had a graphic description of the wedding. It was quite a charming function without any starchy people about & everyone enjoyed it immensely. Well we should like to think that the time will be short ere we see you again with us but matters drag on so in this struggle that we can do nothing beyond hoping for the end. You at any rate will be one of those in for a hearty welcome . . . Well now keep hopeful & as you have pulled thro' so far do your best to keep up until you hear the 'welcome home' ringing in your ears – and may I be there to greet you . . .

Bernard Johnson, Liza's brother, also wrote to his future brother-in-law:

> How we all wish you were back in Blighty with us! But by Jove, it's a comfort to know you're alive – tho' having an awfully thin time, I'm afraid. You can't know the terrible two months you caused over here – but your mother and Liza happily had impregnable hope.

Bernard's reference to Norman 'having an awfully thin time' was quite an understatement. Norman no doubt wished he was indeed back in Blighty with the family, for it had taken four months for Red Cross food parcels to start reaching him in July 1917.

About the fuss over his missing-in-action status, Norman merely commented, 'Not many of us are privileged to read our own obituary.'

In September 1917, six months after being taken prisoner, Norman and John were deemed fit enough to be sent to a POW camp. As their uniforms had virtually rotted away, they were given Russian uniforms and processed through Karlsruhe. It was here that Norman met Lieutenant Brian Manning of the Irish Guards, another officer who was to become a lifelong friend. Manning was later appointed Camp Adjutant at Holzminden.

During his incarceration, Norman wasn't to know that his father, Walter – who had been working as an attendant at the Nottingham County Lunatic Asylum – was tried, sentenced and imprisoned for twelve months in Nottingham Prison for a grim sexual attack on a seventeen-year-old epileptic male inmate.

On 3 October 1917, Norman, John and Brian were transferred to Holzminden, arriving only three or four weeks after Holzminden opened for business.

Two months later, John – who had been imprisoned for a great deal longer by this stage – was repatriated out of Holzminden via the prisoner exchange program and had safely reached England by Christmas 1917. Now free to write without the restrictions of German censorship, John wrote to Mercy Birks on 2 March 1918, offering her a blueprint for assisting her son to escape:

> By the way, your son asked me to let you know that he would very much like a compass sent out. He thought, as I also do, that the best way to get it out would be in a cake of soap. An ordinary toilet tablet would be the best. If you decide to send it, do not on any account send it in a tin, as in most camps (and certainly in Holzminden), the tins are emptied by the German authorities . . .

Norman, meanwhile, had set about making his own compass out of odds and ends – a pickle jar cork and a magnetic needle, which worked a treat (and still did so a century later) – but he made no further attempts to escape.

Eager to get Norman out by whatever means possible, John also wrote to Mercy advising her how she might influence the authorities to consider her injured son for the prisoner exchange program, which had formally commenced in July 1917. In the following excerpt, he encourages Mercy to embellish Norman's injuries for greater effect:

> I wonder if you are trying to work an exchange? If so, things to go for are these – a damaged hip joint and a weak heart resulting in poor circulation. There is a very small groundwork of truth in the last, but if it can be of any use to you, I am perfectly willing to give a detailed account of his wound and disabilities. If you consider that I can be of the slightest use in this matter, please let me know what I can do.

John did, in fact, provide a statement to the War Office in London on Mercy's behalf, requesting a medical assessment for Norman on the basis of his injuries. The War Office then duly referred the matter to the medical commissions responsible for examining POWs for possible repatriation to a neutral country. Norman travelled to Aachen, near the Dutch border, on 22 March 1918 for the assessment; however, it was found that his wounds were not severe enough for recommendation, and he was ordered back onto the train bound for Holzminden.

The prospect of returning to prison was too much for Norman. Exactly one year to the day after his initial capture on 5 April 1917, he made good his escape by scrambling out the toilet cubicle window when the train slowed down. He was spotted by a German soldier leaning out of a train window but, thanks to his Burberry coat, he was mistaken for a civilian dodging the train fare.

Norman rolled down an embankment and took off across the fields. With only a railway map pilfered from the train station waiting room and no compass, he soon got himself lost.

As far as escape bids go, Norman's was destined to be short-lived.

The next day he took cover in an old windmill but word was out that an escapee was on the run. School children were often given the day off school to help search for escapees, so it was unsurprising that it was a young boy who climbed the internal staircase of the windmill and spotted him. Before long, the windmill was surrounded by women, children and old men who kept up a barrage of stone-throwing to drive him out.

Norman was marched away by a German soldier at the point of a fixed bayonet and returned to Holzminden, where he was placed in solitary confinement. He was sentenced to fourteen days for the escape, and a further eight days for having a map in his possession. On release, he was greeted by Niemeyer, who slapped his hand to his chest, declaring, 'All my boys come back to me!'

Unaware that freedom was only eight months into the future, a disheartened Norman settled once more into the humdrum of prison camp life, the tedium alleviated only by activities the prisoners managed to organise for themselves, with the assistance of the Red Cross.

Six

Art and Entertainment

Although orderlies like Dick were kept busy from dawn to dusk, the privilege of rank afforded officers exemption from work detail.

With many long and vacuous daylight hours to fill, the men quickly grew bored. They were permitted to write to the Red Cross to request not only food and clothing items, but also for entertainment supplies, so Mary and her team found themselves sourcing and placing orders at musical instrument suppliers such as Edison Bell and Hawkes & Son for items like melodians, mandolins, concertinas and accordions with which the POWs formed in-camp bands and orchestras. As these were not deemed survival items, the more unusual requests were funded from the wallets of the inmates or their families.

Brain-numbing boredom was the overarching reality of POW life. Mary and her staff processed requests for playing cards, games, footballs, cricket sets, soccer balls, chess boards, draughts and boxing gloves. Books were another way of alleviating the monotony of everyday POW existence, and appeals for reading material such as *The Man From Snowy River* and other titles by Australian literary luminaries such as Banjo Paterson were common. Disappearing into an Australian story or book of poetry allowed homesick prisoners to blissfully escape the reality of their barbed wire prison for a short time. Holzminden eventually boasted a library of several thousand books.

Art and Entertainment

Inmates with one eye on their future civilian life often requested books relating to new careers they wished to pursue on their service discharge; others simply pursued topics of interest – orders for *Jamesons' Manual on Magnetism & Electricity*, *The Complete Motorist*, *The Electrical Ignition of Petrol Engines* and books on wireless telegraphy came across Mary's desk. On one occasion, she fielded a request for a book on shorthand.

Mary and her team ensured that parcels were sent to the POWs regularly and that their requests were fulfilled to the best of their ability, including one from Dick for a book on hypnotism and 'a game of Housie, a large one if you can get it, so that we could all join in'. Gramophones and shellac turntable records found their way into camps – anything to while away the long hours of nothingness. Debating societies were formed, church services were conducted and prisoners with expertise in certain subjects offered lectures to reactivate idle brains.

Soon an in-camp theatre group was formed – the British Amateur Dramatic Society (BADS) – instigated by incoming POWs who had been involved in similar ventures in previous camps. They called their production house the Gaiety Theatre, after the theatre in London's West End of the same name. In the absence of women, men in dresses played female roles – some so successful that they occasionally found themselves on the receiving end of amorous glances from affection-starved POWs who had forgotten that a fellow inmate was hidden beneath the wig and makeup.

Preparation for performances in the second-floor dining room distracted the POWs from the monotony and depression that were a part of camp life. The group busied themselves sewing their own costumes out of scraps begged from the locals, fashioning sets, printing programs and rehearsing for shows such as *Home John* and *The Ballet Girl*.

One POW, twenty-nine-year-old Lieutenant James Whale of the Worcestershire Regiment, later admitted that despite his loathing of his incarceration, his love of all things drama came from his involvement in the Gaiety Theatre at Holzminden, where he threw himself into every facet of production.

Max Gore had vivid memories of one inmate who could impersonate the Kommandant with such precision 'that it would have been hard to tell the difference but for the uniform'. During one stage revue, at which six or so of the *Kommandantur* staff attended, the fake Niemeyer strode onto the stage resplendent in uniform bellowing, 'I guess you know who I am!' Instinctively the German staff leapt to their feet in a show of servility, only to discover their fearless leader was a convincing imposter. They resumed their seats to enjoy the rest of the show, during which 'Herr Hauptmann' was mercilessly mocked; his subordinates found it difficult to hide their delight.

Gaming with playing cards could often be taken very seriously, as was the case with Lieutenant William Hodgson Sugden-Wilson of the RFC and Captain Eric Tollmache of the Sherwood Foresters. During the course of their imprisonment, Eric incurred a gambling debt of £84.3s but William wasn't prepared to let the debt slide. After the war, he pursued the outstanding amount vigorously. When the hapless Eric attempted to pay the debt twice with bank cheques, both cheques were dishonoured. Fearful of losing his commission if reported to army authorities, Eric negotiated an arrangement to pay the amount in instalments, but could only manage £15. The matter rose to a crescendo until it was heard before the High Court of Justice in 1920, fifteen months after the end of the war. Eric was ordered to discharge the full debt – minus the £15 he had managed to repay.

William Sugden-Wilson wasn't the only one who took card games seriously. As well as developing a love of theatre in

Holzminden, James Whale also developed a talent for poker, accruing around £4000 worth of IOUs in his favour during his fifteen months in the camp. His Scrooge-like determination to collect on bets long after the war possibly stemmed from the fact that as the sixth of seven children, he had left school early to aid the family finances and never took money for granted. His working life began in the cobbler trade, where his enterprising ways saw him saving leftover shoe nails to sell for scrap money, which he used to support his art studies.

Thirty-year-old Lieutenant Frederick William 'Will' Harvey was a different kettle of fish entirely. The son of a Gloucestershire farmer and horse-breeder, Will possessed the heart of a poet and a way with words. Although he could have enlisted as an officer, initially he had joined the ranks, where he felt a kinship with other 'citizen soldiers'. A search for officer-quality recruits among the ranks saw him commissioned shortly thereafter. He thrived in the companionable environment that military service afforded him, thoroughly entertaining his battalion of more than a thousand men by lampooning officers and aspects of military life in the trench newspaper, *The Fifth Gloucestershire Gazette* – and getting away with it. He had also been called upon for more serious editorial duties, such as composing moving commemorations about comrades killed in action.

Will was awarded the Distinguished Conduct Medal in early 1915 after a skirmish in no man's land, but on 17 August 1916 – a year after volunteering – he was captured after he was caught showing himself around a German frontline trench.

Over the next two years, Will was transferred through seven POW camps, involving himself in several escape attempts. He filled in his time by writing poetry, giving lectures, performing in plays and advocating for his comrades at military courts instigated by German authorities. En route from Schwarmstedt to Holzminden, he made an escape bid from the train but was recaptured, earning himself a month in the Holzminden cells for his trouble.

Given Will's sociable demeanour, it wasn't long before he was buddies with the other seven inmates in his barracks room. One of his bunkmates, the artistic and arachnid-obsessed 'Mossy',[1] had covered the walls and ceilings with chalk prehistoric creatures, and kept a large box of live spiders.

The chalk rendering of a pond of ducks over Will's bed that Mossy drew inspired Will to write a poem that, almost a century later, in 1996, was voted one of England's most beloved. Compelled to 'explain the secret beauty and humour of that bird no less than its relationship and significance to the heavens above and the hell underneath', Will wrote a three-stanza poem, which in part reads:

> From troubles of the world
> I turn to ducks,
> Beautiful, comical things,
> Sleeping and curled,
> Their heads beneath white wings,
> By water cool,
> Or finding curious things
> To eat, in various mucks
> Beneath the pool.
> Tails uppermost or waddling
> Sailor-like on the shores
> Of ponds or paddling
> – Left! right! – with fanlike feet
> Which are for steady oars

> When they (like galleys) float,
> Each bird a boat
> Rippling at will the sweet
> Wide waterway . . .

The poem goes on to make many observations about the amusing habits of ducks, concluding with humorous sparkle and whimsy, typical of Will:

> And as for the duck,
> I think that God must have smiled a bit,
> Seeing those bright eyes blink
> On the day He fashioned it
> And He's probably laughing still
> At the sound that came out of its bill!

As in many other camps, the prisoners of Holzminden kept autograph books to document this extraordinary time in their lives and the men with whom they shared it. Autograph books became treasure troves of artwork, poetry, quotes and photographs, indelibly capturing a picture of life behind barbed wire. Signature entries generally consisted of initials, surname, rank and the place and date of capture and often a home address. Prisoners referred to each other by their surnames, as per the military custom. In fact, they could go through an entire internment and never know their first names.

Will wasn't the only budding poet at Holzminden. A playful Captain A. Armstrong of the 1st Scottish Rifles responded to a request by a fellow Scotsman, 2nd Lieutenant Angus McPhail of the Royal Highland Regiment (4th Black Watch), to record a poem in his autograph book. Titled 'Gelangenen Gibberish!', the tongue-in-cheek seven-verse Scottish ode reads, in part:

> This braw young laddie's ask it me
> Tae write a wee bit poetry
> I'll scribble just a line or two
> Much worse nor any ye iver saw.
> Here in our lordly domicile
> In various ways the time we while;
> Some pass the time in learnin' French
> And others studyin' for the Bench.
> And some can't cook and ithers can
> Fry even soup in the frying pan
> But noo we hope for a quick release
> From Auld Nick's toils and our togs o' grease.
> Tae string ae verse ontil anither
> I couldna doe it for ma brither
> Sae, if thae lines don't please ye well
> Here's ma bit scrawl and go to PAISLEY.

It is often said that necessity is the mother of invention. Confined behind barbed wire with little to do, some POWs who otherwise had no creative inclinations turned to artistic pursuits to entertain themselves.

Seven

Barbed Wire Disease

In July 1917, around the same time Dick Cash was recovering from his wounds in the Hameln hospital prior to entering Holzminden, the British and German governments signed an agreement on combatant and civilian prisoners of war.

One of the paragraphs of that agreement dealt specifically with the issue of 'barbed wire disease', a euphemism for mental illness affecting POWs who had been held for long periods of time. Prisoners with serious injuries resulting from their capture (gunshot wounds, amputation of limbs etc.) or sufferers of tuberculosis, pneumonia and severe psychiatric conditions could be eligible – irrespective of rank – for medically supervised internment in Switzerland or Holland for the remainder of the war.

Reg Gough noted that several officers in Holzminden had become 'mentally unbalanced', remarking that succumbing to depression was an inevitable reaction to spending long periods of time in the restriction of POW camps. Some had been languishing in confinement since the beginning of the war and had clocked up more than three years of incarceration. He was to later count himself among those who suffered bouts of depression in Holzminden, adding that he had made it a point to extract 'as much humour as possible from prison life'. He did not, like some others, feel humiliated at being captured and imprisoned, observing matter-of-factly that he 'had no control over the circumstances', but was proud of his considerable contribution up to the point of capture.

As a direct precaution against barbed wire disease, those who had spent up to eighteen months in German prison camps could apply to be interned in Holland if the German authorities considered them at risk. Men with severe injuries passed through Holland or Switzerland and were repatriated to Britain; the less serious cases sat out the war interned in either neutral country.

For many, the agreement came into effect too late. Those captured and imprisoned at the beginning of the war, having languished in POW camps for three long years, were at real risk of burgeoning psychiatric conditions and illness from poor nutrition and/or injuries.

Another threat was sexually transmitted diseases such as syphilis and gonorrhoea (colloquially known among servicemen as 'the clap'), which were prevalent as soldiers, aviators and sailors availed themselves of the services of prostitutes while on leave, or arrived in Europe with pre-existing conditions. Left untreated for long enough, a disease like syphilis could develop to the tertiary stage, where the neural pathways to the brain were affected, leaving the sufferer vulnerable to psychiatric conditions.

A POW or a governing authority might apply for an individual to be assessed for repatriation to Switzerland or Holland, but if the neutral assessing body deemed the applicant to be mentally and physically fit enough to see out his imprisonment, he was rejected as an exchange candidate.

The German authorities were wary of prisoners who faked psychiatric conditions to manipulate a transfer out of a prison camp. It was often hard to convince them of the genuine ailments of the mind, as in the tragic case of Lieutenant Sidney Stewart Hume.

By the time Sidney, of No. 66 Squadron RFC, reached Schweidnitz POW camp by way of Freiburg and Holzminden camps, his concerned cousin, 2nd Lieutenant Roland Cunningham Hume – whom he coincidentally met in Schweidnitz – knew there was something irrevocably shattered in the fragile mind of the thirty-two-year-old officer.

So broken, in fact, that, at Roland's behest, several English officers approached the German camp authorities, requesting Sidney's repatriation back to England for psychiatric treatment. Initially they were refused as the Germans believed his display of damaged mental health to be a clever deception to flee the camp. In the face of overwhelming evidence, they finally relented.

Three months later, and at the mercy of vivid delusions that refused to loosen their tormenting grip, Sidney sparked a tragic chain of events that left an innocent man dead.

When Sidney Stewart Hume was born on 1 September 1886, his birthplace of Buenos Aires, Argentina, had been federalised only five years but was already flexing its impressive economic muscles to an admiring global community. Immigrants flooding in from Europe saw the port city quickly develop into a multicultural hub, booming off the back of thriving industry and hefty customs duties.

Sidney was the third son and fifth child of the University of Glasgow-educated Alexander Hume and Marie Henriette Adelaide Mundt, who was of French descent. Alexander ran a thriving railway engineering partnership, Hume Hermanos (Hume Brothers), with his brother Washington and was responsible for raising several of the city's more impressive building structures, including Palacio Hume (Hume Palace), on the city's ritzy Alvear Avenue. He was also a co-founder of the Argentinean Jockey Club.

In the wake of political unrest in Argentina, Alexander Hume's fortunes plummeted and he had no choice but to sell up and relocate to England. He passed away in Deal, Kent, in 1911 at the age of sixty-seven.

In May 1894, when Sidney was eight, his elder brother (the second son of the family), Albert Edward – nicknamed 'Prince' – died of diphtheria at the age of eleven, leaving Sidney with four siblings: Alexander Scott (b. 1875), Mary Elizabeth (Daisy) (b. 1880), Agnes Lilian (Lily) (b. 1885) and Violet Theodora (b. 1889).

Little is known of how Sidney spent his childhood, although his cousin Roland, twelve years his junior, recalls Sidney's excellent horsemanship and slingshot marksmanship skills in his memoirs, *A History of Two Families: The Origins of the Hume Family in Argentina* (1975):

> I have seen him place a wax ball in a plate of soup, put out to cool on a window sill, on the other side of the street! My mother did not regard this attraction in such a good light as she thought he was too naughty and bumptious.

Sidney, who had suffered smallpox at age fifteen, was partially educated at St George's College, Quilmes, outside Buenos Aires, at the turn of the twentieth century. For whatever reason, he did not finish the course.

By the age of twenty-one, Sidney had been conscripted into the Argentine Republic National Army. The training was rigorous, entailing a three-month period during which he worked with horses and undertook gymnastics, as well as theoretical and combat instruction. Weekends were assigned to committing to memory the Code of Military Justice, military inspection and housekeeping.

He was promoted to the rank of corporal on 25 October 1907 in the 1st Line Regiment of the Mounted Grenadiers. Under the command of 1st Lieutenant Tesandro Ramón Santa Ana, Sidney and his regiment were part of a unit appointed as the presidential escort when José Figueroa Alcorta, President of Argentina, undertook an eight-day journey by train to the city of Córdoba in November 1907.

Sometime between his army service and the outbreak of the First World War, Sidney secured himself a position on an *estancia* (a rural estate or ranch) in southern Argentina.

A relocation to Paraguay for several years preceded thirty-year-old Sidney's enlistment in the 1st County of London Yeomanry, Middlesex (Duke of Cambridge's Hussars) around March 1915. Only seven years previously it had become part of the Territorial Force, amalgamating with other London Yeomanry units to form the London Mounted Brigade.

With his superior horseman and marksman skills and mounted national service experience, the mounted cavalry unit at first seemed a natural fit for Sidney. However, soon after he arrived in Alexandria, Egypt – by Christmas 1915 – feeling restricted and bored by the tedious routine of training and patrols, he transferred to the Camel Corps. Here he earned attention and praise from his superiors for his excellent ability to locate Turkish and German positions while on reconnaissance patrols in the desert.

Sidney served at Moudros on the Greek island of Lemnos, where, due to its proximity to Gallipoli, a sizeable British camp was located, its troops playing a vital role in the campaigns against Turkey.[1]

Sidney was admitted to hospital at Moudros for an undisclosed illness, and then transferred to a more established hospital in Giza, Egypt, for further treatment for four months. Upon his discharge in February 1916, and still feeling constrained by patrol duty, he sought the excitement of action by exchanging a saddle for the cockpit of a biplane.

In June 1916, he applied for attachment to the RFC and by August, he had joined No. 14 Squadron, undertaking a flying officer (observer) course, which entailed learning the art of directing artillery fire, navigation, map-making and other requisite skills. When he qualified, later in the month, he became a fully fledged member of the RFC.

According to Roland, by November Sidney had made:

> ... 38 sorties over enemy positions and had taken part in several air battles ... he was sent to England to do a course on fighter aircraft.

When Roland trained as a fighter pilot – at Central Flying School in Upavon, near Stonehenge – he found that cousin Sidney had done the same course a short time before him and was remembered by his fellow officers. Sidney claimed his Royal Aero Club certificate on 23 March 1917.

Three weeks later, Sidney joined No. 66 Squadron and on 26 May 1917 took his first cross-country flight with Major Owen Boyd – both flying Scouts (single-seat fighters) – for a 1 hour 40 minute familiarisation flight over local terrain. The same day, Sidney went up again for a 45-minute solo practice run and once more at 3.50 pm, when he led his patrol over France in a Scout formation, returning to base two hours later.

The following morning he went up in a Sopwith Pup with patrol leader Captain J.D. Latta, 2nd Lieutenant A.V. Shirley, Lieutenant R.M. Roberts, 2nd Lieutenant A. Robertson and 2nd Lieutenant J.W. Boumphrey,[2] but was brought down near Croisilles-Hermies in France by enemy fire and taken prisoner.

Roland said this about his cousin's capture:

I found out later that on a patrol with his squadron in France his machine-guns had jammed. He was isolated from his companions and chased by a German fighter and a two-seater aircraft. He tried to escape from their harassment by doing a nose-dive, but the enemy followed him until he went into a corkscrew spin. He fell in no man's land and was taken prisoner.

After capture, Sidney's first stop was the newly opened Freiburg POW camp in Germany.

Roland vividly describes his cousin's first escape attempt:

The camp in which Sidney was held was in the very centre of the town. It was an enormous warehouse of three storeys, with a central courtyard, completely occupying a block and surrounded on all sides by streets of the town, which were closed to local civilian traffic. These streets were brightly lit with street lamps except when there was an air-raid warning.

All the windows had heavy iron bars, and sentries patrolled the surrounding streets day and night.

Sidney was a solitary individual who did not want to join the official escape plans then being thought out in the camp. He worked entirely secretly. In one of the rooms on the 3rd floor there was a wardrobe which almost touched the ceiling. With great patience, he made a hole in the plaster and succeeded in getting into the attic between the ceiling and the roof, where there was an empty space.

Somehow he made a long rope using canvas from folding armchairs. The architect had designed the roof so that it was wider than the outside walls, leaving eaves which over-hung the front wall. By making a hole in the eave at a place where the wall had a small indentation, he was able to hang the rope down the three storeys from the roof to the street in such a way that it remained shaded from the street lights.

Sidney had already studied the movements of the sentries. Between the time that the guard in front passed by and returned on his beat, the agile lad went down the three storeys on the rope and landed momentarily in a doorway where the light from the street lamp did not reach him. The second time the sentry passed, he crossed the street and disappeared in the labyrinth of streets of the town.

I cannot exaggerate the daring of this remarkable feat, as nobody had been able to escape from that camp until then. Sidney was wearing British uniform and at all times, except when he hid in the doorway on the footpath, he was in the light of the street lamps. To come down three storeys by a rope in minimum time is not something which can be done without making a noise. If the sentry had seen him he would have been killed instantly.

In the darkness of the night he left the town and reached the woods of the Black Forest. It was extremely cold and there was still snow in the ditches beside the forest tracks. He was carrying very few rations. He could not rest nor make a fire while he tried to get as far as possible from the town. The Germans did not discover his absence for two days. Then there was a tremendous row. Patrols were sent out to follow him, using tracker dogs.

The martyrdom of his escape must have been terrible, as he had nowhere to shelter. He slept shivering on damp pine needles. Nevertheless, he avoided being caught for two weeks. He was captured in a wretched condition and was terribly badly treated in the filthy cells of the German Military Police . . .

Barbed Wire Disease

Although the exact nature of the treatment Sidney may have endured at the hands of the German Military Police is not known, it is probable that this is where his mind may have begun its irrevocable dark journey.

After his interrogation, Sidney was transferred to Ratschkau POW camp, then Holzminden, then to another *strafe* camp, Schweidnitz in the region of Silesia, near the Polish border.[3] He was there for some time before his cousin Roland was coincidentally admitted as a POW. It was clear to Roland that something frightening had happened to his cousin between his capture and his transfer to Schweidnitz. He found that Sidney had 'completely changed' and became deeply disturbed by his cousin's fantastically obsessive behaviour. Sidney was convinced there were German spies planted among the camp internees with murder on their minds.

In a display of what Roland later described in his memoirs as 'pathetic loyalty', Sidney appointed himself his younger cousin's protector – to the extent that his actions began to isolate Roland from the other POWs. Sidney was consumed by thoughts of escaping and when he wasn't protecting Roland in his imaginary role of bodyguard, he was spending every waking moment concocting daring plans to flee.

Sidney was thin, highly strung and nervous, and complained that the other POWs – dating back to his Holzminden days – were trying to 'make a fool' out of him. He was convinced he was being watched all the time – in this he was probably correct, but not for the reasons he imagined.

His unsettling behaviour was disturbing the other POWs.

One night, as he lay awake in his bunk, his whole body began to tremble, his heart began to pound, he began perspiring and he was wracked with nervous tension. He felt he was 'half dead' and experienced extreme pain in the kidney region, as though someone had punched him.

The next day, he heard his fellow POWs discussing private matters that he himself had not divulged to them. Recalling the previous night's events when his body had spasmed, he was convinced he had been hypnotised. Although it was later to be revealed in the Breslau hospital notes that Sidney talked in his sleep, he could not be convinced that those around him were not trying to possess his mind.

He also believed that his fellow POWs were out to murder him and pleaded with the guards to put him in a single room and lock the door against his imagined attackers.

By this stage, Sidney had been a POW for thirteen months. Concerned, Roland asked the senior British officers to present his cousin's case to the camp authorities in the hope he would receive the help he desperately needed. The Germans refused to send Sidney back to England, but on 1 July 1918, they transferred him to a hospital in Breslau,[4] 21 miles (34km) away, seeking an official medical verdict. Sidney was admitted 'on the suspicion of paranoia', remaining there for two months for observation and diagnosis.

The German doctor observing Sidney on admittance recorded in his *Krankenblatt* (medical notes) that Sidney appeared calm, but 'he cuts himself off completely from his surroundings'. Over the following weeks, Sidney's behaviour became agitated, and he often complained of being persecuted by those around him. He was acutely sensitive to noise, maintaining that the patient snoring in the next bed did it deliberately to annoy him. When he was being particularly difficult, only the threat of being moved to a noisier ward seemed to pull him into line – at least temporarily – as he feared the hustle and bustle of a busy room.

Sidney accused the Germans of disrupting his sleep in order to induce him to a slow mental and physical decline. He also entertained delusions of grandeur, insisting that he possessed a greater intelligence than those around him, and was certain that a great power or person was determined to drive him to madness.

The German doctor had noted that Sidney could not be convinced otherwise of 'the absurdity of these ideas'.

Sidney began a campaign of letter-writing to the Kommandant of Schweidnitz, complaining of withheld food parcels. He imagined an enemy in every person with whom he crossed paths, including fellow patients.

The German doctor concluded that Sidney was 'self-pitying' and made special mention of his nervous tension, which manifested as moderate eyelid-fluttering, heart fluttering, insomnia and a head sensitive to the touch. Sidney spent much of his time in the hospital, listless and bed-ridden, hiding under the blankets.

When Sidney returned to Schweidnitz, he was worse. Roland had no idea what had happened in the hospital, but he was alarmed by how 'dangerous' his cousin had become. Sidney's animosity towards the Germans was so vitriolic that Roland and the other officers feared he might attack one of the prison guards.

Once again the camp authorities were asked to repatriate Sidney back to England.

This time, with the supporting evidence of a report from the hospital detailing Sidney's genuine psychiatric condition, the camp authorities were convinced and signed his release.

Along with fifty-two stretcher cases and four psychiatric cases, Sidney was exchanged with German hospital cases and arrived at the military hospital at Netley in Hampshire, England, on 25 August 1918, fifteen months after he had first been taken prisoner.

Two days later, he was referred on to Latchmere House Military Hospital at Ham Common, a facility that had been opened by Lord Knutsford's Red Cross Committee to care for shell-shocked officers. It was staffed by seven women and twenty-three men – eight trained civilian attendants and fifteen Royal Army Medical Corp (RAMC) orderlies.

On admittance, Sidney was examined by RAMC Medical Officers Major Norman Oliver and Captain Harvey Baird. They diagnosed delusional insanity and over the course of the following three months Sidney seemed to improve, his fantasies appearing to have substantially subsided. Major Oliver concluded that Sidney's delusions no longer influenced his behaviour, and he was deemed well enough to be sent to the convalescent side of the house to continue his road to recovery.

An article, called 'Psychoses in Officers in 1914–1918', written by Baird twenty-three years after his Latchmere House service, gives us a glimpse of Latchmere House patient treatment of the day:

> The general treatment consisted of rest, fresh air, good feeding and discipline with treatment of symptoms as required. Every case was kept in bed at least a week, lying all day on a veranda. Those with exhaustion symptoms were usually kept in bed much longer. Rest is, of course, essential in the treatment of exhaustion cases, and one can often almost note a daily diminution of the headache, tremor, exaggerated reflexes and so on, while getting a case up too soon, or allowing him too much parole after getting up, is apt to be followed by a recrudescence of the symptoms. Later they were allowed to be up half the day in the grounds. When the exhaustion symptoms had gone they were encouraged to work half the day at gardening, which had a most beneficial effect. Later they were allowed out in Richmond Park and district, first with an

attendant, later with other officers who were convalescent, and last by themselves . . . When the cases became convalescent they slept in more or less ordinary rooms . . . The convalescent patients were allowed out daily from roughly 2 to 6 p.m., but each had to ask a medical officer for permission on each occasion . . .

Recovering patients in the convalescent annex, where Sidney was moved due to his apparent improvement, experienced more freedom. Whereas in the high-care ward, a body search for dangerous weapons was conducted on patients, here the patients were subject only to room and locker searches.

What no-one knew was that on one of his escorted trips home to St Johns Wood with his mother, Marie, and older sister, Lily, Sidney had, on the pretext of wanting to gather some warm underclothes from a chest of drawers, removed an ageing service revolver and smuggled it back to Latchmere House.

Marie was to later make a statement to police that the revolver had been there for a few years and had started to rust, despite her taking it out to oil it every so often.[5]

Influenza had struck Latchmere House, resulting in a staff shortage, which meant that Sidney was not searched on his return to the hospital. He immediately took to his bed and stayed there for three weeks.

The delusions had returned, worse than ever, and this was noted by the hospital at the time, yet the staff remained unaware of the secreted revolver in Sidney's possession.

Sidney's 1984 death certificate describes him as a chronic schizophrenic. This is a complex psychiatric condition and difficult to treat. Characteristically, sufferers experience hallucinations, delusions and paranoia and the feeling of being persecuted or hunted; they often hear voices instructing them to commit aggressive or violent acts, become obsessed with an event or person, and have disordered thoughts and speech. Without the appropriate treatment, schizophrenic sufferers are incapable of separating fantasy from reality.

However, this was 1918. It was an era in which there was still much to be discovered about troubled minds and psychiatric hospitals were officially referred to as mental or lunatic asylums.

On the night of Saturday, 30 November 1918, at around 10.30 pm, Sidney had a brief chat to the head attendant, George Fryer. There was nothing in Sidney's demeanour that tipped Fryer off to the tragic drama that was to unfold only moments later.

Next Sidney went into the toilet, summoning a thirty-eight-year-old orderly by the name of Private John Aldridge of the RAMC with a bell. Aldridge, answering the call for assistance, was confronted by Sidney pointing a revolver at him. The orderly was instructed to raise his hands. Aldridge then made the fatal mistake of lunging at Sidney, with the intention of disarming him. Sidney fired the revolver at close range.

Later, when Sidney was being charged with murder, he described the moment matter-of-factly:

> I pointed the revolver at the orderly and told him to put his hands up; he was braver than I thought he was and refused. I fired and he fell to the ground and I walked out.

After shooting Aldridge at point blank range, Sidney escaped in his pyjamas down a fire escape.

Possibly it was the gunshot that brought him running, but another orderly, Corporal Jarrett, found Aldridge's body on the toilet floor. He reported his discovery to Fryer, and both men rushed back to the scene to find Aldridge bleeding profusely from a wound above his eye. Fryer immediately called for the Medical Officer, Baird, who arrived on the scene, examined Aldridge and declared him officially dead.

The alarm was raised that an armed and dangerous psychiatric patient escapee was at large, and the constabulary was put on high alert.

An hour and a half later – at 12.15 am on 1 December – Sidney was found by Police Constables Malcolmson and Moore wandering Queen Street in Hammersmith, wearing his pyjamas with a khaki bed jacket and slippers. The loaded 38-calibre Webley service revolver and rounds in Sidney's pocket was the smoking gun needed to convince the two constables they had found their man.

When Detective Inspector John Ferrier of V Division arrived, Sidney insisted he be taken to Scotland Yard first to vitally inform the authorities that he:

> . . . did it for reasons so important that I have put myself in this situation. I did it for the reason that my statement could not be suppressed; it was for the benefit of England.

Sadly, Sidney's delusions had him convinced that Aldridge had been a German spy, who was part of a bigger plot for Germany to rise up and dominate the world.

Sidney was officially charged with the murder, and Aldridge's wife, Matilda, and two young sons, only eight and nine, were informed of the tragedy at their home in Reading.

In a police statement, Detective Inspector Ferrier said:

> I was desirous of ascertaining how Hume became possessed of that revolver and I saw his mother – who was very much

upset – and she identified the revolver as the one belonging to her son . . . She informed me that had she suspected for a moment he had taken that, she would have at once informed the authorities at Latchmere Hospital.

The coroner's inquiry resulted in a verdict of wilful murder against Sidney Stewart Hume. He was then remanded to Brixton Prison and committed for trial in February 1919. However, the authorities concluded that Sidney was unfit to stand trial, being of unsound mind, and he was removed to Broadmoor Lunatic Asylum under the *Criminal Lunatics Act 1884*. Sidney – whose psychiatric volatility had ironically begun with imprisonment – was incarcerated in the sinister-sounding Cell 10, Block 6 of the high-security facility.

The media of the day sensationally reported that the perpetrator of the Ham Common Murder, as it became known, had been 'driven mad by the Germans'. Certainly the trauma of Sidney's treatment at the hands of the Germans – real or imagined – remained deeply embedded in his psyche. His obsession with non-delivery of food, a feature of his POW days, still plagued him decades after he was last a prisoner in a German camp.

The family, far from turning their backs on him, continued to keep in contact. In 1942, shortly after their mother, Marie, passed away, Violet wrote to her eldest brother, Alexander (Sandy). She refers to their sibling's still fragile state of mind twenty-four years after his committal:

Have had three letters from Sidney in answer to a birthday present and also some chocolate I had sent him and he is just as bad as ever and the doctors says no sign of any hope or improvement. He is very suspicious of the news of Mama and thinks the whole thing a hoax by the Germans . . .

Sidney made no substantial improvement over the years. In 1968, still not deemed fit to be released into the community nearly five decades after he had shot dead Private Aldridge, Sidney was transferred from Broadmoor and went to live out the rest of his life, without drama or fanfare, at the Priory, a psychiatric hospital at Roehampton.

Although he consistently refused family visits, his sister Lily nonetheless sent a Christmas hamper from Barkers of High Street, Kensington, every year. When Lily passed away in 1966, Hume's niece and grand-niece sought to carry on the tradition. One year, the pair made the trip to the hospital to deliver his Christmas hamper to his new address at the Priory, rather than having it delivered as was the usual custom.

They remember Sidney, who would have been in his early eighties by then, as 'looking like Methuselah, with a long white beard down to his waist'. Having not had direct contact with him for many years, they introduced themselves as family, to which Sidney responded, 'Off with your heads!'

Sidney passed away on 20 September 1984, shortly after his ninety-eighth birthday. As well as noting chronic schizophrenia and senile dementia, on his death certificate the cause of death was given as bronchopneumonia.

★

Upon arrival back in England, psychiatric cases like Sidney were transferred to one of the nineteen English hospitals designated for shell-shocked servicemen. In those days, little was known of this condition and one popular theory was that sufferers had incurred mental repercussions as a result of the physical effects of bomb blasts, hence the term 'shell shock'.

In 1917 and with a growing number of psychiatric cases to

treat, Colonel Rogers, the Regimental Medical Officer (RMO) of the 4th Black Watch, instructed frontline officers:

> You must send your emotional cases down the line. But when you get these emotional cases, unless they are very bad, if you have a hold of the men and they know you and you know them (and there is a good deal more in the man knowing you than in you knowing the man) . . . you are able to explain to him that there is really nothing wrong with him, give him a rest at the aid post if necessary and a day or two's sleep, go up with him to the front line, and, when there, see him often, sit down beside him and talk to him about the war and look through his periscope and let the man see you are taking an interest in him.[6]

During the First World War, the condition was sometimes labelled a character weakness, even cowardice, by the military. London-born journalist Philip Gibbs served as one of five official war correspondents during this period and observed afflicted servicemen with a compassion that was largely lacking in military ranks.

He wrote:

> Something was wrong. They put on civilian clothes again and looked to their mothers and wives very much like the young men who had gone to business in the peaceful days before August 1914. But they had not come back the same men. Something had altered in them. They were subject to sudden moods, and queer tempers, fits of profound *depression* alternating with a restless desire for pleasure. Many were easily moved to passion where they lost control of themselves, many were bitter in their speech, violent in opinion, frightening.[7]

Almost a century and many wars later, the condition – which would now most likely be diagnosed as Post Traumatic Stress Disorder – is far better understood. Support services are offered to afflicted military personnel returning from active duty. For those who fought in the First World War, however, it was a condition that was greatly misunderstood.

Eight

Crime and Punishment

Below ground, under both the barracks buildings at Holzminden, the camp boasted its punishment cells, known to the POWs as 'the jug' – a prison within a prison.

Each cell was small, damp and partially subterranean. The only glimpse of the outside world was afforded through a small window near the ceiling, through which confined inmates could see only the boots of men walking by – at ground level – outside. Basic necessities were provided: a mattress-less bed, a water jug, a wash basin, a stool and a table. Being located below ground level, the cells were subject to the seasonal effects of the weather: summer prisoners sweated their way through their sentence in stifling heat and winter prisoners virtually turned into blocks of ice during the freezing European winter – all subsisting on meagre rations. Any British prisoner who happened to have a German surname could expect harsh treatment from their captors for they were considered a traitor to Germany.

Officers could look forward to a stint in the jug as punishment for infractions ranging from attempted escape to insolence or sloppy salutes directed at a German officer. On the other hand, men of other ranks (ORs) were subject to a different and inequitable set of rules. While officers routinely tested the patience of their captors, men of other ranks like Dick Cash were far more likely to toe the line to avoid serious punishment.

Crime and Punishment

Max Gore recalled a fellow officer named Fullarton who was:

> ... an engineer in civil life with a brilliant mathematical brain ... he could give you from his head the square root of any figure in a matter of seconds ... in the same manner, he could give the cubic content of any area to be excavated ...

Depriving a brilliant mind of mental stimulation generally leads to trouble. Fullarton and some accomplices circumnavigated Niemeyer's newly declared rule outlawing the 'wretched quality' canteen wine by raiding the potato stores and concocting their own alcoholic beverage. The resultant drink, which Max declared 'fantastic', packed such a punch that their drunken rampages alerted the Germans to their covert activities.

Max noted wryly:

> Fullarton and his cronies spent a period of solitary confinement far in excess of that needed to sober them up.

A newly arrived Holzminden inmate could expect a welcome that entailed being marched directly to the jug to begin his sentence for a previous escape attempt from another camp – a short or long stint at Niemeyer's pleasure.

And so it was for twenty-two-year-old Lieutenant Hector Fraser Dougall. By the time he reached Holzminden, the red-head – later dubbed 'Fiery Red Dougall' by a fellow POW – had managed to jump from not one but two moving trains as the Germans transported him between POW camps.

The week of his arrival at Holzminden coincided with the celebrations of Victoria Day in his home country of Canada. In the year of 1918, it fell on 24 May. Locked in his dark cell, Hector's thoughts flew back to his childhood when, as a young boy in knickerbockers, he mischievously let off firecrackers to frighten the girls. Memories from his past warmed him as he recalled the fireworks display, the noise, laughter and dousing of rain that always seemed to accompany the celebrations back home.

Recollections were all he had until letters and parcels from home started to flow through to Holzminden.

Hector was born on 23 August 1896 in Winnipeg, Canada. The only son of William C. Dougall and Jessie Isabella McFadyen, he joined elder sister Mabel, with whom he was to remain close all his life. Ten years later, youngest child Isabelle was born.

Hector graduated from Kelvin High School in Winnipeg and began working in his home town for the Bank of Ottawa. On 7 March 1916, at the age of nineteen, he enlisted in the Royal Winnipeg Rifles of the Canadian Expeditionary Force and was commissioned a lieutenant on 8 May 1916. Like so many others, a brief taste of an infantryman's life in the trenches persuaded him to transfer to the Royal Flying Corps in May of 1917. Years on, Hector was asked what prompted the transfer from foot soldier to aviator during the war and he replied, 'So I could shoot back.' In the air, Hector felt that at least he had a fighting chance.

Nine months after joining the RFC, on 26 February 1918, Hector was flying a mission with No. 54 Squadron when his Sopwith Camel (the successor to the Scout, or 'Pup'), engaged in strafing a German observation balloon south of Laon in France, took enemy fire. The bombardment shattered the cowling and prop and tore at the fabric of the plane, fragments hitting Hector in the forehead and neck. As blood ran like a river, he fought to keep control while the Camel was relentlessly attacked. The valiant engine, which had taken a direct hit, sputtered to a

Crime and Punishment

complete halt and as Hector attempted to level out at around 100 feet (30.5m), the Camel rolled in the opposite direction, and the aircraft slammed into the ground.

The next thing the dazed Hector remembered was staggering to his feet 15 feet (4.5m) from the decimated plane. Seeing his Camel lying in pieces, he realised how lucky he'd been – the safety belt snapping and the act of being thrown from the cockpit had saved his life. But before he was able to set his plane alight as per regulations, he found himself surrounded by German troops.

Questioned over two days at Korps HQ without his wounds being treated, Hector was in a bad way. One eye had completely swollen shut, his injured side was giving him merry hell and breathing was a chore. Finally, after much arguing with the guard, he was taken to a doctor, who removed glass from his forehead and straightened his nose. Then he was shown to his quarters.

Hector was the fifth POW to be packed into a cell space built for one; the food was inedible; his wounds were aching. The miserable existence was made a little more bearable by the discovery that one of Hector's cell-mates was a fellow Canadian – from Peterborough – and a fellow No. 54 Squadron RFC member. Their spirits lifted when a German guard agreed to secure them decent food, books to read and a transfer to Karlsruhe, but it proved to be a cruel lesson in empty German promises.

The cell-mates were given vegetable soup from a wash basin, coffee and a tiny amount of bread and sausage. Hector kept to his bed, nursing a bowling-ball head, a swollen eye and deflated lung, remarking drily in his diary that he 'was not the man' he was a week ago. He loathed his captors' insistence on lights out at 9.30 pm; he felt that the men were being treated like a gaggle of school children. In a matter of days the freedom-loving

Hector was beginning to understand – and resent – the realities of POW life.

On 3 March 1918, Hector and his cell-mates were transported by train to another French town, Montcournet (Mt Coronet), 20 miles (32km) back from the lines and marched to a nearby prison camp that held civilians of various nationalities. The condition of the prisoners horrified Hector, but he wasn't in a position to object – he and his companions were locked in a small room and if it wasn't for the kindness of a fellow POW, a Frenchman who had been incarcerated for fourteen months, who gave them some of his French relief biscuits, they might have starved attempting to digest the substandard food provided by their captors. The officers demanded better food and were finally rewarded with a little butter, sugar, jam, coffee, sausage and soup. The cell rats were equally delighted for during the night they took off with whatever they could get their hairy little paws on.

It was bone-chillingly cold in the cell despite there being a small wood stove and a wood supply; the mattresses were wet; and each man had been allocated only two threadbare blankets apiece. None of them could get comfortable enough to fall asleep.

To their huge relief, the group were marched to the train station five days later, on 8 March, and loaded into a third-class carriage for the all-stops trundle across the Alsace-Lorraine countryside en route to their next destination: Karlsruhe in south-west Germany, near the Franco-German border.

In his diary, Hector expressed ironic humour about the freezing cold:

> Give me 40-below weather in Canada with only a shirt on rather than be cramped up in a third-class European railway compartment coach, travelling about ten miles an hour with no heat.

Crime and Punishment

They were all distracted from the freezing cold momentarily when Doyle, an Englishman from Liverpool, who had climbed up in the luggage rack to relieve the monotony, came crashing down on top of the German guard accompanying to them to Karlsruhe. Hector was convinced that Doyle was not going to see out the journey alive, but the hapless Liverpudlian managed to survive the furious guard's wrath.

The POWs found that Karlsruhe was the Carlton Ritz compared to their previous incarceration experiences and rejoiced in receiving clean separate rooms, decent beds, edible supper and books to read.

Hector felt 'almost respectable' after a good night's sleep, and a wash and shave in the morning. It was the first time he'd removed his clothes in nearly a fortnight. He was questioned by the authorities, then released into a larger room with seven other RFC pilots, among them a flier from his own squadron.

It was here in Karlsruhe that Hector met Lieutenant Sedley Gerald 'Willo' Williams, a twenty-four-year-old fellow pilot. The two hit it off immediately and, fuelled by a shared loathing of the prospect of life in captivity, they began to hatch a plot to flee at the earliest opportunity.

As Karlsruhe was a POW processing camp, it was inevitable they were to move on. On 18 March, Hector, Willo and some other officers were marched to the train station and boarded a train at 6 pm for an unknown destination. Hector noted in his diary that they were travelling 'west and slightly south through very hilly country'.

His sense of direction proved to be accurate for the train was clattering towards another POW camp, Landshut, which was 213 miles (343km) south-west of Karlsruhe.

Unknown to his German captors, Willo had a tiny compass

burning a hole in his pocket and a fire in his belly. At 4.30 am on 19 March, after travelling through the night, Hector, Willo and Australian Alec Couston jumped the train and immediately headed for the French border. With no map and little food, but driven by a sense of youthful determination, the trio travelled on foot by night and hid by day in the woods.

In a letter dated 16 July 1918, written by Willo to Hector's sister, Mabel, in Winnipeg, he recounts their adventure on the run:

> On the second night, Dougall went into the farmyard and pinched a duck . . . We cooked the bird by day and enjoyed it immensely. It was very cold travelling in the bush; in many parts of the ground, the snow was very thick. Water was sometimes scarce so we had to drink the melted snow . . .

By the third day, Alec had struck out on his own. Hector and Willo kept going, following the railway line. Willo began to fear they were heading in the wrong direction but Hector, with his acute sense of direction, was certain their aim was true.

On their fifth day on the run, they happened upon a farmhouse where a sympathetic German householder showed them a map of the district; the escapees realised they were only 15 or 20 miles (24–32km) from the *Frontier* (border). After bidding goodbye to the German woman, they stole some beetroot from the village and hid under a railway bridge, where they lit a fire to reduce the beetroot to soup. This is where a railway worker found them and raised the alarm. Hector opted to make a break for it, but the only escape route was across the icy river. Willo resisted, and the duo were locked up in the railway guardhouse.

The guard had barely left them when the two began ripping up the floorboards in an effort to burrow their way out. Given a little more time, Willo felt sure they would have made it, but the guard returned and they were sent directly to Landshut, from which the pair had just spent an agonising five days running in the opposite direction.

Initially Hector and Willo were held in a civilian prison. Before a search by the Germans, Hector slipped the tiny compass into his mouth to conceal it. It was never detected.

Upon arrival at Landshut POW camp, where they rejoined their fellow officers, for their escape effort both men were sentenced to eight days in a cell without mental stimulation or decent food.

On 31 April, Hector and Willo were put on a train for a three-day journey to their final destination – Holzminden. In an effort to prevent another escape attempt, they were made to take their boots off. The German officer-in-charge had strict instructions to keep an eye on the two with a gift for Houdini-like disappearances.

Their boots were returned to them when they were required to walk the platform to change trains. Hector was the first one to enter the carriage and, with lightning speed, he snatched the railway map off the door, pocketing it without attracting the guard's attention.

At 9.30 am and in broad daylight, Hector and Willo jumped the train, their movement too sudden for the guard to fire upon them. They rolled down an embankment, making for the nearest cover. Consulting the railway map, they were shocked to discover they were further away from the Dutch border than ever before – 300 miles (482km) – but with the aid of the tiny compass, which had evaded detection so far, they pointed themselves north and began to walk.

They stole whatever they could to stay alive – eggs, milk and bacon – by house-breaking. The pair found they enjoyed the thrill of the steal and although they were caught in the act three times, they made good their escape albeit with an angry German in hot pursuit each time. During one wild chase, Hector and Willo were forced to plunge into the river, emerging on the other side to give their furious pursuers a cheery wave of farewell.

However, the jubilant pair's luck was poised to run out. After seventeen days on the run and at the early morning hour of 2 am, they ran straight into a German sentry on the main road. Hector called to Willo to disarm the enemy soldier, but reinforcements had already been called from the guardroom and Willo knew it was hopeless.

Willo recounts in his letter to Mabel Dougall:

> As we were being marched to the guardroom, I bolted. It was very dark at the time and I did it so on the moment that I had no time to tell Dougall of my intentions. The sentry fired at me but missed and I was once more 'free' again . . .

Taking the utmost care to avoid detection, Willo continued to walk for two more days, making it to the safety of Holland on 19 May and, finally, to the safety of Mother England on 24 May.

It stands to reason that despite feeling elation at Willo's successful escape, Hector must have felt deep disappointment for himself. He'd managed to escape twice and had been caught twice, and now here he was en route to Germany's most notoriously inescapable camp, Holzminden.

Much later, Willo received a postcard from Hector, now interned in Holzminden POW camp. As he had suspected, his loyal escape-mate had interfered with the sentry's aim:

> Dear Willo – Good old boy, darn glad you made it. Did the best I could, prevented the point blank. Write to my sister, Mabel K.

Crime and Punishment

Dougall of [address] and give her a full account, something to cheer them up to home. And don't forget the sausages and eats and a big long letter.

Yours as ever, H.F. Dougall

Meanwhile, during the long journey of 18 May 1918 to Holzminden, the ravenous Hector found himself accepting a kind offer of pancakes and sweetbread from an elderly German woman, a passenger on the train. He was very conscious of how he must have looked – two weeks of beard growth, boots barely staying together, ripped trousers and grubby, torn puttees.[1] He was also able to solicit a bowl of stewed vegetables and meat from the guards accompanying POWs to Holzminden, though he was required to compensate them.

Upon reaching the camp at 11 pm, Hector was immediately transferred to a punishment cell under Kaserne B for his part in the escape attempt with Willo.

He later recorded this description of his surroundings:

> ... a 12' × 10' cell about six feet below the ground, one small window, pretty dark and cold.

On his first day, the disheartened Canadian was delighted to receive a visit from his 'long lost friend and brother, Bobby Cowan',[2] who came bearing gifts – a loaf of white bread, a tin of English bully beef, sweet biscuits and jam. Hector would have given anything for Bobby to have sat down for a good long talk, but as he was under punishment conditions, it wasn't permitted.

Also that day, Hector was interrogated by a German officer, the details of his escape attempt were recorded, then it was back to his gloomy cell. Over the ensuing days, he started to clean himself up, scraping the beard from his face in a painful shaving session, followed by the first bath he'd had since leaving Karlsruhe. He noted how rakishly thin he had become, but was pleased that his foot and leg wounds were not giving him too much trouble.

A steady stream of books was supplied to the gaolbird and, with not much else to do, he ripped through each one in no time at all. Volumes of the era – *A Woman of No Importance* by Oscar Wilde, *The Blazed Trail* by American author Stewart Edward White and *Richard Carvel* by Winston Churchill, which Hector described as a thrilling book, not unlike 'hanging upside down or doing a spin inside out' – helped to distract him from the long hours of nothingness.

Hector had no desire to complain about the food he was given, describing a breakfast of porridge, fried bread (a regular inclusion) and chocolate as 'princely'. The good stuff was coming from fellow POWs from their own Red Cross food parcels. An entry in Hector's diary reads: 'Where would I be if it weren't for the generosity of my friends?'

In the cell across the way was a POW whom Hector dubbed 'the Skipper'. The Skipper had been incarcerated for three and a half years, virtually since the beginning of the war, and Dougall never discovered the transgression he had committed that had landed him in the punishment cell. The Skipper had a copy of the *Continental Times*, dated 27 May 1918, which Hector devoured, eager for media reports of what had been going on in the last month. He learned that the Germans had crossed the Aisne and were holding the old Somme line, Paris was under bombardment, German submarines were sinking anything found bobbing on the ocean and lynchings of African Americans were rife in America's Deep South.

Nearly two weeks had gone by and Hector had yet to be told the length of his sentence, but a short time later he received his first letter in Holzminden. Excitedly he opened it, only to discover with tremendous disappointment that, in a case of mistaken identity, he'd received a letter for a Charles R. Dougall. The frustration was offset by a visit from the interpreter, beaming from ear to ear, who told him that he would be released from the cell on 13 June – music to Hector's ears. But he still had nearly a fortnight of torturous solitary confinement to get through. He could hear strains of the camp band playing jaunty little tunes in celebration of a sports day the POWs were staging in the *Spielplatz* outside his window. After glumly listening to the boisterous sounds and cheering, he made his daily diary entry:

> . . . just champing to get out of here into the sunshine and for a good romp around the camp.

The monotony was finally broken on 2 June when the cell door opened and in walked Hector's new cellmate, a Lieutenant Richmond of a Scottish regiment. Things began to look up: Richmond received a steady stream of food parcels, which he gladly shared with a grateful Hector, whose own food parcels had still not caught up with him. There were beans, meat, chocolate, Scottish shortbread, dripping, white bread and honey. Besides the mouth-watering picnic, Hector was thrilled to be talking at length with another human being from the same side. The two cellmates exchanged reminiscences and information about their respective homelands of Canada and Scotland.

The following day, Hector was granted permission to take a walk outside. A combination of his injuries, inadequate diet and the sedentary lifestyle forced upon him by his incarceration made him feel 'pretty weak at the knees' afterwards, but he did feel better for the stroll.

More letters started to find Hector; his mate Bobby Cowan delivered a handful to him in his cell, which Hector fell upon with gusto. He devoured the contents; the mundane details from home were like manna from heaven after weeks of news deprivation.

The hours rolled by in an endless litany of boredom and monotony as Hector counted off the days until his expected release. Finally, on 13 June, five weeks after his arrival at Holzminden, he was led from his cell and could begin to familiarise himself with his new surroundings. He was duly transferred to the same barracks floor as Bobby. Of the twelve others in the barracks room, seven were fellow Canadians, and all of them were flying officers.

★

Hector may have vacated his cell but there were plenty of others to take his place.

Max Gore recalled:

> As escapees, we were ensconced once more in cells: underground ones in the basement with walls so thick that one could only communicate with a person in the adjoining cell by shouting at the full capacity of voice and lungs. It was the means by which Baker and I were able to communicate, but not for long; the effort took too much toll.

Reg Gough described, with dry humour, the incident that led to his only spell in solitary confinement.

Occupants of Kaserne A were distinctly disadvantaged by their position at roll-call, which placed them farthest from the parcel room. The parcel queue was relentlessly long after every delivery, snaking through the camp. One by one, each man shuffled towards the hut at a snail's pace, and it often took hours to get to the head of the queue. The moment roll-call was dismissed, the inmates of Kaserne A would surge towards the parcel hut to attempt to gain pole position, which sent Kaserne B – Reg's barracks house – racing to head them off in the queue.

One morning A surged slightly early, triggering Reg and five others from B to instinctively race for the parcel hut as usual, only to turn to find the rest of the parade laughing at them. He realised they'd been victims of the rival barracks' payback practical joke.

As roll-call had not yet been dismissed, a furious German NCO charged towards the six bolters. Even though the crowd of inmates surged around Reg and the others to give them a chance to melt into the mêlée, he had been singled out and the livid guard chased him through the crowd back to his barracks room, hell bent on collaring him.

Reg was sentenced to three days in the punishment cells and he made good use of his time by goading the cell guards until his release. Nevertheless, in his memoirs he mentions the 'absolute loneliness' he felt in solitary confinement. It was an effective form of punishment: such forms of deprivation were not for the fainthearted, and being in the cells was particularly dangerous for those who endured it for months at a time.

Reg spent nine months as a POW in Germany in the last stage of the war, but he later mused that he:

> . . . cannot express adequately the fits of depression and feeling of monotony that overcame me at times, so what those prisoners [who were captured in the early part of the war and endured the harsh treatment meted out to them when things looked rosy for the Germans] must have felt like it is hard to imagine . . .

Despite the risk of being subjected to long stints in the gloomy cells, most of the imprisoned officers continued on their path of passive resistance in a bid to defy their captors. They knew that Niemeyer intended to break their stubborn collective spirit and they were just not going to have it. Knowing they were protected to a certain extent by their officer status, they pushed the boundaries as far as they dared, taking every opportunity to defy, resist and turn a serious occasion into a farce.

Max Gore recalled a particularly noisy *Appel* when Niemeyer, furious at their raucous conduct, ordered several men to the punishment cells at bayonet point. As they were marched away, the rest of the company whistled the 'Colonel Bogey March'[3] in time to the culprits' rhythmic steps, then burst into laughter. The rest of the prisoners, too many to be gaoled, were locked in their respective barracks for a few days as group punishment.

Said Max:

> When Niemeyer locked us in barracks for the first time, he swaggered up and down the roadway alongside the barracks, looking up at the windows and gloating. It nearly cost him his life when a house-brick, thrown from an upstairs window by an overzealous youngster, missed his florid countenance by inches . . . as a result, what would have been a strafe for a couple of days at most continued for more than a week because the Senior British Officer refused to hand over the culprit . . . Thereafter, although Niemeyer openly continued to swagger and gloat, he did so at a distance of about a hundred yards and with the parade ground in between.

Solitary confinement was something the POWs accepted as part of prison life; it was the withholding of the invaluable Red Cross parcels – a punishment in which Niemeyer indulged whenever he wanted to turn up the heat – that had the worst effect on the inmates. There was no point complaining of ill treatment in a letter to the Red Cross, German or British authorities, as the inmates knew their letters would be censored or destroyed before they even left the camp. Official grievances presented by the senior British officer to the Kommandant fell on deaf ears.

★

No executions took place in Holzminden, but one might argue that, in the tragic case of young Captain William 'Billy' Leefe Robinson, they might as well have.

Born in India in 1895 to a coffee plantation owner, Billy was the youngest of seven children. A Sandhurst military academy graduate, he was a moderate student in the world of academia but later found his calling as a pilot, gaining his wings as a flying officer with No. 19 Squadron RFC on 15 September 1915. Dark-haired and sporting his moustache in the fashionable style of the day, the twinkle-eyed charmer began his career in delivery – flying aircraft to designated locations – before he was seconded to B Flight of No.10 Reserve Squadron, a home defence unit set up to defend the country against the expanding threat of German zeppelin attacks, with a special emphasis on night flights.

During a routine patrol in the early hours of 3 September 1916, Billy – who was, by then, a lieutenant – caught sight of an enemy zeppelin (Schutte-Lanz SL11) making its treacherous journey over London under the cover of darkness. Billy watched as anti-aircraft ground fire barely made an impact on the sinister airship; the scene illuminated by search lights trained at the night sky out of Finsbury and Victoria Park. Despite being low on fuel, the plucky young pilot went in for the kill, tailed by two other night fighters determined to take down the enemy aircraft. Billy blasted the great monster with machine-gun fire – all to no avail until he approached the vast underbelly, firing into the twin rudders with the last of his ammunition. The zeppelin collapsed into a blazing fireball and plummeted into a field outside the village of Cuffley, Hertfordshire, killing all sixteen crew on board, including the experienced, Kent-born German commander, Wilhelm Schramm.

Despite the hour, many Londoners witnessed the fiery downing of the airship and the night was filled with cries of jubilant cheering at Billy's direct hit. On the ground, he was mobbed as a hero by the ecstatic crowd.

In the days and weeks to follow, Billy was showered with gifts from a grateful nation. He was awarded the Victoria Cross by King George V at Windsor Castle, which was reported in the *London Gazette* of 5 September 1916 (in part) as:

> Lieutenant William Leefe Robinson, Worcestershire Regiment and Royal Flying Corps. For most conspicuous bravery. He attacked an enemy airship under circumstances of great difficulty and danger, and sent it crashing to the ground as a flaming wreck . . .

The nation went mad for Billy. He was bombarded with letters and telegrams of gratitude from the public, some containing small gratuities. Businessmen sent him huge sums of money amounting to thousands of pounds, as well as gifts and, in one instance, a gold watch.

Billy's swashbuckling feat also made him a target for swooning women, including French actress Alice Delysia, a dancer at the Folies Bergère and Moulin Rouge in Paris, who sent him a steady stream of adoring – but unrequited – letters.

Crime and Punishment

Seven months later, Billy – now a captain – was in command of No. 48 Squadron RFC. His observer/gunner, New Zealander Lieutenant Edward Darien Warburton, wrote of him, 'Capt. Robinson VC is my flight commander. He seems quite a decent sort.'

In a postwar letter to his mother in 1919, Darien recalled the moment their Bristol F.2 fighter was shot down during a decoy mission over France in April 1917 by German air ace Vizefeldwebel Sebastian Festner of the *Luftstreitkräfte*.

The RNAS Scout aircraft expected to turn up as air support failed to show, leaving the squadron exposed. New guns had been fitted but an incorrect oil had been used, resulting in poor performance. Consequently, Billy only managed to fire off one shot.

The British novice pilots were no match for the might of Jasta 11's highly trained Albatros D.111 fighters, but the Brits put up a valiant fight for an hour, sustaining a loss of three or four planes. The decision had just been taken to return to base when Billy's aircraft took crippling artillery fire in the engine from German fighter pilot Vizefeldwebel Sebastian Festner, resulting in complete engine failure.

Observer/gunner Darien wrote:

We were 25 miles [40km] over the line so there was no chance of getting back and down we went, followed by a German machine who tried to shoot up a little more. Robinson threw the machine about and I let off some of my few remaining cartridges whenever he became too aggressive. When we landed the machine turned turtle. I was cut a bit above the face and head and jammed under my gun. Robinson got out and helped me out. When the machine that had followed us down started firing on us from the air.

I soaked my handkerchief in petrol which was pouring from the machine, lit it and threw it on when the machine went up in a blaze of flame. Also my nice fur gauntlets which had also got soaked in petrol. I pulled them off in a hurry and threw them away also my watch was strapped over my glove. We had no time to think of details as we were being periodically fired on from the air and you must picture us dodging backwards and forwards to get out of the line of fire like a couple of bewildered hens. Shortly after a mounted Boche rode up, pointing a revolver, and took us in charge.

It was clear that Darien admired Billy as a pilot, although in his letter he expressed disappointment that Billy had been pitted against experienced German pilots before the young pilot was ready, believing that:

> . . . his mistake lay in adhering too strictly to his orders to cruise over Douai for 2 hours when he found the RNAS scouts had not turned up.

Billy and Darien were transported to Douai, where they were kept in solitary confinement for five days and interrogated by an 'oily, affable German intelligence officer' who clearly felt that playing the 'good cop' role would achieve a better result. When he was unable to extract intelligence from the pilots, they were sent to Karlsruhe processing camp in Germany via a tedious fourth-class train journey during which they found themselves packed in with 'stinking German soldiers' and little food.

The aviator duo was separated, with Darien transported to Heidelburg while Billy was eventually transported to Freiburg. It was here he joined other officers in three escape bids that failed, before a fourth attempt – a window scramble – succeeded. Freedom was theirs for four days before they were recaptured and returned to Freiburg. Darien was sentenced to a month's solitary confinement in Zorndorf's fortress prison camp before being sent to Clausthal by train. Again he tried to flee en route but his effort was thwarted by prison sentries.

Shortly after, Billy found himself in Holzminden and at the mercy of Niemeyer, who knew the new arrival to be a 'zepp killer'. What's more, the Kommandant claimed to have been a personal friend of Commander Schramm, whom Billy had sent to a fiery death over London a year before. The young pilot's heroic reputation – for which he had been feted and adored in Britain – had preceded him but he was now incarcerated in enemy territory with a target on his forehead. Known as the 'English Richthofen' – a nickname that probably would have made him smile back in England – here there would be no adoring fans.

Determined to escape Niemeyer's clutches, Billy attempted escape with a Canadian officer, Captain William Samuel Clouston Stephenson[4] of No. 73 Squadron RFC, but they were unceremoniously recaptured. Now Niemeyer's full fury was brought to bear on the young pilot. From that point on, Billy was imprisoned in a solitary confinement cell of Kaserne A where the windows were kept sealed and a guard was assigned to wake him up with a flashlight at regular intervals to induce sleep deprivation. Food rations were minuscule. Next Billy fell prey to the global pandemic of the Spanish flu that killed millions across the world. This substantially weakened him and left him more susceptible to the ongoing campaign of persecution levelled against him by Niemeyer. Billy grew weaker and weaker in the oppressive, airless environment.

The entire camp was aware of the ace pilot's ill-treatment in the cell that had become known as 'the chamber of horrors'. He was occasionally allowed out for a walk around the compound, but he existed more as a ghostly presence whom the prisoners hardly ever saw.

As the POWs were prevented from complaining directly to British authorities, the senior British officer arranged for a message to be smuggled out in the handle of a tennis racquet via an officer en route for exchange. The exchanged officer managed to get the message to the War Office in London, who complained to the German War Office. The Germans duly dispatched an inspector to Holzminden for whom Niemeyer conveniently acted as interpreter.

The German inspector returned to report to his superiors that he had not observed any evidence of ill-treatment, even remarking on Niemeyer's 'pleasant' disposition.

The POWs knew that Billy – hero of the hour – was as good as doomed. Upon release after the Armistice, Billy ran into his old observer/gunner, Darien, by chance. In Darien's eyes, Billy had come through his ordeal reasonably well, for he noted in a letter home that his former pilot 'looked very fit and was in mufti, having spent several very gay days staying at a hotel in Berlin'. The journey back to England took them through Copenhagen, Denmark, and they landed in Leith on Saturday, 13 December 1918.

In his letter Darien added:

[We] were taken south to the Reception camp at Ripon where after filling up a lot of medical forms and going before a medical Board we were sent off on two months leave. I was going to travel up to town with Robinson but missed the train we had arranged to go by.

Only two weeks later, on 31 December 1918, a weakened Billy succumbed to the effects of the Spanish flu. He died at his sister's home in Stanmore.

Darien wrote:

> I never saw him again as he was taken ill and died on the 31st December. It was appalling bad luck after getting home again.

Billy was twenty-three.

NINE

Unbreakable Spirit

A successful escape attempt did not necessarily mean return to home and hearth. If a prisoner managed to flee to freedom – and if he was fit and healthy – this generally entailed return to active duty.

For this reason, many prisoners were content to sit out the war behind the barbed wire. They were poorly fed, but at least they weren't being shot at.

Others, however, had no sooner been recaptured or transferred to another camp as punishment for an escape attempt than they were plotting yet another breakout. Boredom was a driving factor – scheming their way over, through or under the wire provided stimulation in an otherwise dull existence, and the serial escapees were relentless in their efforts to display their unbreakable spirit to their captors.

Many breakouts were attempted from Holzminden.

Reg Gough remembers the diligent but comical efforts of the nineteen-year-old flying officer in the bunk next to his own:

> . . . he and a companion rigged up a jumping pole from spars of deck chairs tied together with string . . . They had hopes that the pole would be long enough to carry the jumper over the outer railings. The weak spot in the plan was that the pole was to be steered by guys [ropes] from a lower window. The whole plan

sounded crazy to me and I did my best to persuade the lad to give up the idea . . . Apart from the very fragile condition of the pole, windows had to be opened after dark on two landings and that was a proceeding for which one might get a bullet if the sentry was on the alert. Anyhow, the preliminary steps went off without a hitch and the fellow took off . . . the pole at once snapped where the guy ropes were attached lower down. The would-be escaper fell, luckily between the railings and the building and the Commandant and three or four men were on the spot at once . . . Although the fellow dropped about 20 ft [6m], he was only dazed.

Reg also witnessed the failed – and almost fatal – escape attempt by Alec Couston:

[He] was carried out in the laundry basket to the laundry, which was outside the wire mesh. He waited till night but was spotted by a sentry and was hit in the jaw with a bullet, after he had surrendered. We actually saw this as we were watching, without being seen, from our windows to see how he got on.

Alec was, in fact, surrendering at the time the sentry took aim and fired, striking him once through the arm and also through the jaw. He later reported that the German sentry grunted, 'That's good!' in German after shooting him at close range.

A determined Colin Laurance broke out three times. During an escape attempt with one accomplice, heavy fog descended. Finding a large, leafy tree, they scaled it with the intention of sitting out the bad weather. When the fog finally lifted, the pair found they were perched in the only tree for miles around and within yards of the main road. Quickly detected, they were returned to camp.

During his second escape attempt, Colin and two companions discovered their route barred by a river. Despite chilly winter temperatures, the trio stripped, holding their bundles of clothes over their heads as they negotiated the icy water. Wading out on the opposite bank, they were bailed up by an individual bearing a German Landsturmer's rifle, and he would not allow the shivering trio to dress for several hours.

However, the escapees seized an opportunity to repay their captor in kind several weeks later. Requested by the camp's administration to identify the Landsturmer in order for him to receive a reward for their recapture, the trio claimed never to have seen the man before.

The fact is that numerous POWs escaped the confines of the camp and were recaptured on the run. So how did the prisoners manage to get through the wire in the first place? Theoretically, Niemeyer was running the ultimate inescapable camp. But Niemeyer was no student of human nature.

The worst kind of thuggish tyrant, it never occurred to him that the abhorrent treatment of his subordinates would leave him in a loyalty void of his own making. His guards and staff, who loathed the sight and sound of him, became susceptible to bribes from the POWs. There wasn't much the starving camp personnel would not do for a juicy tidbit from the prisoners' Red Cross parcels, or even for a few cigarettes.

Charles Bernard had this to say:

> Bribery and corruption were brought to high pitch of excellence in this camp, and many of the German under-officers were well in our pay, the main article for bribery being soap. This commodity being unobtainable in Germany, it was considered worth its weight in gold . . .

★

The duty of guarding the camp fell to the Landwehr-Infanterie-Regiment Nr. 77 of the Imperial German Army. The 1st Landwehr division, ranking third in importance behind the regular army and reservists, had formed in August 1914. The 77ers were part of the 38th Mixed Landwehr Brigade and had been raised from the Xth Army Corps to fulfil occupation and guard duties. Many were ex-reservists – from an older generation of soldier and no longer fit for a combatant role as they were too old, sick or physically incapacitated.

The Holzminden guards were a mixed bunch. Those who were sitting out the war tended to have benign opinions of their charges; those who took their jobs very seriously favoured aggression towards the prisoners.

An old boy of the prestigious English boys' school Blundell's, Lieutenant Robert Milner 'Bob' Paddison, of the Duke of Cornwall's Light Infantry, reminisced about a 'stout old gentleman', a kindly farmer of around sixty years of age who wore gold-rimmed glasses. He lived not far from the camp, smiled benevolently and often asked the POWs if all was well. The farmer-guard never seemed to lose his temper and took to expressing concern for POWs who had fallen ill. Bob admitted that he regarded the German to be such a 'good man' that he almost felt bad about deceiving him when it came time to participate in the big breakout.

Bob could have possibly been describing Feldwebel Kasten, who often accompanied the POWs on their parole walks outside the wire. After Armistice, when the POWs were virtually free to do as they pleased while awaiting their official release, Kasten was not at all averse to having his photo taken, and posed with his bicycle and dog for any POW with a camera.

Then there were the guards who made it their business to wreak misery upon the men. Often POWs were shot at, kicked out of bed, insulted and sentenced to unreasonably long periods in the cells; their requests would be denied and their possessions smashed or confiscated.

The name of the game was survival: the POWs made it their business to familiarise themselves with each guard's personality in order to know who they could bribe and who they could not.

Starving and underpaid, the German guards and staff feared and despised their Kommandant in equal measure. According to the German military code, an officer was permitted to strike a subordinate and Niemeyer often took full advantage of his superior rank by cracking men across the face with his hand, or using the toe of his boot with full force to express his displeasure at a minor or imagined infraction. Many of the aged camp guards, who had grown weary of the war and resentful of their dictatorial Kommandant, found their allegiances shifting to the British prisoners.

Charles Bernard gave the matter some thought:

> Our guards, in all the camps, were a sorry crowd, and owing to the lack of food, for they were fed abominably – the policy being that while the troops at the front required the best of food, those on home duty had to put up with anything – were weak and lethargic. In fact, the food that was served to us, which we could not and would not eat, was the regulation ration served to the troops in Germany. The [guards] were in a state of semi-starvation and looked it. It is a fact that, in the evenings, when we were shut up indoors, we could see these men prowling round the rubbish heaps whereon were thrown our empty food cans, in the hope of picking out bits of food left in them . . .

Bribing also placed the prisoners in an unusual position of power.

They worked hard to win over their gaolers but this did not stop at the human variety.

Besides being seen with a retriever puppy, which didn't seem to like him any more than did his own men or the prisoners, Niemeyer kept two 'police' dogs. At night, he sometimes stalked the compound with the reluctant pair in tow, employing his usual cruel techniques in his quest to turn the animals into snarling, merciless POW predators in the event of an escape.

The prisoners counteracted Niemeyer's efforts by employing a 'hearts, minds and belly' technique on the canines similar to the one they used on the starving guards – when the Germans weren't looking, they fed and lavished affection upon the dogs, who were starved for both a decent meal and attention.

One Sunday afternoon in May 1918, two British officers, twenty-three-year-old Lieutenant Harold Medlicott of No. 2 Squadron RFC and Captain Joseph Walter of 7th Queen's Royal West Surrey Regiment, staged a dash for freedom from Holzminden. Harold in particular was revered by other prisoners, who were astounded by his brazen fearlessness. And for good reason. With the utmost ingenuity, he had managed to escape from every camp in which he had been held, employing such means as a bathroom tunnel and a ladder from a window; he had also constructed an improvised drawbridge to escape from a prison fortress, hidden under a pile of rubbish waiting to be removed from a camp and cut the bars on a window in order to flee across an iced-over castle moat.[1]

Harold's breakout with Joseph – by going over the fence in broad daylight – was his twelfth escape attempt.

This is Max Gore's account of how the pair went about it:

They both wore civilian clothes that they had either made from scraps or bribed one of the camp staff to bring in. They could have been theatrical props. They had timed the sentry on this particular beat as to how long it took him to reach one end from the other, and they had gauged the distance from the edge of the neutral zone to the iron railed stone wall which was topped with three strands of barbed wire leaning inwards. By meticulous calculation as to how long it would take them to cover the space of the neutral zone, climb the wall, cut the barbed wire, climb over the top and drop down the other side, they judged they could do it with one second to spare. All this they accomplished and nonchalantly strolled past the sentry when they met him on his return beat . . .

Spotted by a guard who raised the alarm, Harold and Joseph made a dash across the countryside with the elderly camp guards in doddering pursuit.

According to Charles Bernard, as the dog-handler released the hounds, the German gave the urgent command for them to give chase but Niemeyer's 'killer' dogs turned and trotted back into the camp with wagging tails to the calls of the cooing inmates: 'Good doggies!' and 'Come to Papa!'

Charles added:

Above the noise of cheers and catcalls, Niemeyer's voice could be heard roaring like a demented bull, giving orders to the sentries who had been posted in the square, to fire at the windows. He was running hither and thither, his face livid with rage, and brandishing his revolver. I was looking out of the window at the end of the passage, together with about thirty other fellows. As the sentry below raised his rifle to fire, we all fell in a tangled mass of arms and legs and bodies onto the floor, and the noise

A group of officers photographed in front of one of the Holzminden barracks by Otto Liebert. *Courtesy John Hawkins*

Sketch of Kaserne B by C.H. Leach. *Courtesy L and T Vaughan (The Angus McPhail Collection)*

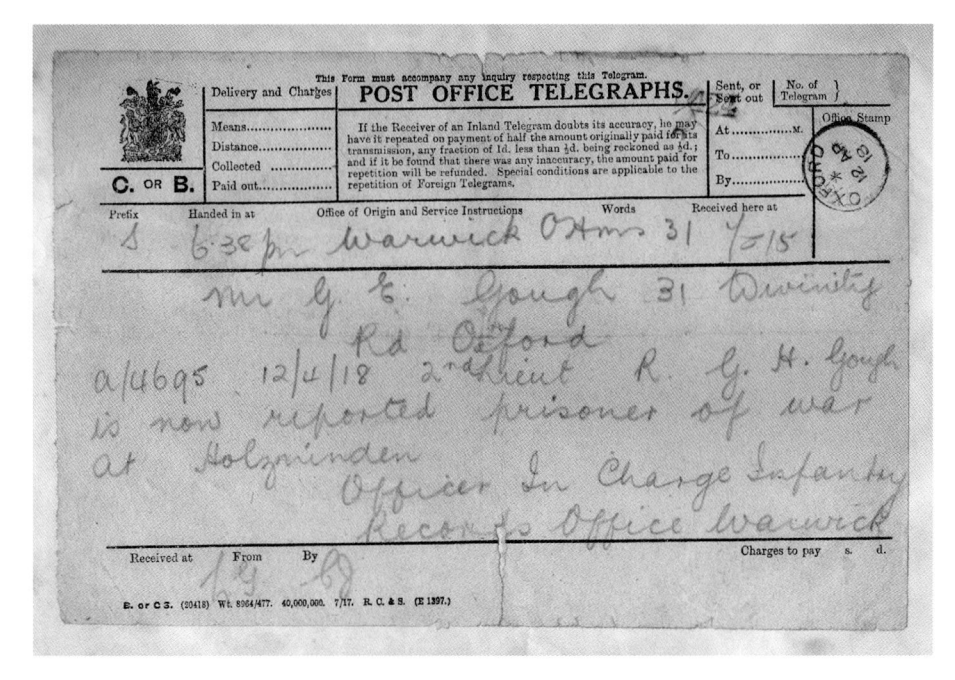

Telegram received by Reg Gough's father on his son's internment. *Courtesy Michael Gough*

Algie Bird (right) after being shot down by Manfred Richthofen (left).
Courtesy Peter Bird

A typical *Appel* on the *Spielplatz. Courtesy Oliver Harris*

Bread ration card.
Courtesy Michael Melching

Rupert Hawkins's alcohol ration card.
Courtesy John Hawkins

Holzminden camp currency.
Courtesy Michael Melching

The Kommandant, Karl Niemeyer.
Australian War Memorial P03473.001

Dean Gardner's parole card. *Courtesy Ron Gardner*

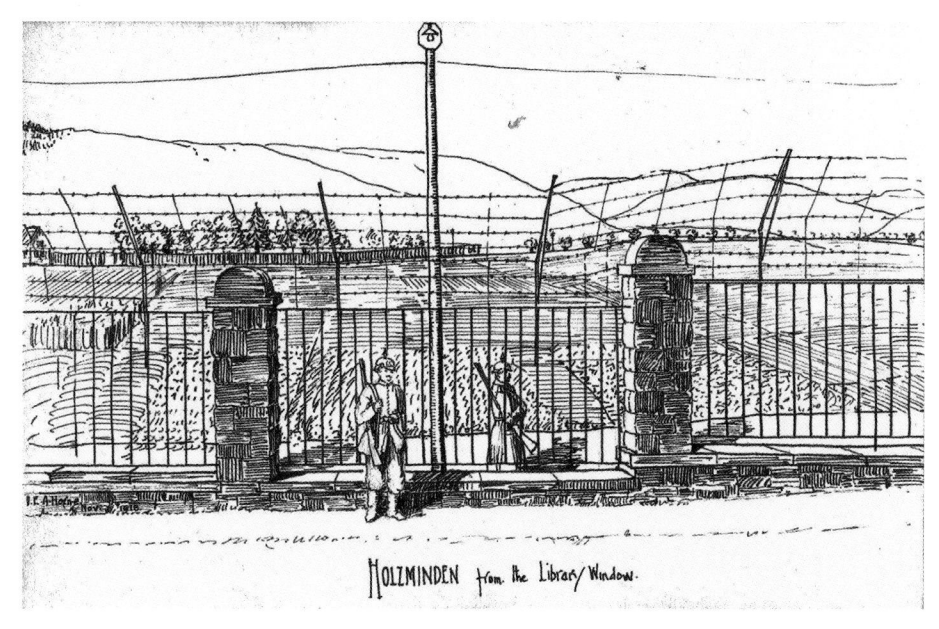

The view from the library window by David Horne. *Courtesy Lesley Moore*

"PARCELS!"
OR
"IF YOU DON'T WANT THE GOODS
DON'T MESS 'EM ABOUT!"

A MUSICAL COMEDY,
IN A BOX CONSISTING OF A LID AND
A BOTTOM CONTAINING FOUR TINS

BOOK AND LYRICS BY { D. G. GOLD.
G. R. EDWARDS.

PRODUCED BY G. R. EDWARDS.

UNDER THE MANAGEMENT OF THE B. A. D. S.

AT

THE GAIETY THEATRE
HOLZMINDEN.

NOTE: — THE PRODUCTION IS IN **NO** WAY INTENDED TO REFLECT UPON THE EXCELLENT WORK DONE BY THOSE WHO SEND US PARCELS FROM HOME.

A Gaiety Theatre program. *Courtesy Peter Clouston*

The cast of the *Home John* revue in July 1918. *Courtesy L and T Vaughan (The Angus McPhail Collection)*

Errol Sen (front) and Brian Manning (back, right). *Courtesy Oliver Harris*

Sidney Hume. *Courtesy Royal Aero Club, UK*

Edgar Garland poses for art students prior to leaving for the war. *Alexander Turnbull Library, Wellington, New Zealand (SP Andrew Collection) ID 1/1-013963-G*

A satirical sketch of a Scottish officer by A.F.G. Clarke. *Courtesy L and T Vaughan (The Angus McPhail Collection)*

The propaganda postcard by T. Carnel depicting Edith Cavell's death.
Australian War Memorial P03087.002

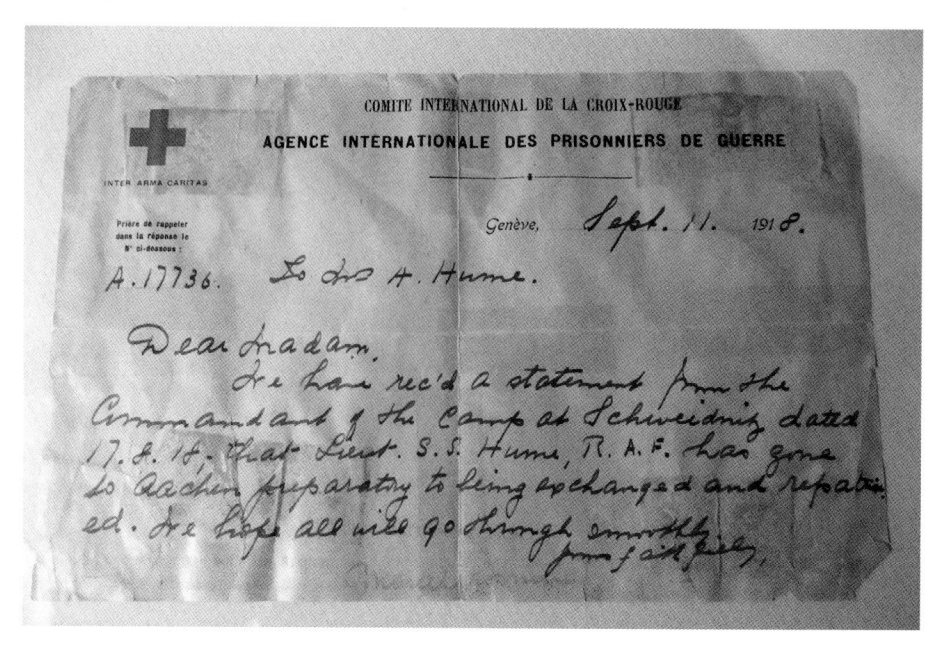

The Red Cross telegram advising Sidney Hume's family of his repatriation to England. *Courtesy Inés Menendez Behety*

Stacked sacks of excavated dirt under the stairs. *Otto Liebert, courtesy Ron Gardner*

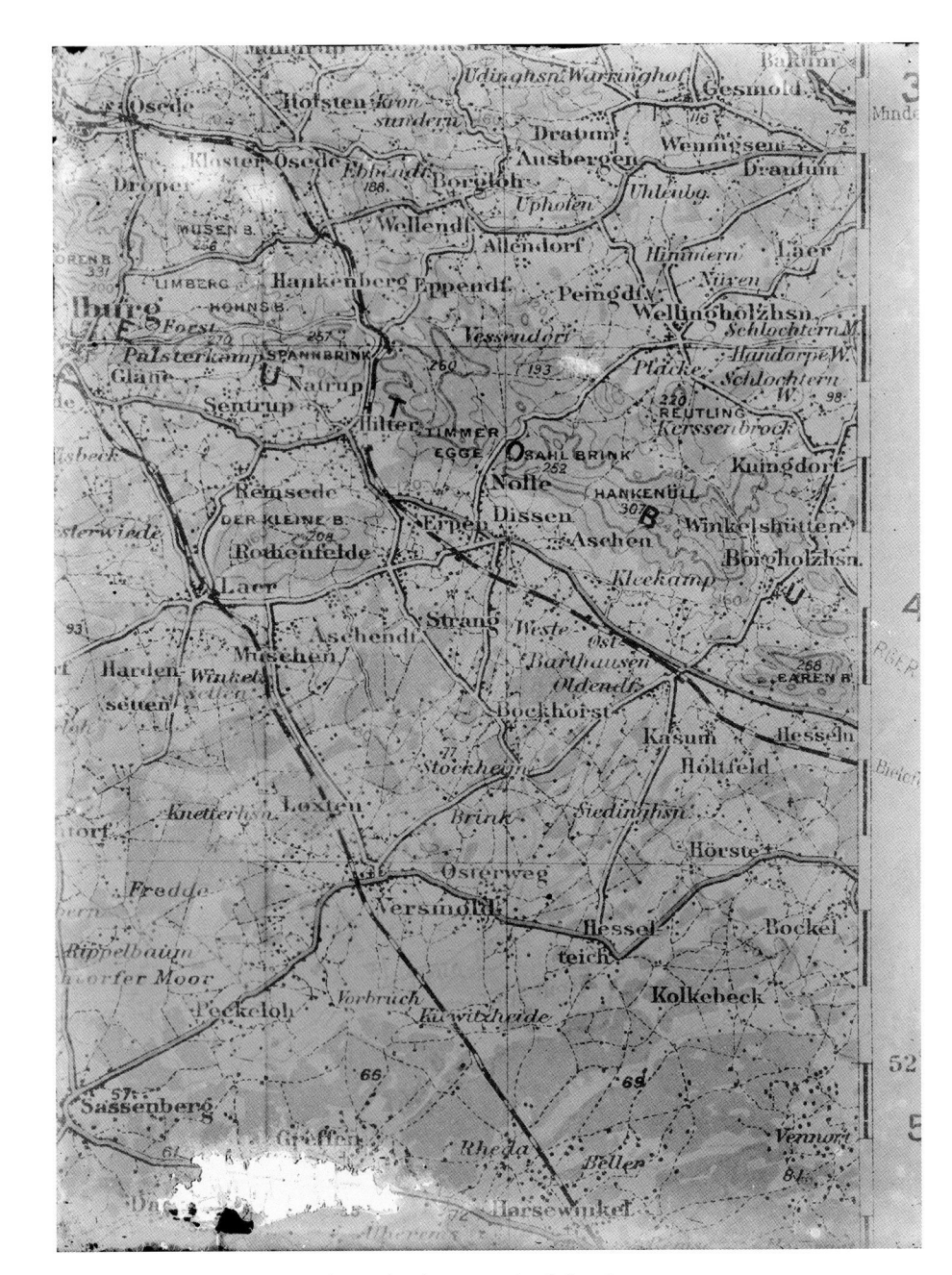

A portion of the map Dick Cash photographed for the escapees.
Australian War Memorial P03473.012

The tiny compass used by Hector F. Dougall and Sedley Williams during their escape. *Courtesy Jeremy Williams*

An escape encampment sketched by E.W. Leggatt. *Courtesy Alec Purves*

The excavated tunnel. *Otto Liebert, courtesy Ron Gardner*

Ten of the recaptured tunnellers. *Courtesy Peter Clouston*

Blain, Gray and Kennard in their asylum disguises. *Courtesy Diana Gillyatt*

Successful escapees Gray, Leggatt, Purves, Kennard, Blain and Tullis pictured with a guard and a nurse in the Dutch camp. *Courtesy Alec Purves*

A staged photo commissioned by a panicked Niemeyer at the close of the war. Otto Liebert, courtesy Ron Gardner

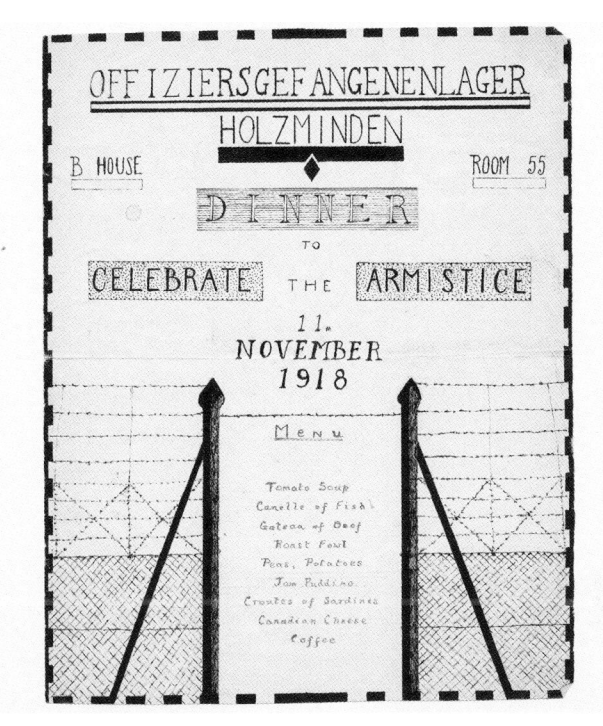

A menu celebrating the Armistice. *Courtesy Alan Mumford*

The camp flag seized by Hector F. Dougall after Armistice.
Courtesy Fraser Dougall and Brenda Dougall Merriman.

A 1939 newspaper article about the 1918 escape. *Courtesy Will Hare*

of splintering glass and crack of the bullets as they hit the ceiling above us was drowned out by the curses of those on top of the seething mass, and the groans of those underneath!

Despite the farcical tone of the duo's escape attempt, it had a tragic ending. Harold Medlicott and Joseph Walter were transported to Bad Colburg POW camp, from which they once more attempted escape, but were recaptured. On the return trip to Bad Colburg on 21 May 1918, they jumped from the train in yet another bid for freedom.

In a letter to the Medlicott family dated 15 May 1936,[2] nearly twenty years after the event, Major M.R. Chidson, who had been at Holzminden with Harold, shared his understanding of what happened to the doomed pair.

He wrote:

A day or two later the bodies of the two officers [Medlicott and Walter] were brought to the camp and the Germans stated that both of them had made a sudden dash for freedom whilst being marched from the railway station nearest to the camp, where they had been brought by train, to the camp itself and, after having ignored several challenges of the guards in charge of them, had been shot down ... it is said that the Senior British Officer in the camp requested formally that the bodies should be seen by himself or other British Officers and examined by a medical officer: this was refused, without any reason being given, though I believe that permission was given for the faces of the two dead officers to be seen for the purposes of identification. It was also alleged and commonly believed at this time that a British soldier who was employed as an orderly at the camp in question succeeded in visiting the mortuary and examining the bodies and that he later testified that both had numerous bayonet wounds.

Major Chidson went on to say:

> I myself have never met a more fearless or unassuming man than Medlicott: his escapes often succeeded only owing to their literally incredible daring. Only a man of very unusual modesty would have resisted the temptation to rest on his laurels long before he reached the almost inevitable end, since, young though he was, he already was a figure known to every officer prisoner of war by repute, if not personally. Even at the time when acts of gallantry were commonplace all over the world and when examples of devotion to duty were frequent, Medlicott stood out above other men and was a constant, if unconscious inspiration to his comrades.

Harold was just one of many prisoners who exhibited admirable cunning and creativity in their escape attempts from German POW camps. When the self-educated twenty-six-year-old naval pilot Flight Sub-Lieutenant Harold 'Gus' Edwards of Squadron 3 Naval Wing was sent to Holzminden as an incurable escapee, he had notched up two daring escapes from previous camps.

Harold's parents were English emigrants who in the summer of 1903 had begun a new life in Canada. His father, William 'Will' Edwards, had been the manager of an underground coal mine in England until times became tough and the mine closed. Will and his two brothers, James and George, faced unemployment. James sailed to Canada to investigate opportunities within the mining industry there, and Will followed. Together with his wife, Kate Louisa Warburton, and their two young sons, Harold, aged eleven, and Benjamin, twelve, the family moved to Glace Bay, a mining town on Cape Breton Island in Nova Scotia, Canada.

Underground mining at the turn of the twentieth century was a grim business. As the provider of housing and stores, the mining company virtually owned the lives of its employees. Miners attempted to address poor working conditions and slave wages by staging strikes but their employer was a powerful one – where else would they find work?

Will could only find work as a miner, rather than resuming the role of a manager, and with the drop in wages, the family found themselves once more struggling for every penny.

Harold was educated at the New Aberdeen Public School until 1907, and then at the age of fourteen, and against his mother's wishes, he left school to join his brother, Ben, in the mine to help his family out financially. He took on the role of coal-mine trapper, which entailed opening the ventilation door for the mine ponies to pass through as they hauled trolleys filled with coal to the surface.

Unlike many of the other boys – some much younger – Harold knew that his salvation lay in education. As he kept up the ten-hour-a-day routine in the dismally dark, wet and rat-infested environment to help supplement the family's income, he plotted his eventual escape. He and his mother mapped out a study routine that saw him hit the books after his shift, from 6 pm until 8 pm. He would then go to sleep, rising at 3 am to continue studying for another three hours before his shift started.

His mother agonised over her son's gruelling regime, but the self-motivated lad kept it up for seven long years. And his dedication bore fruit. By the age of eighteen, Harold Edwards had secured himself a position as the chief electrician at the British Empire Steel Corporation at the Glace Bay mines. Ben had also taken on an electrician role.

Harold stood out from the crowd. Thanks to his adherence to his study routine, he was possessed of knowledge – particularly about electricity and aviation – far and beyond many of his colleagues. It was an era in which pioneers in both these fields were beginning to make the world sit up and take notice, and Harold was enamoured of the startling inventions which were to become the forerunners of modern-day technology.

After all these years, both the Edwards brothers had begun to rise up through the ranks at the mine, and the family's financial position steadily improved. Many years later, Ben's daughter recalled how the two of them would mischievously wire a chair with an electric current: the innocent sitter would leap up, shocked, at first touch. Family and friends had to be forever on the lookout for pranks pulled by the pair.

The outbreak of the First World War in 1914 coincided with Harold's coming-of-age. He was twenty-one years old and his years of self-study and commendable work ethic had paid off. He was well educated and ready to face the world.

The call to arms saw many young Canadian men front up to recruiting offices all over the country. Harold had his eye on a career as a naval pilot, but a lack of the all-important aviator's qualification, issued as the Fédération Aéronautique Internationale Certificate, stood in his way. He enrolled at the Curtiss Flying School in Toronto, but applications were so numerous that the school could not possibly accommodate all. Further limiting admissions, weather forced the flying school to shut down over the winter, leaving Harold and other disappointed applicants on a very long waiting list.

The Department of the Naval Service (DNS) at Ottawa identified the shortfall in training opportunities as a serious issue and came to the rescue. The DNS instigated a program by which young men could enter the Royal Canadian Navy and start their basic naval training aboard the depot (fixed base) ship HMCS *Niobe*,[3] until they could be sent to Britain to undertake their flying instruction. In August 1915, Harold joined the Royal Canadian

Naval Volunteer Reserve as an aviator candidate, which afforded him the entry rank of able seaman.

Finally Harold was on his way, leaving the dark coal pits of Glace Bay far behind him.

In February 1916, he sailed for England, receiving orders from the Office of the Admiralty to report to the Portsmouth Navigation School. It was here that he was asked by a messmate if his Edwards surname meant that he was related to American songwriter and vaudeville legend Gus Edwards. When he quipped, 'I am Gus Edwards', the nickname simply stuck. He spent the next six months in classroom training at various locations, including White City, Eastbourne, Cranwell and East Church. However, the training was biased towards theory. Handed control of an aircraft after accruing less than an hour of airborne training with an instructor and barely six hours in the air, it was more than likely that he was doomed to crash at least once (at Ewell) and force a landing (at Headcorn); one of these incidents resulted in the loss of the little toe on his left foot.

Inadequate training notwithstanding, Flight Sub-Lieutenant Edwards was posted to Luxeuil-les-Bains in north-eastern France with 3 (Naval) Wing, where 75 per cent of pilots were Canadians. From here he undertook several missions, including a number of repeat bombing raids on an ironworks and blast furnace at Saarbrucke-Burbach. On 22 March 1917, he was the only pilot out of a formation of nine to return to base safely – and his Sopwith Scout was down to five of its nine cylinders.

Not long after, 3 Wing was ordered to disband and the aircraft were reassigned to the Royal Flying Corps for Western Front air support. The Wing undertook one last mission – a reprisal attack on Freiburg for the recent German torpedoing of the hospital ship *Asturias*.

On the afternoon of 14 April 1917, the twenty-five-year-old Gus took off with B Flight, the second of two formations – the earlier one having left that morning – but they were engaged by German fighters in savage aerial combat and hit by a blast of gunfire from a German Albatros D.111. Gus's observer, J.L. Coghlan, was killed and the Sopwith Strutter sustained damage, forcing him to crash-land behind enemy lines at Schlettstadt.

Gus became a prisoner at the military detention barracks at Colmar, France, along with thirty-two-year-old Lieutenant Colonel Charles Edward Henry Rathborne, who had lifted off in the first formation that morning. Unknown to them at the time, the pair were ultimately destined for Holzminden.

Gus and Charles were imprisoned in opposite cells. From his cell Gus signalled Charles by waving his hand across the peephole, which served to stagger the light signals in a pattern of Morse code. The two spent the next eight days signalling to each other from across the hallway; once interrogation was completed, Gus was permitted to visit Charles's cell.

After a daring escape attempt from the Colmar detention cells that involved bribing a guard for a hacksaw in return for a bar of soap, Gus and two fellow POWs made good their escape, remaining on the run for ten days. They had covered 175 miles (282km) on foot before they rounded a corner and walked straight into the path of a German military provost marshal; he was decent enough to buy them beers at the local pub before surrendering them to his superior officer. The trio were punished with two weeks of solitary confinement back where they started – Colmar.

Gus was sent to Karlsruhe camp in Germany, from where he wrote to a friend, J. Murphy:

> I am a prisoner at Karlsruhe. I was shot down after lengthy engagement with several enemy machines . . . My controls were

shot away and I fell all the way completely out of control. Luckily we struck the ground in such a way that I was unhurt. Since then I have sombered away with a gnawing in my stomach like many others who have shared this fate.

As it turned out, he had been shot down by a nineteen-year-old German pilot who was to die ten days later – on his twentieth birthday – during an aerial battle.

Another enemy pilot dropped word to Gus's commanding officer, Captain W.L. Elder, of the young Canadian's fate.

Gus was then sent to Freiburg, from where he made a further unsuccessful escape attempt, in the company of two others. This time it involved a frayed clothesline draped from a third-storey window; the line snapped, sending one of his escape-mates plummeting to the ground.

Gus was to also spend some time in a converted Catholic poorhouse prison, most likely Neunkirchen, before being welcomed to Holzminden by a strutting Niemeyer on 3 December 1917.

But Niemeyer's inflated ego and blindness to basic human nature was to ultimately be his downfall, setting in motion the greatest humiliation of his career in the dying months of the war.

PART II

THE REAL GREAT ESCAPE

Ten

The Tunnel

Dashing RFC fighter pilot thirty-two-year-old Captain David Benjamin Gray had a swarthy complexion, dark hair neatly parted down the middle and a clipped moustache. He spoke several languages fluently, a talent that earned him the Hindustani nickname 'Munshi'[1] in Assam, India, where he was born to British parents on 29 July 1884.

Munshi was a long way from his birthplace when, on 17 September 1916, his squadron was charged with escorting twelve No. 16 Squadron bombers on a mission in northern France. The bombers' orders were to decimate the strategic railway junction at Marcoing, and it was the duty of Munshi's No. 11 Squadron to defend the formation if they came under attack from the enemy.

That morning, Munshi was nervous. He was piloting a new FE2b biplane that had only just rolled out of the factory, arriving at his base at Izel-les-Hameaux in France the day before. At the best of times, First World War pilots were mistrustful of newly constructed aircraft, as the haste with which the beasts were being built left alarming room for error. However, Munshi had even more cause for concern: the base mechanics had not had a chance to perform a safety check on the aircraft as his squadron was dramatically behind schedule. He had no choice but to proceed to the mission's rendezvous, taking off with Lieutenant Helder in the observer/gunner's position in the forward cockpit.

To Munshi's relief, the bombing raid went without a hitch, but no sooner had the two British squadrons turned towards base than nine German Fokkers descended from above like a swarm of angry wasps. In the heat and smoke of the ensuing dogfight, Munshi's engine was peppered with machine-gun fire, sending the two-day-old FE2b into a downward spiral. Fuel streamed from the disabled aircraft as Munshi fought to pull up the nose; all the while, Helder continued to blast their relentless German pursuer with machine-gun bullets.

They were just 500 feet (152m) from slamming into the ground at full force when Munshi regained some measure of control. In complete engine failure, Munshi managed to level off the aircraft, bringing it in for a rough landing in a field near the French town of Bapaume. Shaken but unhurt, the pair only had a moment to set the plane alight, as per regulations, before they were surrounded by a large contingent of German infantry.

Their lives as prisoners of war had begun.

The German-speaking Munshi arrived in Osnabrück via Gutersloh quarantine camp, where he had continually feigned a lack of understanding whenever given an order in German by his gaolers. While this ploy may have deceived his captors, before long his fellow POWs had caught on and were approaching him for German language lessons in preparation for the many and varied escape bids under preparation. Munshi's sharp mind and leadership skills were outstanding. Along with his proficiency in the German language, these were to become crucial components in the first and greatest successful mass escape of the First World War.

As with many POWs, Munshi was possessed of an unremitting determination to slip the choke-chain of his German captors. He was also a particularly clever strategic thinker. In Osnabrück he began covertly observing incoming POWs to identify willing and skilled escape accomplices.

His eye fell on two promising potentials.

The first was blond, blue-eyed twenty-two-year-old 2nd Lieutenant Cecil Blain of No. 70 Squadron RFC. Here was a young man who saw daring and challenge rather than risk. With the flippancy of youth, he undertook feats of derring-do with little consideration for the consequences. Munshi, during his surveillance, had noted that Cecil spoke fluent Afrikaans (Cape Dutch) and understood – although did not fluently speak – German. After studying Cecil closely for compatibility, he approached the youngster with his proposal to form an escape team.

The third member of the team was as different from the puckish, good-natured Blain as was humanly possible. Captain Caspar Kennard of No. 16 Squadron RFC was a tall, dark and brooding twenty-seven-year-old lone wolf who was inclined to be strategically antisocial. He was often seen with a pipe between his lips, but it was rarely lit. His previous escape attempt from Gütersloh POW camp had impressed Munshi. It took the escape leader some time to break through the newcomer's defences and get to know the man behind the standoffish exterior.

Both Cecil and Caspar saw the value in joining forces with the German-speaking Munshi but shortly after they began to put their first escape attempt into effect, a loathed French officer by the name of Capitaine Allouche tipped off the Osnabrück camp authorities to a stockpile of tools Cecil and Caspar kept hidden in their room. For reasons unknown, Cecil was specifically targeted and was sentenced to solitary confinement. There he had ample time to glower over the betrayal. And to plot revenge.

But by the time a seething Cecil was released, in February 1917, Caspar had already amassed a reprisal team. With a band of willing accomplices, Cecil and Caspar crept into Allouche's quarters one night clutching a tin of treacle and a pot of human waste and ashes. Held down and his clothes ripped off, the widely despised French officer was 'tarred and feathered' with the foul mixture for snitching to the Germans.

The following day, Cecil and Caspar were officially identified, with ten others, as members of the previous night's retaliation party. Munshi had also been involved but had miraculously avoided being identified by the outraged victim.

If Cecil and Caspar had suspected that their punishment would entail separation from their leader, they might have thought twice about the reprisal attack. The pair were unceremoniously transferred to Clausthal POW camp – commanded by Heinrich Niemeyer, the equally repugnant twin brother of Kommandant Karl Niemeyer of Holzminden. All Gray could do was farewell two-thirds of his escape team at the gates as they were driven away to their new prison – and perhaps to inwardly curse their rash act of vengeance.

Within a year, the trio were fated to reunite.

★

Later in 1917, a group of resolute serial escapees was engaged in reconnaissance of the Holzminden compound, spearheaded by twenty-six-year-old officer Lieutenant William Gourlay 'Shorty' Colquhoun[2] of Princess Patricia's Canadian Light Infantry. The Ontario-born Shorty held the distinction of not only being the first Canadian captured but also the first of his countrymen to be awarded the Military Cross.

Shorty and fellow internee Lieutenant Ellis discreetly began reconnaissance of the compound, seeking a potential starting point from which to burrow their way to freedom. Immediately it was clear that the orderlies' end of Kaserne B, which sat closest to the perimeter wall, offered the most potential.

To investigate more thoroughly the officers needed to gain access but this presented the first of many challenges: although the orderlies were permitted to enter the officers' quarters to perform their duties, conversely the officers were not permitted to enter the barracks of the enlisted men.

A solution had to be found.

A concrete wall down the centre of the barracks separated the officers from the orderlies. The POWs were under constant surveillance by the sentries and any attempt by an officer to saunter in via the orderlies' entrance would be instantly spotted. Further, Niemeyer had the disconcerting habit of materialising in the barracks unexpectedly, in the hope of catching the POWs indulging in *verboten* activities.

An officer conceived of the idea of disguising themselves as orderlies, which would afford them the freedom to enter off-limits territory. The officers consulted some trusted orderlies, who gathered together spare sets of the hated black and yellow uniforms, which were then smuggled into the officers' quarters.

Now to test the plan. The officers recruited some willing lookouts, positioning them at strategic locations around the barracks exterior with instructions to covertly signal the all-clear. The sentries detected nothing out of the ordinary when the officers disguised as orderlies, faces hidden by pulled-down caps, sauntered out of their end of the barracks and in through the orderlies' entrance at the opposite end.

Their relief was no doubt short-lived when the officers found themselves faced with their second and more daunting challenge. Just inside the orderlies' entrance was a set of stairs leading down to the basement, where the underground rooms had been converted to a potato cellar, solitary confinement cells and storage rooms. But there was a problem with access: at the bottom of the stairs, not only was the door locked but also there was a wooden barricade affixed to the side of the stairs, barring their way.

The officers reconvened to discuss their options. They assessed the probable layout of the space under the stairs and were convinced it was the closest accessible point to the outer wire.

Now they needed access to the space to test their theory.

During a further reconnaissance, members of the escape team closely examined the barrier and saw that it was possible to cut a doorway in the wooden palings. But how to get their hands on the necessary tools? Finally it was agreed that they would deliberately damage a door in their own quarters to draw a civilian carpenter and his tools to their lair.

When the carpenter duly arrived, the officers staged a pre-arranged fight to attract the attention of the contractor and the guard. The diversion allowed a POW to snatch a cold chisel from the toolbox and then vanish. When the contractor and guard returned to the job and found the tool missing, it didn't take them long to work out what had happened. It's more than likely the guard was reluctant to report the theft to the Kommandant for fear of being blamed and punished; or perhaps, like many of the other guards in the camp, he was happy to turn a blind eye in return for morsels from Red Cross parcels. The carpenter was most likely silenced the same way, for the incident was never reported, leaving the officers free to continue their efforts.

As guards were often on cellar duty, the tunnelling crew surmised that they had to synchronise their return to the orderlies' quarters with the much-anticipated midday meal. At a precise time each day, the hungry German guards left the basement to hurry to lunch in another building, leaving the cellar area unattended.

The Tunnel

With the guards at their midday meal, the officers quickly cut a doorway in the wooden barricade with the pilfered tool, then prised off the panel. One of the officers climbed over the staircase railing, dropping the short distance to the floor below, and disappeared into the semi-darkness. The other officers waited anxiously on the stairs for his return.

Had their hunch been right or would they have to start again in another location?

The tunnelling team were elated when the reconnaissance officer returned with the news that the cavity under the stairs was the perfect place to start the tunnel.

So far, so good. At work on the wooden barricade earlier, the officers were gratified to discover that the secret door they had fashioned could be easily slotted back into place. Only on very close inspection could the saw joins be detected.

Work on the tunnelling project began in earnest, with solutions to logistical challenges discussed at length and agreed upon by the team.

The limited hours the tunnellers could work on their project were challenging. Since a POW absence at the twice-daily rollcall would be noticed, work could not start until all the prisoners were dismissed from the 9 am *Appel*. Similarly, at the other end of the day, the men needed to be out of the tunnel, cleaned up and ready to present themselves at the afternoon's *Appel* at 4 pm. Digging would have to proceed as noiselessly as possible so as not attract the attention of the Germans on duty in the basement.

The area under the stairs – having been blocked off for a lengthy period of time and by virtue of the fact it was located underground – was dark and damp, the air fetid. The men had to work by the light of candles received in their Red Cross packages, using any primitive tool they could get their hands on: their collection consisted of kitchen cutlery, sharp edges of tins and a poker from the barracks stove. The only professional tool to hand was the chisel stolen from the carpenter's box.

They rolled up their sleeves and started digging. At this stage the details of the operation were known only to a select few. Based on their collective wisdom accrued from many escape attempts at many camps, the men knew better than to broadcast their plans.

Rather than dig down through the concrete floor, the escape team opted to drive the chamber straight towards the outer wall. Although it was the fastest route to freedom, it had a major drawback: the tunnel roof would only be 3 feet (0.9m) below the surface, meaning that an alert guard with sharp hearing might detect the tunnelling activity. Consequently, the plan was to descend the chamber to a more secure depth once they were clear of the outer wall. The team agreed that this plan would cost them the least amount of valuable time.

With determination and ingenuity, the officers negotiated every manner of solid barrier during their digging – concrete foundations, steel reinforcing rods, rock, clay and alluvial soil from the trajectory of the nearby River Weser. The more resistant material, such as the steel, was doused in acid obtained by bribing a civilian camp contractor, who smuggled in the corrosive substance in his kit.

Working inside the tunnel was not for the faint-hearted. Luxuries like wriggle room were not an option: there was neither time nor resources. The chamber was claustrophobic – only as wide and as high in diameter as the average fireplace; there was no room to stand or even kneel.

Finding ways to discreetly disperse the soil excavated from the absolutely basic tunnel the men carved was a constant headache. Anything bag-like, such as pillows and mattresses with the stuffing removed, was pressed into service to hold the excavated earth. Bulging bags of debris began to build up at the tunnel entrance and inventive ways had to be found to dispose of it. The officers began hauling it upstairs to the empty attic rooms and dumping the contents on the floor.

A relay system was devised. Only three officers worked on the tunnel at any one time – one digging at the tunnel face, one at the tunnel entrance to remove the excavated debris and the third keeping the others to a tight schedule. The tunneller could only dig for around an hour in the confined and airless conditions before wiggling backwards out of the chamber, exhausted, to swap over with his replacement. A lit candle at the entrance provided a modicum of light, and the officer on digging duty would crawl the length of the tunnel in the pitch dark holding another candle, which he would light once he arrived at the tunnel face to begin work.

After many weeks of digging for three hours daily – surprisingly without incident or even a hint of detection – the tunnel reached slightly beyond the outer wall. They would shortly be angling the tunnel towards the surface: freedom was tantalisingly close.

Such a milestone should have been cause for elation, but Niemeyer instead gave the men cause for anxiety. The Kommandant had a habit of bolstering the number of guards at strategic locations without warning, and suddenly he focused his attention on the very area outside the perimeter wire targeted by the tunnellers. This immediately thwarted the plan to break through the surface a little outside the camp wall; detection was assured. The escape team would have to divert the tunnel to an alternate exit point.

While the hard grind of tunnelling proceeded, the rest of the team were working out the details of how to make good their escape once out of the camp. German guards and staff deemed susceptible to bribery were identified. The pressure was on to forgo items in the prisoners' Red Cross parcels that could be used as inducements, such as chocolate, which was considered a luxury item to the German staff. The inmates were prepared to part with any item of food in exchange for information and useful materials.

Niemeyer retained a young soldier who acted as the conveyer of his instructions and also assisted with distributing the mail. The Kommandant had no idea that 'the letter boy' harboured a loathing for both his own country and Niemeyer, making the youth a willing accomplice when approached by the prisoners to supply camp intelligence and minor items smuggled into the barracks in the pockets of his military coat.

Other German staff who had suffered at the hands of Niemeyer were equally pliable. The only female in the camp – the Kommandant's secretary – had become besotted with an Australian flying officer and fed him camp intelligence via notes dropped from the window to a waiting guard who was in the POWs' pay.

The line of willing German accomplices grew longer and included a camp interpreter, a parcel room attendant, a canteen attendant and the camp dentist – not to mention civilian contractors who came and went, such as carpenters and the sanitation contractor.

And then in February 1918, in a series of coincidences and unforeseen events, the tunnelling operation began to lose its momentum.

★

In a move that seemed to indicate that Niemeyer's suspicions had been aroused, seven of the men were suddenly transferred to another camp in February 1918. The remaining tunnellers waited for the axe to fall but, to their relief, the tunnel remained undetected and the rest of the team resumed their backbreaking work.

Shortly after, more POWs began to flood into the camp in the wake of a successful German battlefield offensive called *Kaiserschlacht* on 21 March, in which more than 100,000 British troops were captured in one day. Some of them ended up in Holzminden.

Further, in response to the prisoner exchange initiative, which had been activated the previous July, large groups of long-time prisoners were transferred out of Holzminden to the neutral territories of Holland and Switzerland.

The dwindling team and the floundering progress left the rest of the tunnellers demoralised. Subsequently, most opted to enter the prisoner exchange program rather than take the risk of pushing on with the tunnel, which they believed had a very slim likelihood of success.

After the mass departures, the three remaining team members cast around for reinforcements.

Meanwhile, in the weeks the Holzminden moles had been burrowing their way towards the outer wall, Munshi, Cecil and Caspar had continued to dedicate themselves to the art of escape from other camps. Cecil and Caspar had made several unsuccessful attempts together from Clausthal and Ströhen, which led to their eventual separation: Caspar had been transferred to the subterranean fortress prison of Zorndorf for a dark, damp three-month stint in solitary confinement. The duo was to be reunited at Neuenkirchen POW camp before they were to unexpectedly join Munshi in Holzminden.

During this time, Munshi had also been kept on the move, and had done stints in various camps: initially in Gütersloh, followed by Crefeld, Clausthal, Zorndorf and Schwarmstedt. And like Cecil and Caspar, the first thing he did upon arrival in each new facility was to assess the viability of escape.

In January 1918, shortly after the majority of the original Holzminden tunnellers had been transferred out, Munshi, Cecil and Caspar were reunited as guests of Niemeyer. All three brought with them tunnelling experience from previous camps and had learned from their mistakes and miscalculations.

In written testimony by the effervescent Cecil, made shortly after the war, he explained his attraction to the Holzminden tunnel:

> From Neuenkirchen, all flying officers were removed and were taken to Holzminden on the River Weser. It was not long before I got busy again here, for I was admitted to the working party of another tunnel which had been running for some months, and it certainly looked a very promising thing. For the time being, all other schemes for escape were forgotten and work carried on steadily. After each tunnel I worked on before, I swore stolidly that I would never work in one again, but these vows were of no use – amusement had to come from somewhere and I enjoyed this sort more than any other. It was a slow job, but in a cheery working party I found the work great fun.

It didn't take long for the trio to be recruited by the three original tunnellers, who brought about the formation of a new thirteen-man working party. The new group consisted of Lieutenant Andrew Clouston of the Canadian Army's Royal Newfoundland Regiment 1/1; Lieutenant Colin Laurance and Lieutenant Frederick Mardock of the Royal Naval Air Service; Captain William Henry Langren of the British Army's Prince of Wales' Own West Yorkshire Regiment; Lieutenant David Wainwright of the Royal Navy; Lieutenant Robert Milner Paddison of the British Army's Duke of Cornwall's Light Infantry; Lieutenant Walter Butler;

The Tunnel

Lieutenant Arthur Morris; Lieutenant Clifford Robertson and Lieutenant Neil MacLeod.

With a fresh and eager team in place, work on the tunnel resumed in earnest. The willing orderlies once more resumed their support duties as look-outs.

The approach of the previous tunnellers had worked so well that the new team adhered to the same routine, though they made refinements. The officer at the tunnel face worked on his belly, scraping chunks of dislodged material into an enamel basin. When the basin was full, the tunneller tugged on one of the ropes attached to a handle and raised himself on all fours, as far as the chamber ceiling would allow, so the basin could slide under his body and out between his splayed ankles. At the tugging signal, the officer waiting at the entrance would haul on the rope until the basin appeared. He would transfer the contents into a bag, then tug on the opposite rope to indicate that the basin was ready to be pulled back down the tunnel to be filled again.

When Niemeyer had reinforced the perimeter guard a few weeks earlier, the team had been forced to redirect the tunnel, which had been curving west, to the north, where the crops could provide cover at the exit point. But crops – in this case rye and beans – are eventually gathered in, so the men had to reach their target before the mid-year summer harvest – no later than August. Smuggled compasses guided their way as they burrowed under the very feet of their German captors and fellow POWs.

By now, progress had slowed to around two feet – less than a metre – per day, sometimes much less. Not only was it taking longer to clear out the debris but also there had been several tunnel collapses. The diggers had been shoring up the length of the tunnel at the weakest points with wooden slats collected from prisoner bunk bases but, given that many of these had been burned as fuel during winter, there were never enough to do the job properly.

As the tunnel lengthened, it took on even more of a tomb-like quality. With no small measure of relief, the digger would wiggle his way backwards out of the shaft at the end of his shift, taking three times as long to get out as he had to get in. Nevertheless, heartened by the fact that the operation had not been detected, the tunnellers chipped away with relentless determination.

★

Another change occurred that was to have a bearing on the eventual escape.

During a second round of prisoner exchanges, the camp's senior British officer (SBO), Major Haig, who had been keeping a detailed diary of Niemeyer's offences, left Germany. His replacement as SBO was Wing Commander Lieutenant Colonel Charles Rathborne.

Born on 17 February 1886 in the north-eastern seaport of Trieste, Italy,[3] Charles was blessed with a placid, kind temperament, a quality that served him well both as an officer and a human being. With eyes sparkling with warmth and a rare inability to lose his temper, he was once described as possessing 'the face of an archbishop'.

Charles had begun his lifetime military career as an eleven-year-old student at Littlejohn's, a naval crammer.[4] As a seventeen-year-old, he joined the Royal Marine Light Infantry with the rank of 2nd lieutenant. Ten years later, he was attached to the Royal Naval Air Service as a flying officer and by 1917 had attained the rank of wing commander.

Then his life took a turn towards the unexpected.

It began with the German sinking of an unarmed hospital ship; the full fury of British wrath was then brought to bear on the enemy. On 14 April 1917, Charles was flying escort on a successful reprisal bombing raid of Freiburg. They were heading for home when a squadron of German Albatross Scouts intercepted the British bombers. With his engine disabled by gunfire and his observer/gunner mortally wounded, he was forced to land and was immediately taken prisoner.

Of his new status Charles later quipped:

Prisoners of war are a distinct type of being. This condition is brought about by a lack of mental exercise, insufficient physical exercise and in many cases, malnutrition. Before one can aspire to being a Prisoner of War, it is necessary to go through the unpleasant state of being captured . . .

Charles, who was a qualified German interpreter, was transferred between Holzminden and other camps three times in quick succession over a period of three months. He had already been through the camps of Colmar and Karlsruhe before he found himself in one of the first intakes to Holzminden. But in November 1917, he was suddenly transferred out of the camp for a brief incarceration in Freiburg before being returned to the 'hateful' Holzminden. He was back for barely three weeks before he was sent to the newly opened Schweidnitz POW camp, from which he attempted escape before being recaptured – he had presented incorrect forged ID papers – and sentenced to twenty-one days in solitary confinement. During his incarceration, he was not permitted to exercise and he emerged from the darkness physically weakened.

That unsuccessful 'stunt' was also the trigger for Charles's transfer back to Holzminden – his third time there.

Back in Holzminden, Charles was once more SBO. Here is how he eventually recalled this role, which he had also performed in Karlsruhe:

> This Office is a most thankless one and consists of prefering [sic] a string of complaints against the German authorities in the hope of obtaining better treatment. In a prison camp the Senior Captive Officer acts as the prisoners' spokesman. I happened to be a German Scholar and consequently I was fairly well fitted for the work.

Despite any reluctance he may have felt at finding himself lumbered with this 'thankless' role yet again, he was cheered at discovering that several POWs he had befriended since his capture had also found their way to Holzminden.

Charles had been aware of the existence of the newly started tunnel when he first arrived at the camp but had not sought to become involved. Upon his return to Holzminden for a third stint, three months later, he discovered it had lengthened to an impressive 40 yards (nearly 37m) and, extraordinarily, remained undetected by the Germans.

He began to view the tunnel with new eyes.

By this time, a supplementary party had formed, made up of individuals who were allocated positions on the escape list after the working party. This team consisted mainly of those who had previous escape experience or had refused to be transferred via the prisoner exchange program. They were responsible for any task that did not require the physical hard labour of digging – lookout coordination, gathering local topographical and transport intelligence and smuggling in escape tools such as compasses. As the operation evolved, they set up an escape factory in the windowless attic spaces overhead in the barracks roof, where they managed support activities.

With the working party already well established, Charles joined the supplementary party, which included Lieutenant Stanley Stuart Beattie Bruce Purves of No. 19 Squadron RFC;

The Tunnel

2nd Lieutenant John 'Jock' Tullis of No. 70 Squadron RFC; Captain Edward Wilmer Leggatt of No. 2 Squadron RFC; Lieutenant Pierre (Peter) Clifford 'Cliff' Campbell-Martin of No. 25 Squadron RFC; Lieutenant Douglas Clarkson Birch; Lieutenant John Keith Bousfield of the Royal Engineers; Lieutenant Leonard James 'Jim' Bennett of the Royal Navy Air Service; Lieutenant Peter William Lyon of Australia's 11th Battalion; Lieutenant Thomas Frank Burrill of the Montgomeryshire Yeomanry; Captain Philip Norbert Smith; 2nd Lieutenant Fred Illingworth; Captain Frank Sharpe; Lieutenant Bernard P. Luscombe and Major John Morrogh.

A third group of potential team members was then identified – those who had an excellent chance of successful escape due to their fluency in German and their finely honed survival skills.

The escape list grew with each passing week. Those who were involved in the tunnel project were sworn to secrecy. Given the hundreds of POWs in the camp and the scale of the operation, it was extraordinary that the majority of the Holzminden internees did not know of the existence of the tunnel that was snaking its way beyond the outer wall.

Detection by the Germans was a constant concern and despite meticulous planning, there were several heart-stopping close calls. The dreaded day arrived when their captors woke up to the disguise ruse as the fake orderlies hurried from one end of the barracks to the other.

In his memoirs, Charles explained how the Germans then set up a watch to catch out the POWs:

> . . . but we discovered this and suspended operations for a week. The Germans searched the entrance Hall to the Orderlies quarters carefully examining all the barred windows, but they did not

succeed in discovering the tunnel. When at length we decided to continue operations, we came to the conclusion that it would be unsafe to enter through the Orderlies door. As our quarters were in the same building, though separated by walls, we decided to knock a hole, through the wall. To cover the hole up for night inspection a filling piece was made . . .

Creating that new access point wasn't quite as straightforward as Charles made it sound, however. After knocking a hole in the officers' barracks wall, it was discovered there was nothing but solid concrete behind it. Undaunted, the officers turned their attention to an attic wall. When they cut a hole in it to reach the spaces beyond they discovered that from under the attic eaves, they could make their way down, floor by floor, between the walls, to continue their work on the tunnel on the orderlies' side of the barracks.

The attic wall hole played a second, vital part in the operation: it was to provide a route to the chamber entrance on the night of the escape, after the men had been locked in their barracks for the night.

There were other hair-raising close calls, as Jock Tullis recounted:

Sometimes we had bad scares and thought it must only be a question of minutes until the whole thing was discovered by the Hun . . . Once or twice it was a near go, especially on one occasion when a newly captured Padre in the hearing of two of the German interpreters asked another Officer what he knew about the tunnel.

One orderly we were not too sure of who used to receive presents of wine from Niemeyer in the hope that he would give him information in return. This orderly got very drunk one night shortly before the completion of the tunnel and fell downstairs, fracturing his skull, accidentally of course, so that was another danger removed!!

The Tunnel

★

The tunnel grew so lengthy and claustrophobic that the lack of oxygen at the tunnel face became a serious hazard. A creative solution was needed urgently.

Attempts at fixing the suffocating conditions inside the tunnel delivered mixed results, as Jock described:

> . . . an air pump was made, something after the shape of a village blacksmith's bellows to which lengths of pipes made of twisted wire, covered with canvas were attached, having for their joints Colgate's shaving tins which . . . have a screw on the lid. But even with this, which at the best was far from perfect as the air got out all along the pipes, I have known air to be so foul at the tunnel head that if a match were struck it would only glow a dull red, and a candle would not think of burning.

In a variation of the pipe, shaving tins and Red Cross biscuit tins were fashioned together in a long tube that stretched from the tunnel entrance to the working face. A POW was assigned to pump air with the homemade bellows – constructed from an aviator's leather jacket – to the digger on duty. As Jock attested, the air that travelled through the makeshift pipe was foul and the tunneller at the face struggled to breathe. When their hour's shift was up, the exhausted digger would emerge crusted in filth and nursing a thumping headache.

Over the following months, the tunnel inched painstakingly forward under the noses and feet of their captors. Each day the operation remained undetected by the Germans was a victory as the men chipped away in the dark, airless space towards the predetermined exit point in the rye field – and what they hoped would be freedom.

Eleven

Flight Plan

As the now rat-infested tunnel lengthened, the pressure mounted on those above ground who were hard at work planning for the flight across Germany.

The safety of the Dutch border lay 150 miles (241km) to the west, and the POWs had calculated that it would take them fourteen or fifteen days to walk the distance. They acutely understood the need to thoroughly prepare if their plan was ever going to have a chance of succeeding.

Even some prisoners who had arrived a little too late to participate in the digging of the tunnel, such as young Canadian Ian Cameron, made significant contributions. He had no intention of escaping but Ian happily signed the parole card and used his strolls outside the wire to gather intelligence about the terrain, pinpointing landmarks and the location of the train station.

A particular strategy the men used involved writing home in code, hoping that the anomalies in their sentence structure would alert their families to the hidden requests for small objects like compasses. As English was a second language for the German censors, dropped letters or 'mispelled' words were often overlooked during the inspection for *verboten* content. Families often received what appeared to be bizarre chit-chat in letters from their imprisoned loved one. Although initially this was puzzling, it usually wasn't long before a bright spark made the connection and the family set about code-cracking letters received from Holzminden. Contraband items began arriving in the camp, hidden in the handles of sporting equipment or in ingeniously hollowed-out objects such as bars of soap and false-bottomed containers, which sometimes avoided detection, but at other times did not.

From Ströhen POW camp Jock had carried in his pocket a tiny compass, which he described as being a 'little bigger than a sixpenny piece'; prior to the search upon arrival at Holzminden, he had placed it under his tongue. Although he had been made to open his mouth for a search at least once, the German guard did not think to insist on Jock lifting his tongue. The compass slipped undetected into Holzminden, and he kept it on hand for the big breakout.

No creative method of smuggling was off limits – other than the sacrosanct Red Cross parcels. The POWs, grateful for the solicitous care they received during their incarceration, respectfully refrained from using Red Cross parcels for their shady smuggling activities in order not to indict the good name of the organisation, nor risk having food parcels stopped.

The camp guards were also keen smugglers and it wasn't long before the POWs had an astonishing supply line running into the camp under Niemeyer's nose – compasses, maps, cameras, public transport timetables, torches and wire-cutters. Over the construction of the tunnel, the POWs amassed enough escape tools to open a hardware store.

Some ingeniously made their own tools – functioning compasses were cobbled together from magnetised needles and other bits and pieces like cork and paper, every bit as good and reliable as a store-bought one.

Every nook and cranny of the barracks was transformed by the resourceful POWs into secret storage compartments for contraband. For some unexplained reasons, the barracks already contained many false compartments, which the prisoners carefully disguised and blended in any disrupted surfaces or structures to evade detection. When an object was hidden, the other internees were set the task of finding it to test the viability of the hiding place. It was surmised that if those who knew the barracks so well couldn't find a secreted object, then the German guards certainly wouldn't.

Searches by both camp guards and police detectives were commonplace. Occasionally the prisoners would deliberately plant items they could afford to sacrifice. This allowed the Germans an occasional victory, which served to throw them off the scent. Furthermore the guards involved in smuggling escape paraphernalia to the POWs overlooked contraband they might have found during the searches to avoid being blamed – and incurring Niemeyer's fury – for allowing it through in the first place.

With a steady stream of items coming into the camp, the officers turned their attentions to implementing the next stage of the plan – the establishment of a secret escape factory. They had previously broken into an attic room on the very top level of the barracks by simply unscrewing the screws that fastened the lock to the door.

The windowless attic room became a hotbed of activity. In one area, the supplementary party fashioned old uniforms into German civilian clothing by removing insignia and dyeing the fabric. In another, a group painstakingly forged travel documents, copied perfectly from the identification papers pick-pocketed from visiting tradesmen. Occasionally documents were also daringly lifted from the local police detectives called to conduct snap inspections of the barracks. Some Holzminden staff willingly handed over their IDs in return for food or money.

Flight Plan

The POWs were remarkably resourceful. In a camp of several hundred men who had come from professions and trades before the war, any manner of skill could be found among them to assist with the tunnel project – from the soil and strata analysis of archaeology expert and Bombay-born Brit 2nd Lieutenant Osbert Guy Stanhope Crawford to deft lock-pickers and forgers.

Despite the high level of activity, the operation remained top secret. Given the size of the project, it is extraordinary that the rest of the camp remained oblivious to the tunnel's existence. A POW was only made aware of the escape project if the strategists running the show had identified him as a potentially useful contributor.

★

One such man with invaluable skills just begging to be utilised was Dick Cash, whose talents with the camera were destined to serve a critical yet largely invisible role in the escape plot.

It was only shortly before Dick had arrived in Holzminden that the ambitious escape plan had leapt into action. Dick's internal injuries, incurred on the battlefield, had left him in a weakened state and this precluded him from doing any actual digging. Despite orderlies being offered escape positions in return for contributing to the operation, the other ranks like Dick knew that execution awaited them if they were captured following an escape attempt. Although this served as a disincentive in terms of accepting an escape position, many orderlies were more than willing to assist the officers with the project in different ways and would play an invaluable supporting role in the unfolding drama.

At forty-two, Dick was older than many of the prisoners, who were mostly in their twenties and thirties. As a quiet, salt-of-the-earth family man from country New South Wales, he was not given to drawing attention to himself. A non-smoker, he often distributed his allotment of cigarettes to fellow internees. He had managed to bribe a German guard with food in exchange for a pair of wire-cutters, which he gladly loaned to anyone who wanted to attempt going through the wire. This was on the understanding that the escapee was to throw them back to a waiting accomplice inside the camp, who would then return the wire-cutters to Dick.

As the supplementary party continued to identify necessities for the flight across Germany, someone reasoned that the escapees would have a better chance of reaching the safety of the Dutch border if they were equipped with maps. Getting their hands on a map was the easy part; it was making multiple copies of it for each escapee – and there were now upwards of eighty on the list – that presented a challenge.

In their survey of POW skills within the camp, Dick's talents as a professional photographer came to light. In short order he was entrusted with the task of securing the equipment needed and producing multiple photographic copies of the map.

After singling out one of the guards susceptible to bribes, Dick proposed a covert courier service in return for Red Cross goodies from comfort parcels. His shopping list included a camera, a military map of Germany, plates, chemicals, developing paper and a carbide bicycle lamp. Before long, the items Dick had requested were stealthily finding their way into his hands. How his German accomplice managed to secrete such bulky items without detection is not known, but he most likely delivered them to Dick in a Red Cross parcel box.

Discovery by their captors was an ever-present threat, so Dick found a place in the orderlies' quarters in which he hid the equipment. He then set his room-mates the challenge of finding the contraband. A search high and low turned up absolutely nothing, leaving him confident that in the event of a snap search, the equipment would remain hidden.

Dick was assigned a small attic room, where he set to work photographing the military map. It was too large to be photographed in one piece, so he first cut it into twenty-eight sections, carefully numbering each one. Night after night he worked – photographing, developing over and over again, sorting and numbering more than 300 prints into organised piles, until he had enough complete sets to distribute to the men about to escape through the tunnel.

The tunnel mission was so covert, even with more than eighty men directly involved, that each potential escapee was operating on the most basic of information about who was actually involved – all to reduce the risk of discovery. This is never so evident as in Dick's case. In *The Tunnellers of Holzminden*, Hugh Durnford references the escape factory operating in the secret attic rooms, making an incredible claim that in part reads, 'Here maps were photographed without cameras and developed without solutions . . .'

Of course, the map reproduction could not have been achieved without a camera and chemicals, but in Durnford's account, escape maps seemingly appeared out of nowhere. Which is the way the escape team preferred it: the clandestine plan's success depended on the silence of those involved.

Although numerous POWs appear by name in *The Tunnellers of Holzminden* and subsequent books about the escape, Dick does not.

Durnford and many others simply had not been aware that overhead in a dark attic room, an unassuming Australian orderly was risking his life for the officers he served by photographing escape maps with an illicit camera and making multiple prints using smuggled developing chemicals.

★

As the tunnel drew nearer to its exit point, it seemed as though the escape operation had astonishing potential for success. The officers began formulating plans for their flight across the German countryside. The fluent German speakers among them, like Charles Rathborne and David 'Munshi' Gray, plotted conspicuous escape routes that involved German disguises and well-rehearsed stories, should they be stopped by a German patrol or police officer. Although they would be taking the quickest way to the Dutch border, this approach was also by far the riskiest.

Munshi, Cecil and Caspar conceived of a stupendously daring plan. Recalling that there was a genuine lunatic asylum, called Vechta, located close to the Dutch border, the intrepid trio decided to disguise themselves as an escaped asylum inmate and the two guard escorts who had just nabbed the lunatic escapee on the run.

Caspar, who spoke no passable German, was assigned the role of the gibbering inmate, who would almost certainly not be called upon to speak. Cecil, who spoke a little German, was to pose as a junior guard. It was agreed that the German-speaking Munshi, posing as the senior asylum officer, would be their point man on their journey to freedom.

Those who did not have a command of the German language, however, had no choice but to plan a route that would involve skulking their way to the Dutch border via heavily wooded terrain under the cover of darkness.

Jock Tullis, one of the supplementary party, recalled the meticulous planning phase:

> For a week before the great day, my friend [Stanley Purves] and I spent hours studying the best route to follow, preparing

our food, packs, clothes etc. The food carried consisted chiefly of ships biscuits, dipped in molten dripping, stoned dates and great quantities of chocolate melted down into square blocks. In addition we carried meat cubes, Plasmon oats, compressed and mixed with Horlick's Malted Milk Powder, tea, cocoa and soup cubes, two tins compressed meat sausages and 15 or 16 trench cookers; wax blocks with a wick in the middle on which to cook one hot meal per day. Each day's rations were made up in waterproof bundles so that when swimming rivers etc., the food would run a fair chance of remaining dry.

The clothes carried were two spare pairs of socks and some warm underclothes to wear during the day while lying in hiding. I also carried a silk shin and found this a splendid thing for keeping in the heat. We fully expected to have to swim the river Weser flowing about 50 yards wide so some means had to be devised of getting one's food and clothes across dry.

My old Burberry [coat] was treated to a thick coating of molten fat and rubbed well in after which I put my pack and boots in, folding my clothes along the top and tied the Burberry along the top of the bundle with string. We next got a large tin bath and filled it with water and found that the bundle floated beautifully and after a quarter of an hour's immersion everything was still bone dry. We lastly provided ourselves with a loop from the bundle to go round our shoulders, so that when swimming the bundle would tow along behind and not get in the way of arms or legs . . .

The intricate survival plan was duplicated across the scores of officers on the escape list, who planned to travel in pairs, trios or solo.

Then, with the harvest deadline rapidly approaching, there were a number of setbacks – examples of unfortunate timing involving fellow POWs. One was unintentionally triggered by a pair of officers attempting a daring escape of their own, and endangered the tunnel project.

Lieutenant Archie 'Fluffy' Sutcliffe of No. 3 Squadron RFC was often assigned the female role in the POWs' Gaiety Theatre productions due to his uncanny ability to mimic the female form. Nicknamed 'Fluffy' during his school days for reasons unknown, he grew his hair to a convincing length before sashaying his way out of the front gates dressed as the Kommandant's female secretary, on the arm of Lieutenant Timothy Brean, who was disguised as a German.

Max Gore witnessed the brazen escape attempt:

> Together they walked past the sentry guarding the gate from the compound to the *Kommandantur*, the sentry springing to attention and saluting as they did so. They strolled through the headquarters yard, the 'secretary' taking notes and her 'boss' pointing to various objects and dictating to her as he went. Through the main entrance gate they passed and continued leisurely on their way, pretending to examine this and that, till they passed the last part of the wire compound and were halfway up a bit of a hill . . .

The absurd escape attempt would have worked if it hadn't been for a sentry who was glancing out the window of the guardroom at the time and recognised Timothy as a British officer. The audacious pair were detained and sent for the obligatory stint in the jug, but not before a number of appreciative German guards gave them the thumbs-up for the colourful attempt.

Given that any POW planning to escape was required to notify the SBO in advance, either the pair had not consulted Charles with their plan or, having done so, ignored the order not to proceed. At any rate, the pair had been unaware of the tunnel's existence and therefore had not realised they were endangering those involved. Any escape attempt sent the camp authorities into a tailspin and the tunnellers could do nothing but hold their collective breath and wait for the axe to fall.

Around about the same time, the charismatic Munshi was transported to Hanover to answer charges of attempted murder against a parcel-room attendant who claimed the English officer had pulled a knife on him during a heated discussion in the parcel room. Munshi's absence from the tunnel project was deeply felt – in particular by Cecil and Caspar, who were relying on their fluent German-speaking companion to get them across Germany.

Several days in a state of nervous anxiety followed, awaiting the camp guards to descend on the barracks for the inevitable intense camp search in the wake of the Sutcliffe–Brean stunt, and for the outcome of Munshi's trial.

No-one held out much hope for a positive result for their fellow officer but, in an astonishing and unexpected twist, the testimony of the parcel-room accuser was dismissed as unreliable and Munshi was returned to Holzminden, where he was held in the cells for two weeks. Even here, the resourceful POWs managed to work around some of the obstacles placed in their path. Hugh Durnford, who had served in the Indian Army, resided in a barracks room above the cell holding the Indian-born Munshi. He was able to convey news of the tunnel's progress to the imprisoned Munshi in a language the Germans did not understand – Hindustani.

The tunnellers couldn't believe their luck when the dreaded search never materialised. The thought of detection was unthinkable so near to the finish line and the close call saw them throwing themselves into the operation with renewed vigour.

Shortly after the panic subsided, the officers estimated that the tunnel had reached its target exit point under the rye field. To test this theory, Lieutenant Walter Butler – the designated 'cutting-out man' – wiggled along the subterranean chamber all the way to the end. The excavation team had directed the tunnel's trajectory towards the surface in preparation to digging out at the exit point. Walter opened up a small hole over his head with a stick but he was dismayed to discover that several feet still lay between him and a glimpse of blue sky overhead. However, he resolutely kept digging until he broke through to the surface.

Walter then tied a piece of white rag to the stick, poked it up through the hole and gave it a brief wiggle, aware that several officers were standing at the fourth-storey window on spotting duty. To the spotters' dismay, the white rag proved that the tunnel was a good 8 yards (7.3m) short of its target destination in the rye field.

There was nothing to be done. They had to keep digging. It was estimated that they needed to allow at least another month to reach the rye field.

Many of the officers felt they could not risk the extra time – the harvesters would be scything down their protective cover very soon. The decision was made to dig madly for another week, which they estimated should get them just beyond the row of bean plants lining the rye field. Then the escapees would take their chances from there.

Twelve

The Big Stunt

There was a week to go before the scheduled breakout.

It was now time for the escapees housed in Kaserne A to facilitate tunnel access by manufacturing an excuse to be transferred to Kaserne B. This meant dreaming up a convincing excuse for the Germans to authorise the transfer.

Bob Paddison, a working party member, canvassed a 'nasty little beast' of a German officer – who sold jewellery in Hanover and boasted of his ivory matchbox and heavy gold ring – by pleading his case for a 'shadier, cooler room in summer'. The German officer transferred Bob to a 'suffocating room' in Kaserne B; although his intention was to make the prisoner's life difficult, he had no way of knowing that he was doing Bob a favour by giving the would-be escapee access to the finished tunnel and a ticket to potential freedom.

Munshi, Cecil and Caspar were also housed in Kaserne A but successfully applied for a transfer to a twelve-man room in Kaserne B shortly before the scheduled escape. Others working on the tunnel project did the same, applying on various pretexts and were similarly granted permission to move. The sudden flood of transferees from Kaserne A to Kaserne B strangely did not seem to arouse the suspicions of their captors.

Charles Rathborne was monitoring the activity closely. As the escape drew closer, because he was the senior British officer –

and therefore forewarned of any escape plans – he strategically quashed competing plots to give the tunnel escapees, including himself, the best chance for success.

The working party had drawn lots among themselves to determine the order of departure. There was to be a sixty-minute break after the first thirteen to allow them to clear the tunnel and disappear into the German countryside. Walter Butler – who had tested the tunnel a week earlier, only to discover they had fallen short – drew pole position.

It was decided that after the second team, the supplementary party, had gone through, again there would be a break to allow clearance before the rest of the officers on the escape list could take their chances in the remaining time before the sun came up.

More than eighty officers were in the queue to escape.

★

The time had come. It was the night of Tuesday, 23 July 1918, and the tunnel had taken a backbreaking, suffocating, mind-numbing nine months to complete.

Max Gore, listed to escape after the supplementary party, wrote of his memories years later:

> I remember that night very well. There was a thunderstorm and what with the nervous tension and the anticipation of each lightning flash, the following clap seemed to crash and reverberate through the Hartz mountains like the boom of the bass drum, the clash of the cymbals, and the roll of the kettle drums, in the grand finale of a gigantic orchestra conducted by Zeus.

As arranged, each of the escapees had gone to bed dressed in their German disguises, which had been manufactured upstairs in the attic. They all clutched a survival kit containing food, compasses, maps and fake ID. Each was waiting for a tap on the shoulder by Hugh Durnford, the designated 'traffic controller', who signalled the POW to rise and make his way to the secret access hole in the attic room wall.

The officers were all in accord that if they themselves were caught escaping, the orderlies were not to be implicated as accomplices. On the night of the escape, the orderlies were once again on hand as look-outs and guides, rendering invaluable assistance to ensure the operation ran smoothly.

Walter Butler, the first to go, reached the end of the tunnel at around 10.45 pm and used a bread knife to jab a large hole in the roof of the tunnel, right through to the surface. The officers of the working party had the presence of mind to create a receiving pit a day or so previously for the excavated earth in preparation for that last push. This meant that the earth and debris of the final breakthrough would not block the escapees' exit.

When Walter stuck his head out of the hole for a cautious look, he saw to his immense relief that the exit hole had emerged within the cover zone of the rows of bean plants. After enlarging the exit hole until he was able to pass through, Walter crawled out. With a thudding heart, he crouched quietly to assess the camp activity before stealthily moving off into the full cover of the rye field crop under the blessed cover of rain.

Orderly Private Ernest Collinson of the Bedfordshire and Hertfordshire Regiment, who had been standing at a window in the orderlies' quarters, finally spotted Walter's dark form emerge in the rain-swept field. He hurried off, climbing up via the wall cavity to the attic room, where he gave the signal for the next officer to be ushered through.

One by one, each officer escapee – carrying their boots to

reduce noise – received the signal. With the utmost stealth, they then proceeded to the attic room, entered through the hole in the wall, making their way along the length of the barracks via the roof eaves, then dropping down into the orderlies' quarters through the manhole.

Each member of the thirteen-man working party successfully crawled their way down the tunnel, out the exit and melted into the night without challenge.

Then it was the turn of the supplementary party. Charles Rathborne, fourteenth in line, recalled:

> ... I had my kit ready which consisted of two suits of plain clothes – one to look respectable in and the other to keep the inner one clean whilst crawling through the tunnel. Besides this I had a small handbag containing a little food, razor, soap, a towel, hairbrushes and a small looking glass. I wore a felt hat in true German style with a feather at the back and a pair of spectacles which I had obtained from a friend. With this kit on I made my way in my turn through the hole in the wall and then down the Orderlies stairs to the tunnel. The first fourteen now got into the tunnel, which was only just large enough to receive one's body; the kit had to be pushed ahead.
>
> Eventually my turn came to crawl out of the further entrance. I knew the two sentries were only a few yards away and one could almost hear them breathe. I crawled out pushing my kit ahead behind the bean stalks and from there through a corn field. I never imagined it would be so difficult to make any headway through standing corn.
>
> Progress appeared to be very slow and we were a long time clearing the light of the big arc lamps which illuminated the wire round the camp ...

The Big Stunt

All the while, stationed at various points on the way from the barracks to the tunnel entrance, trustworthy orderlies were guiding and timing the progress of officers with the utmost precision. The flow of escapees through the attic wall was being controlled by Lieutenant Louis 'Swaggie'[1] Greive of Australia's 23rd Battalion, who had strict instructions to wait for the signal before allowing the next escapee through. Interval timing was crucial; those in the tunnel needed to crawl their way along before the next one entered the chamber to avoid a traffic jam and asphyxiation in the claustrophobic tunnel.

Jock Tullis, who followed escape companion Stanley Purves, describes the arduous crawl along the tunnel:

> Getting through that tunnel was a nightmare experience, the distance seemed endless as one pushed one's heavy pack along a couple of feet and then wormed after it. It would have been easier had the tunnel been level but in one place where it came from the 30 foot level to within two feet of the surface, the slope was like going up the side of a house. I [got] stuck at the bottom of this slope, as everyone going up had to dig their feet and elbows into the side to get a hold at all and, of course, loosened the sides so that stones and earth rolled down and piled up at the bottom. Sticking wasn't a pleasant experience, one is apt to get panicky, but the thought of others coming behind had a calming effect, and eventually I loosened the rock that was holding me and crawled or wormed my way up with frequent rests to regain my breath.
>
> Once the top was reached, the going was easier and shortly afterwards my head struck solid ground in front, and on looking up I saw a dark blotch of sky and felt the first puff of pure free air in my face. On getting out, my first thought was, 'What was the sentry doing?', so I had a look through the beans and by the

light of the arc lamps I saw him walking slowly up and down, rifle under arm, and coat collar up round his ears as it was raining hard with a strong wind blowing from the south west – a happy occurrence for us as it carried any small noise we did make away from the camp. I soon reached the corn and crawled through a lane as wide as a wagon track made by the fellows in front of us. Once through the corn we paused a few minutes for a much needed breath, and then set off for the river Weser being joined by another officer, a Capt. Leggatt who was going to travel alone . . .

As one by one the officers climbed up through the exit hole and into the rye field, the journey through the tunnel became progressively harder for those coming after. Passing through the tunnel was laborious, backbreaking effort. Stones and earth continued to be dislodged with the constant movement of human bodies.

Unbeknown to them all, the traffic through the tunnel was dangerously compromising its stability. By 4.30 am, twenty-nine escapees had successfully made their way out of the exit hole. The luck of the remaining escapees refused to hold out, for as the thirtieth man was about to emerge, the tunnel finally gave way, collapsing in a torrent of earth and stones. The final section, which had not been reinforced owing to a shortage of timber bunk boards, had finally caved in under the pressure of the heavy traffic.

Several men were trapped at various stages throughout the 60-yard (55m) tunnel by the earthfall and panic ensued as they called to each other. They would have to back all the way out, excruciating inch by excruciating inch.

The man closest to the tunnel entrance heard the shouted relayed message that the tunnel had collapsed and there was no way forward. Slowly he began to back out until he emerged from the entrance and reported the blockage.

In *The Tunnellers of Holzminden*, Hugh Durnford recalled that:

> ... a New Zealand officer called Garland, who was high up on the waiting list, came up to the rendezvous to prospect. He happened to be about as strong physically as any other two officers in the camp, and possessed the biceps of a Hercules. He at once volunteered to go down and try to pull out the rear-most man. After about half an hour he succeeded in doing so, and the two collaborators in this severe physical exercise crawled back through the attic hole completely exhausted and dripping with sweat.

Durnford had certainly described Edgar Garland – the stocky, 'Herculean' aviator – correctly; however, according to the man himself, he was, in fact, one of those caught in the tunnel collapse. Edgar, Wellington's home-grown hero, who had kept up a flow of letters back home describing his wartime adventures, vividly recounted in 1920:

> ... as we had only five minutes' warning, we did not know who was in front or behind. I was summoned about three in the morning. 'Be in the tunnel in five minutes; or you miss your turn.' It was pitch dark when I got inside the triangle room, where the mouth of the tunnel was situated, and there was a gurgling noise, something like the sound water makes just as it runs out of a big tank and down a pipe. It was caused by the people still in the tunnel who were calling out to each other as they wormed along.
>
> The first part of the tunnel was very steep and when I started to push my haversack in front of me, it suddenly disappeared – and rolled down to the bottom. Going downhill was easy enough, but when I got to the bottom of the dip, I found progress very hard work.

The tunnel was so small that I had to lie flat on my stomach with my hands above my head. There was not room enough to pull one arm back or to raise my head far without hitting the roof. There was no such thing as crawling; the only way I could advance was by pushing my haversack along in front of me and then shoving myself forward by my toes.

My electric torch enabled me to see what was in front. I came across tins of bully beef and chocolate, which had been lost out of bags. All the time the awful gurgling noise was going on and the air began to get very bad. It should have taken about twenty minutes to worm to the end of the tunnel, but soon the man in front of me who had been going very slowly stopped and lay still. I thought he had fainted, but when I shook him by the foot he said, 'The tunnel has fallen in and they are trying to clear it. It will only take a few minutes.'

In the meantime, the chap behind me ran into my feet. 'What's wrong?' he gasped. I told him that there was a block somewhere up ahead, but that it would probably be cleared in a few minutes.

The tunnel soon got filled up with men who knew nothing about the block. This was dangerous as it made the air very bad. There was now so much noise that it was not possible to communicate with those behind and tell them to go back. We waited and waited. I could feel myself getting weaker. We had to wait in that suffocating place more than two hours before the man who entered last gave up and got out. The next man then started back, and the next, until I heard the man behind me say that he was returning.

It was terrible work. We had to pull our haversacks instead of pushing them; our coats came over our heads, and it was uphill. When one of the fellows got jammed and could not move, I really thought we should be suffocated. But after a lot of struggling he got his coat off over his head, and that saved us. When I got to the uphill part I thought I should never manage it; but I struggled on, and by and by I felt some one pulling my feet. The men at the entrance had formed a human chain and were hauling us out. It was now almost daylight, so I hurried upstairs to the secret entrance . . .

It's unclear as to why these two such different versions of the same event exist, but it's fair to say that if anyone knew where Edgar was at the time, it would be the man himself. His vivid mole's-eye description of backing out of the tunnel gives us a glimpse of the agony of the backwards journey along a kinking, narrow, airless tunnel clogged with men and debris.

By now it was dawn and the opportunity to attempt escape was gone. The collapse had cost fifty-seven men their shot at freedom.

A valiant effort was made to pull the remaining officers from the tunnel, but two were stuck fast and had to be left behind temporarily as the others rapidly tried to conceal the tunnel entrance and race back upstairs before the barracks was unlocked at 6 am. After the guards had completed their morning inspection, the officers hurried to the tunnel entrance to release the final two from their tomblike confines.

First World War history had just been made: never before had there been a breakout from a POW camp on such a scale. The fifty-seven disappointed would-be escapees had no time to ponder what might have been for them; repercussions were imminent.

★

Niemeyer was inevitably going to discover the mass escape from his 'inescapable camp' during the head count at the 9 am *Appel*. But it just so happened that the pair of officers who were last out of the ruined tunnel exited from the orderlies' entrance in their mud-stained clothes, rather than proceeding upstairs to the manhole that would take them back to the officers' quarters via the roof eaves to avoid detection.

As luck would have it, they ran straight into Niemeyer, who quizzed them on their dishevelled appearance. Moments later, the farmer from next door, who had begun work in his rye field, arrived in a fury to report the trampling of his crops.

When Niemeyer went to investigate, he found the yawning mouth of the tunnel exit and the pathway of trampled grain stalks.

He was famously said to have uttered darkly: '*So, ein tunnel.*'

A rampaging Niemeyer posted a guard at the tunnel exit and ordered an immediate head count of the POWs. Having clearly expected – or, at the very least, hoped for – a modest shortfall in detainee numbers, the Kommandant was visibly shocked when he learned that twenty-nine of his charges had vanished into the countryside. He exploded in a black rage and the men predictably found themselves confined to barracks.

Convulsed in guffaws of laughter, the POWs watched the Kommandant's furious antics from their windows. Niemeyer gave the order for the guards to fire at the windows, but the men knew the drill: they had already taken cover, hitting the floor amid roars of laughter. It was more than likely that the guards – many of whom favoured the POWs over the Kommandant – would have deliberately missed anyway.

The breakout was reported to the local police and to Niemeyer's superiors at the Xth Army Corps headquarters. Immediately, a massive manhunt was launched and a king's ransom of 5000 marks offered for the return of each escapee.

Already in a state, what enraged the Kommandant even more was his inability to locate the tunnel entrance for at least two hours. None of his men was keen to go down into the tomblike depths and follow the trajectory back to its source, and no

The Big Stunt

amount of bribing the orderlies would make them give away the tunnel's point of entry. Finally, powerless to order the interned officers to perform manual labour, he had the orderlies excavate the tunnel under an armed guard; it was days before they tracked the mole hole all the way back to the orderlies' quarters.

Otto Liebert, the local Holzminden photographer, appeared on the scene and took snaps of the excavation. It is not known if he was summoned to document the event or had raced up to the camp after hearing of the mass breakout. Today, three of Liebert's photos are the only existing visual evidence of the incredible feat achieved by the POWs.

If the prisoners left behind thought they had suffered at the hands of Niemeyer prior to the great tunnel escape, they now steeled themselves for serious reprisals: all prisoners – regardless of whether they had been involved in the escape operation or not – were forced to suffer lockdown conditions in the stifling mid-summer heat.

But that was just for starters. Everything was now *verboten*: group gatherings, library privileges, Gaiety Theatre productions and mail call were all cancelled. Officers were deprived of the services of their orderlies while the latter were digging out the tunnel. The cells were boarded up further to prevent the slightest chink of light entering and POWs were transferred to other camps. Roommates were lost, allocated to other parts of the barracks, as Niemeyer attempted to keep an eye on the greatest flight risks. Guards were ordered to take a head count of sleeping prisoners three times a night, purposefully waking them to do so.

Despite the unpleasant conditions, many of the POWs went to sleep at night with smiles on their faces, content in the knowledge that Germany's 'most inescapable camp' had been compromised by twenty-nine of their own in a momentous event that became known as 'the big stunt'.

Thirteen

Flight to Freedom

While an irate and humiliated Niemeyer leapt into action, all twenty-nine escapees had negotiated the River Weser, which ran beside the camp, and had embarked on their own adventures.

They knew that word of the mass exodus would soon be out. This meant that the local population would be on the look-out. It was a safe bet that Niemeyer, desperate to salvage his reputation, would have amassed a mighty manpower contingent for the manhunt and also put up a generous reward for the prisoners' return. The escapees had also predicted the use of bloodhounds, and had pre-emptively employed tricks such as laying pepper trails in the hope of throwing the hounds off the scent.

Charles Rathborne, confident he could pass himself off as a German, did not flee into the countryside. Unlike his fellow escapees, he had packed lightly. His intention was to walk to the town of Göttingen, 45 miles (72km) in the opposite direction, rather than take the arduous trek cross-country on foot, as the non-German speakers had planned. He had correctly surmised that his pursuers would not expect any of the runaways to take a route that led in the opposite direction to the Dutch frontier.

When Charles had emerged from the crop field and checked his watch, it was 2 am. Despite his excellent language skills and bold plan, he was keen not to invite trouble. His previous escape attempt – from Schweidnitz – had ended badly when a German sentry noticed that Charles's forged ID papers bore the Prussian Spread Eagle rather than the required Lion Rampant stamp. It was a damnable error that saw him recaptured and sent to Holzminden for the third time.

Charles passed the darkened windows of the Holzminden township in the wee small hours before he took to the hills, where he found a deserted fir-tree plantation about 5 miles (8km) from the township. Here he hid from dawn until eleven that night before continuing his journey under the cover of darkness, repeating this pattern again the following day and night.

Intermittent rain plagued his journey. Constantly wet, he also had to contend with ants swarming over him as he tried to sleep during daylight hours. By the time he was 15 miles (24km) short of Göttingen, he was fed up. He threw caution to the wind and started to walk by day, trusting that his fresh change of travelling suit and his language skills would deceive any Germans he met along the way. As it turned out, he came across hardly any locals in this time – only a soldier smooching his sweetheart in a local village at 3 am. The lovers barely gave him a glance as he bid them good night in German and continued on his way.

Arriving at his destination without challenge, Charles gathered his courage to enter a tavern. He had resolved to keep his responses in German short and avoid engaging in lengthy conversations. The innkeeper, an elderly woman, did not question the slightly bedraggled stranger who approached the bar at three o'clock that afternoon and asked for a beer. Needless to say, it went down a right treat. Not only that, it also imbued Charles with a newfound sense of confidence.

Leaving the tavern, he picked up a train timetable. Needing to kill time before his train left at 8 pm, he sauntered into a cinema, where he brazenly sat among the local audience to watch a series of 'very interesting pictures' of *Kaiserschlacht,* the German offensive of 21 March that had seen the influx of POWs into Holzminden during the tunnel's construction.

Charles walked to the train station, bought a ticket and boarded the 8 pm train south to Bebra. When he alighted from the train, he had put roughly 86 miles (140km) between himself and the dreaded camp. That night, the rain poured down and he spent it trying to sleep in a pile of stacked corn in a freshly harvested field outside the town.

The next morning, a Saturday, he took the train further south to Fulda, but found he had missed his connection west to Cologne. Unconcerned, Charles again availed himself of the local tavern facilities. He took in every detail of his surroundings, noting:

> There were a lot of infuriated old women in this tavern who were complaining bitterly about the shortage of potatoes in particular and food in general.

After Charles consulted the timetable, he realised that the trains did not run to Cologne, so he altered his route, aiming to get to Cologne via Frankfurt. Upon arrival, he hurried from Frankfurt railway station, knowing it to be full of German secret police. He realised he was looking rather scruffy and his collar was quite obviously dirty. Feeling this might be a giveaway, he attempted to buy a new one. When the shopkeeper demanded a coupon, which Charles didn't have, his heart sank. After some haggling, however, the shopkeeper relented and sold Charles a clean collar without further quibbling.

As the train to Cologne did not leave until midnight, Charles found himself with time on his hands yet again. Beer was about the only thing that could be bought without a coupon, so once more he found a tavern in which to while away the hours. The innkeeper was uncomfortably talkative and, detecting a slight accent in Charles's responses, asked him if he was Polish. A nervous Charles replied in the affirmative and was relieved when the innkeeper appeared to be satisfied with this.

Another trip to the cinema absorbed the rest of Charles's waiting time and he boarded the train to Cologne without challenge. His memoir reads:

> I caught the midnight train for Cologne travelling 3rd class. All my railway travelling was done in 3rd class carriages and by slow trains. Express and corridor trains were subject to frequent search and passengers were generally required to produce passes. Crowded slow trains are difficult to search and consequently the authorities generally left them alone. I passed an uneventful night in the train and slept most of the time, arriving at Cologne at 9 on Sunday morning. Here again I wasted no time in clearing out of the station ...

By now his unshaven and dishevelled appearance was likely to attract undue attention so Charles went to a barber's shop. The chatty barber, who had recently been released from the Imperial Germany Army due to his war wounds, was blissfully unaware he was scraping the whiskers from the face of an escaped British prisoner.

At nine that night, Charles arrived in Aachen (Aix-la-Chapelle), Germany's westernmost city. More than 185 miles (298km) now lay between him and Holzminden, and despite the crooked dog's leg journey he had taken to get there, it had amounted to only a few days by train.

Charles could taste victory. The Dutch frontier lay only a few miles away. He recalled:

I also had a detailed map of this district. Here I waited until 11.30 and then, producing my compass, I started my cross-country journey walking across fields by compass bearing and avoiding all roads. It started to rain, which helped matters. After tramping for about three hours, I heard soldiers talking and dogs barking. I was then in the middle of standing corn, so I got down on all fours and crawled. Progress through standing corn was terribly slow, and as the weather was wet, my clothes were soon drenched to the skin. I crawled for about an hour in this manner and could hear the sentries shuffling about on my right and left.

Suddenly it began to dawn and I came across pasture land. This looked very much like Holland to me as I know that no land was wasted for pasture purposes in Germany. I therefore decided to get up and walk. There was a sign post which told me I was a kilometre away from Bocholz . . .

After questioning a civilian on a bicycle, Charles confirmed that he was, indeed, in southern Holland. He reported to the Dutch Military Police, who extended their hospitality to him. He was given a meal, offered a much-needed bath and presented to the British representatives in Holland.

Charles Rathborne, escapee from Holzminden POW camp, was a now a free man.

The British authorities arranged for his repatriation, and on 4 August 1918, Charles stepped ashore in England.

One can only imagine the look on Niemeyer's face when he received a taunting telegram from Charles from the safety of London: 'Having a lovely time STOP If I ever find you in London will break your neck STOP.'

★

Charles's fellow escapees had altogether different experiences. Jim Bennett and Cliff Campbell-Martin, who had teamed up for the long walk to the Dutch border, had one close call after another during their flight across the German countryside. They had only been on the run for a few hours when they heard a commotion, carried on the wind, from the camp behind them – the sound of guards shouting and bloodhounds baying. With daylight illuminating the countryside, they hid in a crop field until late into the night and agreed to walk in only the darkest part of the night to ensure cover.

To avoid detection, they often perched in trees throughout the day, a tactic that proved agonising for their bodies. They later hid in a rye field, the harvesters coming dangerously close to the place where they lay hidden among the stalks. At one point, they were forced to outrun a police officer; another time they had to evade a cavalry detachment.

The pair also came within a whisker of being found by searchers. The two fugitives were hiding in an area that was drained by a series of parallel ditches when they realised that a group of pursuers were organising the search up and down between the ditches. Taking advantage of the methodical German nature, the escapees waited until a search party passed by, then emerged from one ditch and ran behind the searchers' backs to the next ditch in the opposite direction before flinging themselves down. They continued this pattern until they were clear.

Having run the gauntlet of patrols, police officers, search parties, dogs and harvesters, the pair was faced with the challenge of river crossings. Cliff couldn't swim, so at every body of water, Jim would swim the duo's clothing across, then return to assist his escape-mate.

The River Ems lay beyond a barbed wire fence, guarded by German sentries. If they could make it to the river, they had a good chance of getting away. Aiming for a hole in the barbed wire fence, the pair made a mad dash for it. No doubt the adrenalin was pumping and hearts were thudding as shots rang out around their ears. But by some miracle – or perhaps the sentry was a poor shot – they plunged into the river unscathed, and managed to make it across to safety with Jim assisting non-swimmer Cliff to the other side.

Two hours later, the pair arrived in Holland, exhausted. A combination of drinking brackish water, lack of food and sleep deprivation had taken its toll on both of them. It was Friday, 2 August and they had been on the run for ten days.

Only three days behind them were Munshi, Cecil and Caspar. They had been making their way through Germany without hindrance, thanks to their brilliant disguises as an asylum escapee and his guards. Before leaving the camp, they had forged a German document stating their false identities and the reason for their travel – to escort the escaped 'psychiatric patient' back to Vechta Lunatic Asylum, in Germany's north-west. Caspar's only requirement was to gibber and drool, which he did masterfully, and this had the desired effect of causing curious onlookers or suspicious authorities to beat a hasty and fearful retreat.

They had cause to employ their cover story almost immediately when, on the second night, they took a route through what was supposed to be the sleepy village of Gellersen. It was midnight and, rather than the darkened windows they expected at that hour, every home was lit up and excited villagers were spilling into the streets.

The trio guessed correctly that news of the escape had reached Gellersen. Taking Caspar by the arms, the 'asylum guards' dragged him along as he played the mad lunatic to maximum effect. Munshi explained to the villagers in German that they were transporting this dangerous madman by night to avoid contact with other people and, like magic, the crowd took a step backwards.

Thoroughly enjoying their starring roles before a captive audience, Munshi pretended to administer a sedative to the drooling and violent Caspar, which was really just an aspirin from his kit. Slowly Caspar slipped into 'unconsciousness', leaving Munshi and Cecil free to avail themselves of the villagers' hospitality by accepting bread, cheese and wine.

Their hosts – who had no idea to whom they were talking – unwittingly passed on critical intelligence when they mentioned that the area between Barntrup and Hameln was under heavy patrol.

Taking leave of their unsuspecting hosts, Munshi and Cecil returned to their sleepy charge, rousing him before they thanked the villagers and continued on their way, dragging a drooping Caspar between them. They were elated at how well their ruse had worked – and they would certainly avoid the Barntrup–Hameln area now – but they were cautious enough not to take any more risks. Finding a wood not far from Gellersen, they spent the daylight hours in hiding.

Travelling at night, like many of their comrades, they experienced a close call when they nearly ran into a German patrol, but had pulled back into the woods before they were spotted. Munshi picked up in the conversation as the troops passed that, disappointingly, some of the other Holzminden escapees had been recaptured.

The trio continued onwards, sticking to unpopulated areas, negotiating driving rain and boggy swampland. Their brilliant disguises had turned to muddy rags after two weeks of survival trekking through inhospitable terrain. They realised they needed to take special care; their elaborate ruse would hardly hold up to scrutiny as it had done back in Gellersen.

Exhausted by nearly a fortnight on the run in horrendous conditions, the trio confronted one last hurdle. They were crouched by a low ditch at the side of a road, with the promise of Holland on the other. In between, a patrolling sentry was marching endlessly up and down. Day after day over the course of their mud-encrusted journey, they would have given anything for the driving rain to subside, and now they wished the rain would return to provide them with cover for their final dash to freedom. The sludgy conditions made for a slippery climb. Inch by inch they crawled up the ditch to the road, timing themselves to step onto the road when the sentry was at his farthest point.

Finally Caspar and Cecil reached the top of the ditch. The sentry was about to pivot and return; they had no time to lose. With his ankles gripped by Cecil, Caspar leaned over the side of the ditch and hauled Munshi up.

When the sentry turned, the trio was already across the road and flinging themselves into the sucking bog on the other side. Whether it was the descending darkness, the sentry's poor aim or a combination of both, the escapees were unscathed, though two rifle shots went zinging past their ears. They thrashed through the mire then, realising that the sentry had given up, threw themselves down. They had made it.

Munshi, Caspar and Cecil arrived at the Dutch quarantine camp in the early hours of Monday, 5 August, to be greeted by the familiar faces of Jim Bennett and Cliff Campbell-Martin.

★

Shortly after emerging from the tunnel, travelling companions Jock Tullis and Stanley Purves were joined by solo escapee Edward Leggatt. The duo had no objections to expanding their group to a trio, but the first thing they had to do was get across the fast-flowing River Weser, which ran beside the camp.

During the preparation stages, the enterprising Jock had had the foresight to waterproof his Burberry coat with molten fat and it was into this that he and Stanley placed their clothing, wrapping the items in a bundle to keep them dry. At the river's deepest point, the water surged around their shoulders. Jock held on to Stanley's shoulders as they negotiated their way across the swiftly flowing river. Edward had quickly fashioned himself a makeshift raft, but to little avail. His clothing was soaked by the time they reached the other side. By contrast, Jock's waterproofed coat had served the purpose well, for the clothing contained inside was bone dry. They dressed on the other side and set off, intending to travel by night and sleep by day.

The second night the trio lost their way in the completely starless night. At the Bodexen crossroads, which they were able to pinpoint on their map, Edward decided to go it alone, choosing to take a more northerly route than the ones his travelling companions had selected.

Jock and Stanley hit the track once again, skirting the villages of Fursten and Lowesdorf, and eventually taking cover in a fir-tree forest near Killenbeck. In keeping with their original plan, they hid by day and walked by night, each carrying their 45 lb (20kg) pack. Though they avoided populated areas, they were chased by villagers, hunted by schoolchildren and shared a meal with a stray black cat. On the fourth night they came across two figures, indistinct in the moonlight, whom they presumed to be fellow escapees, but the pair took off into the woods. When Jock whistled the tune 'Annie Laurie' to identify themselves, the pair whistled back but did not emerge. Their identity is a mystery that was never solved.

The following night, Jock and Stanley were taking a ten-minute break when someone walked past them. Stanley greeted the man in German, only to realise that it was Edward, with whom they had parted company on the second night.

Unsettled by his experience of solo travel, Edward asked to rejoin them, giving them a hair-raising account of hiding up a tree to avoid a Boy Scout patrol that had been sent to search for escapees.

The three continued on their way, stopping frequently so that Edward could attend to his aching feet, squashed inside ill-fitting boots.

A week into their travels, Edward sketched the trio's ditch encampment in the woods. The offending boots, which had been rubbed in fat to loosen them up, are pictured in the foreground.

The tenth night saw the trio chased by wolfhounds released by a suspicious German. In their haste to get away, the runaways ended up on the wrong side of a stream, which forced them to take the risk of negotiating a bridge at the village of Rokholt in order to get back onto the right side. They surveyed the bridge for some time for sentries, but none appeared and they decided they couldn't wait forever. They hurriedly crossed the bridge without challenge and pushed on once more.

Their next obstacle was the River Ems, where they spotted an unattended ferry tied up on the opposite side. After losing a toss, Jock stripped and swam the river, untied the ferry and towed it back across the river to collect the other two.

By this stage, food stocks were low so the men dug up potatoes in a nearby field, sliced them thinly and cooked them in a Lyle's Golden Syrup tin, heated by one of the trench cooker blocks they had been carrying.

On the fourteenth day, after stumbling through a blinding white fog into muddy ditches, they took cover during daylight hours. From their position they could see and hear the church bells of Losser, a town in Holland. Aware that they could easily become disoriented during the border crossing and find themselves back in Germany, as other escapees had, they thoroughly familiarised themselves with the route and landmarks to improve their chance of success.

Dodging a bicycle patrol, the trio crawled past a German guardhouse, then under four lines of barbed wire. They got to their feet, walked a bit further, then stopped to check their map. They were elated to realise that they were standing on Dutch soil, and had been for about a mile.

It was Tuesday, 6 August, and they were finally free.

The same day, the tenth and final successful Holzminden escapee, John Bousfield, arrived at the quarantine camp.

Fourteen

Back in Enemy Hands

The ten successful Holzminden escapees returned to England – first Charles Rathborne, then, twelve days later on 16 August 1918, the other nine. It was to be some time before they realised that nineteen of their twenty-nine comrades who had fled that night had not been so fortunate.

In his escape diary, recorded in 1921, unsuccessful escapee Bob Paddison recalled the rollercoaster ride of experiences of his journey across the German countryside with Arthur Morris before their recapture:

> The sunsets & sunrises – Saturday 27th July is know[n] to us as the red morning owing to its sunrise – the moon on several occasions and the awful stuffy blackness of a thunderstorm in a little prehistoric village which frightened us out of our lives ringing in a curfew bell in the roof whose little loft we were occupying – we had climbed in through the belfry but we'd forgotten about that. Then I remember a damp night after we'd been out about a week. We had lost our way and were moving along a soggy sand track when we suddenly stopped under the blackness of two magnificent elms – what stopped us I don't know but we listened for some time to rain drops and certainly the vague enormous shapes of the elms were rather awesome. It was a silly situation – we weren't really afraid of the dark by then and yet there was I at

any rate standing stock still looking up at the elms listening to the occasional pit as one leaf tilted and pitched its burden on to the one below and all the time my heart doing its best to choke me . . .

There was good reason for the runaways to be jumpy. One by one, the nineteen who remained on the loose were recaptured, mostly betrayed by locals who had their eye on the sizeable reward. Search parties arranged by local communities managed to turn up the hiding places of many of the POWs. Heartbreakingly, a few had almost made it to the border before being recaptured.

Once returned to the camp, the nineteen – Paddison, Morris, Wainwright, Clouston, Robertson, Laurance, Butler, Langren, Mardock, MacLeod, Lyon, Burrill, Birch, Smith, Morrogh, Illingworth, Sharpe, Shipwright and Luscombe – resigned themselves to the punishment that awaited them. All were committed to the cells, where their punishment was stepped up to include bread and water rations and the lighting was switched off.

Niemeyer focused his ire on the returned escapees, ensuring that they suffered for their sins. On 27 September 1918, the nineteen were committed for a German military trial, charged with mutiny and destroying imperial government property. A charge sheet was drawn up and when each of the accused was asked for their civilian occupation, some just said the first thing that came into their head, and this was duly recorded as fact.

Even though the British officers were permitted legal counsel, each of them, unsurprisingly, found themselves convicted and sentenced to six months' imprisonment. However, the sentence was never enforced, for Germany was now losing the war.

★

Around the time of the trial, all Holzminden prisoners began to notice a distinct about-face in the treatment they received at the hands of Niemeyer. The reason for the Kommandant's change of heart soon became obvious: Germany was preparing to surrender.

In October 1918, Hector Dougall remarked drily in his diary:

> . . . the Commandant is getting very nice to us. Had a photographer in camp all day, taking our picture in groups and kidding us along . . . everybody arguing about the war . . . the Commandant is trying to get on the good side of us now by doing us little favours, but we don't take any notice of them.

The weeks leading up to the Armistice had every prisoner on tenterhooks – excitement and anxiety ran in equal measure, no-one knowing exactly when that moment of freedom was going to happen.

The balance of power had well and truly shifted. Niemeyer, knowing his goose was cooked, made a desperate but futile effort to turn down the heat on the simmering pot before the red-hot explosion.

Norman Birks noticed:

> . . . a distinct change in the attitude of our captors. They had changed from a bullying to a fawning community. A strange nation: brave and aggressive when winning, but not very admirable when losing.

The photographer mentioned in Hector's diary was Otto Liebert, who had visited the camp on numerous occasions, and had taken the photographs of the excavated tunnel. Niemeyer commissioned the Holzminden photographer to portray the camp in a positive light in a series of propaganda images. Shooting the 'happy snaps' continued on and off for several days. The finished results consisted of uniformed officer groups and candid shots as Niemeyer frantically attempted to represent the camp as something akin to a jolly boys' boarding school rather than the abusive and miserable place it had been for more than a year. Terrified of British reprisals, he buddied up to many of the POWs as though the whole thing had been a terrific joke. Needless to say, his efforts were in vain.

In one photo, more than 140 officers pose – rather resentfully, judging by the unimpressed expressions on their faces – outside a barracks buildings, well turned out in full uniform. In a more casual photo, a large group of POWs is gathered outside one of the barracks as others hang precariously from upstairs window sills, portraying a laxity that had previously not existed in the camp. Most telling is the presence of perhaps a dozen unarmed guards milling about on the left of the group – another of Niemeyer's attempts to improve his 'report card' by falsely depicting a chummy relationship between guard and prisoner.

In the weeks leading up to the Armistice, security became virtually non-existent. Reg Gough recalled in his memoirs that:

> . . . there were signs that the Germans were going to lose the war and their treatment [of us] became much better as things got worse [militarily]. They evidently did their best to make us forget . . . that there had been times when their treatment of prisoners would not be a thing to be proud of and were now inclined to let us do more or less as we liked within the bounds of the camp . . .

Yet amid the POWs' relief at their impending release, tragic events were taking place within a mile of the barbed wire. Chaos reigned in the township of Holzminden; driven to their knees by starvation, like the rest of the country, the townspeople rioted.

The camp quickly began to run out of its already depleted food stocks.

Hector's diary records twenty-one civilian deaths as a result of starvation and rioting in just three days, and an average of eight funerals a day passing by the camp gates in the following weeks en route to the nearby cemetery. Given that the available food was bordering on the inedible, if there was any at all, it probably was no great shock when a wagon laden with 200 Red Cross parcels – on which the POWs were dependent for sustenance – was raided by townspeople from Holzminden. Subsequently, only four parcels reached the camp that week.

In a series of diary entries that amount to an anatomy of the Armistice from a POW's perspective, Hector, practically inhaling the scent of freedom in the air, wrote with hope and despair in equal measure.

On 10 November 1918, he noted:

> Revolution broke out in Holzminden. The revolutionists are in power. The officers have lost their swords and badges. The Red Flag is up. Everybody has wind up around here until we find out whether they are going to be friendly or hostile. The revolutionists are also in power in Berlin. They have the terms of the Armistice and their reply has to go to the Allies before tomorrow noon. Quite a bit of bloodshed in Berlin. No parcels or mail. Guess all our parcels have gone West with the revolution. The Kaiser has to abdicate pretty soon.

Hector and the rest of the world soon discovered that the Kaiser had already crossed the border into exile in the Netherlands – on 9 November – paving the way for the birth of the Weimar Republic.

Revolution, however, was not the only crisis Germans were facing. The Spanish flu, a deadly worldwide pandemic, had begun to strike down victims in January 1918 and would continue to rage across the globe for another three years, killing between three and five per cent of the world's population.

In his diary, David Horne describes a local funeral procession he encountered during one of his walks through Holzminden woods:

> Quite a lot of deaths, the people being so ill fed, that they fall a-prey to any plague. I notice one funeral today, which reminded me of the Highland funerals. Only one woman present, all men in black, silk hats, some of very ancient fashion. The hearse most gaudy, black and aluminium colour. The horses covered with black cloth, so that only their eyes and legs from knees downwards are visible.

The camp was not immune to the virus. Those suffering from malnourishment and mistreatment were particularly susceptible to the highly infectious disease due to their compromised immune systems. Although many Holzminden POWs contracted the virus throughout 1918, there is no record of an internee dying of the disease behind the wire. However, it is unknown just how many might have died from the effects of the Spanish flu on their return home, like young Billy Leefe Robinson.

The moment the world had been waiting for came finally on 11 November with the signing of the Armistice. Within twenty-four hours, the number of *Appels* was reduced to only one per day. With the balance of power shifting within the camp, the prisoners anticipated glorious freedom any day.

Two days after the Armistice and with the threat of war crime charges barking at his heels, Niemeyer took flight from the camp.

Despite the best efforts of the British authorities, determined he answer for his tyrannical reign, he seemed to disappear off the face of the earth and was never brought to justice. His fate was discussed extensively in the media of the day, and the most persistent – although unverified – rumour circulating was that of his eventual suicide. According to another rumour he had been shot, but this was most likely wishful thinking on the part of angry POWs and authorities. It was also suggested that he had fled to the United States to hide out, but Niemeyer's real fate was never established.

With Niemeyer gone, the POWs celebrated in any and every way possible. Inmates staged celebratory Armistice dinners, printing their own hand-etched barracks menus; each signed the back for posterity.

Niemeyer's replacement for the dying weeks of the war was the Kommandant of the civilian camp, Colonel Gallus of the Xth Army Corps. The POWs dubbed him 'the Bishop', a nickname referencing his almost 'holy' style in comparison to that of his predecessor. But by then, even the camp guards were treating those they had closely guarded for the past fifteen months with deference in the hope that things would go well for them.

In stark contrast to the last fifteen months, the POWs found themselves granted liberties they had not experienced since their imprisonment. The men took advantage of the relaxed regulations, wandering about the camp to take photographs without hindrance, something that had not been possible before. Food parcels and letters, no longer withheld, began to arrive in great quantities. Many wandered into town but returned at day's end anxious for official word as to how and when they were to be repatriated.

Rumours of a release date were rife and as each eagerly predicted date came and went, their spirits rose and fell correspondingly.

Still, the prisoners waited.

Hector's hopeful diary entry for 15–17 November 1918 reads:

> Wish a few other sympathisers would send a few cigs. Expect to leave here any day now. Everything all ready. One week of the Armistice is over so just three more weeks to wait at the very most. Then for a grand old time in London.

Despite now technically being liberated a week previously, the POWs felt like hostages of fortune. Patience wore thin.

Camp security had grown lax, if it existed at all.

Hector wrote on 22 November 1918:

> Have had a great time down at Bevern [a local town]. Got a chicken and a promise of rabbits. Had tea there and a jolly good time. Now that we are sending food into the country the people are receiving us with open arms. Five of us and I had dinner at a hotel down town. Chicken, steak, five bottles of bubbly, two red wine, one white wine and about fifty cognacs. Our eats came to 118 marks, wine about 200 marks. Transports are very scarce and they have to sweep the mine fields. The extreme Socialists are rapidly gaining power now and forming a Red Guard. The present powers are organising a White Power to resist them, so if food doesn't come soon there is likely to be serious trouble. The Bosch are squirming and protesting as hard as they can about the terms of the Armistice.

After a parole walk on 27 November with a sympathetic guard, the more restrained David Horne wrote:

> This morning we had the best walk since I came to Holzminden. The Feldwebel said if we promise to keep together (about 60 of us)

he would take us on a 'verboten' walk. Right thru the town across the river Weser, thru the village of Stahle and up to the crest of a hill from whence tho' a little misty, we got a splendid panoramic view of the district and of the winding course of the river. Retraced the same route until we reached the town, when we came thru the High St. Walked about 8 miles [13km]. Two German boys, about Alistair's age, walked beside me and McArthur, jabbering all the time. One was Otto Franck and the other Willy Illeg. Both fine smart laddies.

They were gaily decorated with ribbands and the Town and Villages were everywhere festive with banners and garlands because the German troops were arriving. This piece of ribbon is off Otto's cap. I showed them our family photo group and my sketch book. One of them said 'We no longer say Deutschland uber alles' [Germany rules], it is now 'England uber alles' [England rules]. They walked the whole distance with us in most uncomfortable-looking footwear, of wood and cloth.

David's upbeat mood did not last. A stickler for military regulations and basic human decency, that afternoon, he noted with disgust the impatience of many of his cohorts back in the camp. He wrote:

Great discontent in camp about delayed news of our departure. About a dozen started off last night to walk and quite a number say they are going tonight, including orderlies. This is against strict orders and shows a lamentable lack of discipline.

As the weeks wore on with no definite word of release, chaos reigned throughout Germany and the initial jubilation of the POWs in November turned to anxiety in December.

On Sunday, 1 December 1918, David, who had regularly attended church services within the camp since his arrival, walked into Holzminden with a group of twenty to attend a German Lutheran service in one of the town's ancient churches.

He later reflected with sadness on how Germany had also suffered during the war:

> Not many men, mainly women attended. Service seemed to have some Romish elements but chiefly extreme evangelical character. They sit to sing, stand to pray. Girls' choir in chancel, boys' choir in gallery. Sermon moved both men and women to tears. Pastor referred to the return of soldiers from the Front and to those who would never return. He announced the death of 2 Holzminden lads, brothers killed on 5th Nov, 6 days before the Armistice.

With rumours running rife that they were to be released on the following Sunday, 8 December, the men were required to surrender their valueless Holzminden camp currency on 5 December.

Hector recorded a joyful alcoholic bender on 5–6 December:

> Had a great big binge last night. Terrific time. Lots of wine . . . music . . . had a damn good time, got awfully drunk. Afternoon of the 6th heard we are to leave at 4pm Sunday. Can you imagine the excitement. Everybody mad. Some fellows who have been captured four years cannot imagine getting home again.

It was followed by a more sobering entry for 7–8 December:

> Nothing doing yet. There is great internal trouble here. Bavaria is raising hell. The socialists there are thrashing and spilling blood

right and left . . . no parcels yet . . . everybody in the camp is just about starving . . . nothing to eat but potatoes and cabbage . . . another rumour that we are to go tomorrow at 1am . . . well, when we get on the train I will believe it; haven't packed my things yet. There is a field kitchen across the way here . . . tied to the smokestack of it is a bone of an Englishman, a pelvic bone, and Englishchen Swinerie written on the smokestack.

David Horne, Padre Major Bird and fellow parishioners Lieutenant Clarence Bartlett of the RFC and 2nd Lieutenant Ernest Cooke of the 5th York Lancer Regiment made their way to the men's civilian camp to conduct an open-air thanksgiving service in celebration of the end of the war and the release of all POWs held in occupied territories.

Conditions for the POWs were now grim. Although three weeks earlier a glut of food parcels had been delivered to the camp, the supplies began to dry up and the prisoners resorted to rationing. The day of the rumoured release, Sunday, came and went, and the men were still behind barbed wire.

Hector's entry for 9–10 December reads:

Two long, miserable days . . . they said we might leave Tuesday night . . . no mail and no parcels . . . we don't know whether we are going tonight or not, so am going down town. Had dinner there and just in the middle of it, in rushed a postern and said we were going and had to go back to the camp at once. So back we went. Most of the stuff in camp was smashed up and a great fire going in the Spielplatz. They called out the fire department to put it out and we cut their hose to pieces . . . got beautifully drunk myself . . . so did most of the boys . . . marched down to the station and confronted by third class carriages. After smashing up a few more things, we got aboard and pulled out about 10pm. Lots of refreshments on board and a good glow to start off.

So, cheerio!

As Hector had stated, on Tuesday 10 December – and still waiting for definitive news of their release – impatient POWs began to smash crockery, cooking utensils and furniture to vent their frustration. Combustible material such as clothing and even the meagre food supplies were set alight in a bonfire built in the *Spielplatz*.

When the German guards attempted to water down the blaze with fire hoses, the POWs sabotaged their efforts by slicing through the hose with snatched bayonets.

David Horne, appalled by the breach of discipline and the senseless waste, attempted to salvage what he could, with the assistance of Major Bird, with the intention of donating some clothing to the civilian men's camp and selling the remainder for the benefit of the Red Cross.

Finally, when the exasperated senior British officer took matters into his own hands and threatened the local railway authorities with violence if a train was not provided to transport the men to Holland the following day, desperately needed forward momentum was achieved. Miraculously, a steam engine transport was made immediately available.

Hector – the fiery young red-haired Canadian – celebrated their imminent departure by scaling the huge camp flagpole of the *Kommandantur* to 'liberate' the Prussian flag bearing the eagle emblem.[1]

On Wednesday, 11 December 1918 – four weeks to the day after the declaration of Armistice – the released POWs marched in formation as free men out of the compound and down to the train station, leaving behind the hated prison forever.

On the wall of a dark Holzminden punishment cell below ground level, where so many had been held in terrible conditions, a memento had been left behind. A rebellious Holzminden POW had scrawled these words of resilience from Richard Lovelace, an English cavalier poet from the seventeenth century, who had himself been a prisoner: 'Stone walls do not a prison make, nor iron bars a cage.'

PART III

BEYOND HOLZMINDEN

Fifteen

Life After the War, an A to Z

Four months after the successful escapees had returned to England, Germany was defeated and the process of repatriating thousands of British POWs began in earnest.

The officers and orderlies of Holzminden had come from all over the British Empire to serve their King and country – farmers, lawyers, artists, businessmen, architects, tradesmen, teachers, musicians, sportsmen, clerks, fathers, brothers, sweethearts and husbands.

It is impossible even to estimate how many prisoners entered and departed the Holzminden compound over its fifteen-month lifespan. No definitive records remain of the admittances and transfers during this time, and it was a largely transient population. A prisoner might be held for days, weeks or months before being transferred. Or he might have been a serial guest, as was the case with Charles Rathborne, who was interned at Holzminden on three separate occasions. Often the only evidence that a POW passed through the camp is a brief mention in someone's journal, a signature in a Holzminden autograph book, on a menu, on a Gaiety Theatre program or a tiny notation on a Red Cross index card in the archives of a war museum.

So what happened to the men of Holzminden after the war?

These A to Z entries provide a glimpse of the postwar lives of a small number of the internees following their release.

The Lucky Ten
Lieutenant Leonard James 'Jim' BENNETT (1892–1983)
Royal Navy Air Service

Somerset-born Jim married Edith Elsie Parry in South Wales in 1927. A year later, a son was born to them, followed by a daughter in 1931.

During the Second World War, he co-founded a special section of MI9, the British Directorate of Military Intelligence. His duties included lecturing on escape and evasion tactics to members of the armed forces, to better equip them should they find themselves behind enemy lines. Jim also helped to design a number of gadgets to assist personnel on their escape journeys; one of these was a button with a compass inside when unscrewed. Jim was the recipient of several military orders and decorations: the Military Cross, 1914 Star, British War Medal and Victory Medal.

2nd Lieutenant Cecil William BLAIN (1896–1919)
No. 70 Squadron RFC

Young Cecil, who had escaped with Munshi and Caspar disguised as a junior guard from a lunatic asylum, was not destined to enjoy a long life. Awarded the Military Cross and, in June 1919, the Air Force Cross, he flew with the newly formed Royal Air Force (the amalgamation of the Royal Flying Corps and the Royal Naval Air Service). In 1919, he was test flying a Sopwith Dolphin over Suffolk, England, when a crack developed in the port wing at the height of 450 feet. The aircraft crashed, killing the twenty-three-year-old.

Lieutenant John Keith BOUSFIELD (1894–?)
Royal Engineers

British-born John was awarded the Military Cross and Bar in recognition for dangerous reconnaissance work on the Somme in 1916. In the 1930s he was appointed general manager of the Asiatic Petroleum Company (ASP), based in Hong Kong,[1] and achieved the role of chairman in 1940. He also chaired the Hong Kong General Chamber of Commerce in 1939. By 1941 ASP was the second largest corporation in Hong Kong but business activities ceased with the Japanese occupation of Hong Kong, from 25 December 1941 until the end of the war.

John died in British Columbia, Canada.

Lieutenant Pierre (Peter) Clifford CAMPBELL-MARTIN
No. 25 Squadron RFC

Indian-born Clifford, a non-swimmer who was helped across three rivers during the escape by fellow escapee Jim Bennett, was a descendant of the Augier–Delanougerede family who had settled in Calcutta around the time of the French Revolution. He married twice. The first time was to Monica O'Shea, in London in 1919, and the couple moved to India with their infant daughter.

Clifford worked in the mica mining industry in Bihar, at the Imperial Forest Research Institute in Dehra Dun, then as the forest officer for the Bettiah Raj, one of the great estates of North Bihar. Monica Campbell-Martin's account of life in the provinces of India between the wars, *Out in the Midday Sun*, was published in 1951.

Clifford returned to England in 1939. At the outbreak of the Second World War, he enlisted the assistance of his old escape-mate Jim to secure a commission, but the bid was unsuccessful. Cifford joined the RAF as a rear gunner. He was a recipient of the

Military Cross and Croix de Guerre, but was killed in action on 17 October 1941.

Captain David 'Munshi' GRAY (1884–1942)
No. 11 Squadron RFC

Munshi, who came to be known affectionately as 'the father of the tunnel', remained with the military, fighting in Russia with the British Expeditionary Force. He rejoined the 48th Pioneers, his former Indian Army regiment, newly promoted to colonel.

At the outbreak of the Second World War, he enlisted with the RAF as a flight lieutenant before retiring in 1942. By then he was fifty-eight years old. Although he could no longer fly due to his age, this did not preclude him from joining the Home Guard. Tragically, on his first weekend of duty, he was hit and killed by a lorry.

He was awarded the Military Cross in recognition of his escape from Holzminden.

Captain Caspar KENNARD (1891–1935)
No. 16 Squadron RFC

After posing as a gibbering lunatic to escape Germany, Caspar – along with his cousin Maurice – went to Buckingham Palace to be presented with the Military Cross. But when they saw King George approaching at the end of a long hallway, the pair hid in the ladies' toilet as they had no idea where they were supposed to go or how to behave before royalty. He returned to his life in Argentina, taking up the position of manager of an *estancia* (large rural estate).

Caspar married Evelyn Neild in 1920 and died in a shooting accident at the age of forty-four.

Captain Edward Wilmer LEGGATT (1892–1971)
No. 2 Squadron RFC

The successful escapee who sketched his two escape companions while on the run enjoyed a long career in aviation. After serving back in England until 1919, when he was demobbed, Edward relocated to Australia. In 1920, he was the first to deliver air mail between Melbourne and Traralgon in country Victoria – by throwing bundles of mail tied to small parachutes from the Armstrong Whitworth aircraft at different points along the 100-mile (160km) route.

He married Philomena Mary Lillian Dowling in 1921; the couple's son was born in 1927.

Edward joined the Australian Air Force in 1923 and served for three years, followed by a stint as the chief instructor at the New South Wales arm of the Australian Aero Club. He went on to form his own aviation company and also competed in air races. In 1935, he went prospecting for gold in Papua New Guinea; his diary from that period is full of mining descriptions and sketches of native fauna and indigenous artefacts.

Edward served as a commanding officer from 1940 until the end of the Second World War. He was awarded the Military Cross and Bar, the Victory Medal, the British War Medal, the Star and the Australian Service Medal 1939–45.

The panama hat Edward wore during his escape is held in the Imperial War Museum in London.

Lieutenant Stanley Stuart Beattie PURVES (1893–1969)
No. 19 Squadron RFC

A mechanical engineer by trade, Stanley was engaged to build a rice mill in Bangkok after the war, relocating there with his wife, Sybil, in 1920. A later move, to Australia, saw him take up a position with Dorman Lodge, the Scottish engineering company in charge of constructing the Sydney Harbour Bridge. Stanley was based in Moruya, where the quarrying of granite for the buttresses of the bridge was carried out.

He became general manager, then chairman of the newly formed Goliath Cement Company in Tasmania; Stanley, Sybil and the couple's three children never returned to live in the UK.

During the Second World War, he joined the Volunteer Defence Force – modelled on the British Home Guard – attaining the rank of major before retiring in 1946.

Seventy-six-year-old Stanley, a keen trout fisherman, was killed while driving from Penguin to Burnie, Tasmania, in 1969. It is believed he fell asleep at the wheel.

Stanley received the Military Cross for his role in the Holzminden tunnel escape.

Lieutenant Colonel Charles RATHBORNE (1886–1943)
Royal Navy Air Service

After taking public transport to freedom, following the tunnel breakout, Irishman Charles remained a dedicated military man for the rest of his life. Having begun his career in 1903 as an officer in the Royal Marine Light Infantry at age seventeen, he rose through the ranks, achieving the top position of Air Commodore after the war. He married Olive Alice Raines in 1919 and they had one child.

At the age of fifty, as the Second World War loomed, he was made Deputy Commandant, Southern Area, Observer Corps, and, at the height of the war, took on the role of London Industrial Alarm Controller, Central and East London Area.

Charles was awarded the DSO and Bar, Victory Medal, 1914 Star and War Medal and Military Cross. He died in 1943, aged seventy-five.

2nd Lieutenant John 'Jock' TULLIS (1894–1976)
No. 70 Squadron RFC

Jock was twenty-four when he was demobilised in 1919. After working as a draughtsman and fitter with an engineering firm until mid-1920, he took up a sales position in the family company, John Tullis & Son, in Bridgeton at the east end of Glasgow, drawing a weekly wage of 4 guineas (£4.20s). Jock went on to other roles in the manufacture and sale of disability aids.

He married Ethel Ramsden Feather in Argyll, Scotland, in 1924. As a result of Jock's incarceration in various POW camps, he could not bear being in a room with a closed door; the phobia even extended to his own bedroom. Ethel, who called him Terry, was to remark with a twinkle in her eye that it made for an interesting honeymoon. Nevertheless, the couple managed to have two daughters and a son together.

Jock was awarded the Military Cross.

Some Characters in the Holzminden Story
Lieutenant George Augustus 'Gus' AVEY (1892–1976)
2nd Battalion New Zealand Rifle Brigade

Gus was working as a clerk in the railways when he joined up at the outbreak of the First World War. He served with the New Zealand Rifle Brigade and, in 1916, he was awarded the Military Cross for acts of gallantry in the field.

After he was captured on the battlefield, Gus made several escape attempts – from Freiburg and Schweidnitz camps – which earned him a court-martial and ninety days in the cells at Holzminden. Upon release, he assisted with the tunnel, but at the time of the infamous escape he was being held in the cells for an infraction.

After the war he assisted his father to run a general store in Auckland. Gus married Daphne Annie Masters in 1919 in Hamilton. Together they managed a number of general stores, hotels and milk bars in and around the Auckland area, and produced three daughters and a son.

Gus joined the Home Guard during the Second World War.

Lieutenant Charles Edward Burton BERNARD (1890–1977)
10th West Yorkshire Regiment

Born to an English tea merchant father and Japanese mother in Yokohama, Japan, from an early age Charles showed a flair for art. Before he left for the battlefields of Europe, the twenty-five-year-old had married Lillian Maud Turney, whom he had met at Goldsmiths College, where they had both studied art. They later had three children.

Charles's knack for drawing satirical cartoons lampooning army life often got him into trouble. After capture he utilised his artistic skills in a series of POW camps, designing theatre sets and programs, and became heavily involved in publishing camp magazines. He was sent to Holzminden in September 1917 and was transferred to The Hague via the prisoner exchange program to await the war's end.

After the war, Charles returned to a career in illustration, specialising in whimsical, fairy-like creatures. Today his fine-art paintings and illustrations are collector's pieces, often reproduced in publications, a tribute to the creative genius of the artist known to the world as C.E.B. Bernard.

Lieutenant Algernon 'Algie' BIRD (1896–1957)
No. 46 Squadron RFC

Algie was born into a family of Norfolk millers and, as the eldest son, he was being groomed to run the family business, until the war interceded. When he was eighteen years old he joined the Norfolk Regiment, but by September 1917 he was flying with No. 46 Squadron RFC.

Algie was the young pilot who, on his first offensive mission, was forced to land by the legendary Red Baron and subsequently found himself captured on film with the German flying ace as well as the aircraft designer Anthony Fokker. Algie sat out the rest of the war in POW camps, including Holzminden.

After repatriation Algie returned to study milling at the City and Guilds Institute in London and later took up the reins of the family business, Downham Market Steam Mill (later renamed Eagle Roller Mills).

He married Winifred Richards and together they had a daughter and son.

Lieutenant Norman Arthur BIRKS (1892–1989)
No. 29 Squadron RFC

A proud Yorkshireman, Norman was formally demobilised in February 1919 and returned to his family – who had previously received word of his demise on the battlefield. He and his wife, Liza, had two children and in 1922, Norman established a light engineering business specialising in manufacturing and distributing components for the gas and plumbing industries.

In 1932, popular stage and film actor Tom Walls entered a horse in the Derby Stakes at Epsom Downs Racecourse named 'April the Fifth'. The entry was an outsider, but Norman couldn't resist placing a bet on a horse named for this significant date in his life: April 5 had been both the date of his capture in 1917 and his escape attempt en route back to Holzminden in 1918. The horse won at 14–1.

During the Second World War, Norman served as second-in-command of the Air Training Corps squadron at Leatherhead, Surrey, providing basic training to the young lads preparing for the Royal Air Force.

Norman was a hockey enthusiast, playing for many years at amateur level for the Epsom Hockey Club; he continued as an umpire until he was over seventy. In later years, he volunteered as a fundraiser ('tin-rattler') for various local charities. He regularly attended Officers' Prisoner of War Dining Club events and RFC reunion dinners until he was over ninety.

Captain William Swanson Read BLOOMFIELD (1885–1968) No. 57 Squadron RFC

William was born in Riverslea, a grand Victorian mansion in Poverty Bay, New Zealand, built by his wealthy father, Thomas Bloomfield, and his mother, Mary Swanson, who was of Maori descent. In 1911, he graduated from an architecture course at the University of Pennsylvania, USA, thereby becoming the world's first Maori architect.

After joining the RFC, William was shot down on 6 March 1917 and incarcerated. He was well known for ordering into Holzminden food parcels from Harrods of London, where he operated an account.

Following the Armistice, William made his home in Auckland, New Zealand, and wedded Irishwoman Audrey Rhoda Swift Gribbin, a marriage that produced a son. He designed a series of prominent local buildings: Yorkshire House, Queens Arcade, the Masonic Temple, the Station Hotel, the Titirangi Hotel and St Augustine's Church in Devonport. He co-founded the Auckland Aero Club on 24 April 1928 and went on to design their clubrooms.

At fifty-four years of age, William joined the Royal New Zealand Air Force as a squadron leader at the outbreak of the

Second World War, and was responsible for training air cadets. Later he resumed his career as an architect; his creations regularly featured in the New Zealand Institute of Arts and Architecture's periodical, *Home and Building*.

Lieutenant Arthur Stanley BOURINOT (1893–1969)
No. 70 Squadron RFC

Born to Lady Isabelle and Sir John George Bourinot in Ontario, Canada, as a recent college graduate, Athur interrupted his role as a civil servant to join the Canadian Overseas Expeditionary Force a year after the war broke out, setting sail on SS *Missanabie* for the battlefields of Europe via England. He later transferred to the RFC but was captured and incarcerated as a prisoner of war in June 1917, ending up in Holzminden in December 1917 via Karlsruhe and Freiburg. Throughout his internments, Arthur wrote poetry filled with quiet observations, such as 'Night in Holzminden'.

After the war, he studied law, passing the Ontario Bar examination in 1920. Arthur published several books of poetry in the following decades, taking his place as a prominent Canadian poet, poetry editor and scholar.

Lieutenant Ian Donald CAMERON (1898–1973)
No. 65 Squadron RFC

After Ian's father gave his underage son permission to enlist, the young lad spent twelve months in France in what was considered one of the 'safer' jobs – driving ammunition trucks to the front lines at night. The moment he turned eighteen, Ian transferred to the RFC and was assigned to No. 65 Squadron. He was shot down during one of his first missions over enemy lines and later explained that, as one of the newer pilots, he was assigned an older aircraft, which lagged behind the others. The rapid descent that day caused his heart to enlarge, the effects of which plagued him for the rest of his life. In Holzminden, Ian assisted in the great tunnel escape by supplying reconnaissance information from parole walks.

After the war he returned to Canada, where he and his wife raised their two children. Ian became Sheriff of Elgin County, County Court Clerk, and Registrar of the Ontario Supreme Court. He continued to be active in the military, and during the Second World War was the Commanding Officer of the 2nd (Training) Battalion of the Elgin Regiment, retiring in 1963.

Private John 'Dick' CASH (1876–1923)
19th Battalion, Australian Imperial Force

Dick, the quiet Australian orderly who photographed and copied the escape map, returned to his wife, Cissy, and their four remaining children in March 1919. The following year, he was awarded the Meritorious Service Medal and received a commendation from King George V for his courageous work in support of the escape. He tried to settle back into home life, but was constantly battling health problems related to his wartime injuries, and was in and out of hospital over the next five years.

His decline was exacerbated by actions of the local Orange Lodge[2] (otherwise known as the Orange Order or Orangemen), who had invited Dick to join their ranks. Following Dick's polite refusal, the Orangemen hounded the returned serviceman out of the very businesses he had started and that Cissy had battled to keep going in his absence. Six months later, Dick finally succumbed to the long-term effects of his internal injuries and passed away in Randwick Hospital, Sydney, on 14 September 1923. His body was transported back to Thirlmere, and he was buried next to his brother, Arthur.

Miss Mary Elizabeth Maud CHOMLEY (1871–1960)
Secretary, POW Branch, Australian–British Red Cross Society

After the war, Mary continued her lifelong support for the underdog, mainly in the arena of women's equality. In 1919, and now in her late forties, she was appointed by the British government to a delegation to report on women's working conditions and to investigate possible opportunities for female emigrants to Australia. From 1925 to 1933, Mary chaired the Women's Section of the British Legion – which still exists – at Virginia Water in Surrey, where she also resided. The mission of the British Legion is to assist the welfare of military personnel, both currently serving and ex-members.

For many years after the war, ex-POWs sought Mary out to express their gratitude for her dedication to their comfort and care while they had been imprisoned in German and Turkish camps.

Little is recorded of Mary's life between her return to Australia and her death on 21 July 1960 at the impressive age of eighty-eight. She is buried in an unremarkable grave in St Kilda Cemetery, Melbourne.

Lieutenant Vernon Courtenay COOMBS (1897–1988)
No. 18 Squadron RFC

A keen music student, eighteen-year-old Vernon volunteered for the British Army's Artists Rifles, but then set his sights on the RFC. Determined to be accepted into the prestigious RFC despite poor eyesight, Vernon memorised the bottom two lines on the eyesight chart before taking the test. He passed. On 15 July 1917 he volunteered to test a new gun in a De Havilland DH4 near the front line but encountered enemy aircraft. Shot in the hip, Vernon crash-landed in a field and was taken to hospital, where he underwent surgery; his wound restricted his movement for the rest of the war.

At Holzminden he involved himself in the Gaiety Theatre shows at the camp by orchestrating the music; he also learned to play double bass and trombone on instruments provided by the Red Cross. After the war, Vernon was employed by the Bank of England until retirement.

With an ex-Holzminden POW as best man, he married Selma Lokander in 1922 and together they had two sons. Vernon became honorary secretary of the Holzminden Dining Club. At the time of his death, at ninety-one, only two officers remained, so the role of honorary secretary died with him.

2nd Lieutenant Osbert Guy Stanhope CRAWFORD (1886–1957)
No. 48 Squadron RFC

Bombay-born Osbert, an orphan by the age of eight and subsequently raised in England, assisted on archaeological excavations in England, the Sudan and on Easter Island. At the outbreak of the war, he joined No. 48 Squadron RFC as an observer via the London Scottish Regiment and the 3rd Army Topographical Section.

Osbert and his pilot were captured during a reconnaissance mission in February 1918. His escape attempt from Landshut POW camp was foiled, and Osbert was eventually sent to Holzminden. He utilised his knowledge of soils and strata gained on archaeological digs to assist the tunnelling team; he also smuggled food and news to escapees in detention who had been caught and were returned to the camp. Though he plotted escape, Osbert remained at Holzminden until the end of the war; he spent most of his time reading.

After the war Osbert had a career as the first Archaeology Officer of the Ordnance Survey; he founded the journal *Antiquity* and pioneered aerial archaeology, utilising his wartime experience of flight and reconnaissance. Considered eccentric at times, Osbert never married and he lived alone. He wrote seven books on archaeology and his autobiography, *Said and Done: The Autobiography of an Archaeologist*, was published in 1955.

Captain Gerard 'Gerry' Bruce CROLE (1894–1965)
No. 43 Squadron RFC

From an early age, Edinburgh-born Gerry showed significant sporting prowess in rugby, golf and cricket; he was capped for Scotland in both cricket and rugby in 1920. Serving in the RFC, he was shot down over the Western Front, wounded and incarcerated at Holzminden for the last year of the conflict. After repatriation, Gerry was invited to Buckingham Palace to receive his belated Military Cross. Unlike many RFC pilots, who were keen to remain in the air after the war, Gerry never wanted to fly in a plane again.

He married Katharine Margaret 'Peggy' House, with whom he had three sons. From the early 1920s to the mid-1940s, he worked for the Sudan Political Service; his final career posting was as Deputy Governor of Darfur Province.

Subsequently Gerry went into education, focusing on history, rugby and cricket. He held the position of headmaster at Gordonstoun in Moray and then at Blairmore School in Aberdeenshire. He was a man of varied talents and interests, including tree-planting.

After his death, he was remembered by a generation of 1950s schoolboys as a major influence in their lives – as an inspirational teacher and sports coach.

2nd Lieutenant Ernest 'Ernie' Osmond CUDMORE (1895–1924)
No. 25 Squadron RFC

Australian-born Ernie, a keen horseman, lost his leg at thirteen in an accident, after defying instructions not to go riding by himself. The loss of his limb didn't slow him down one bit: he learned to ride a single-cylinder Triumph motorcycle with a sidecar. In 1917, at the age of twenty-one, Ernie inherited his share of his parents' estate, which enabled him to fund private flying lessons in England – he had discovered that his wooden leg was no barrier to joining the RFC.

Shot down over enemy territory by a German sniper, he ended up in Holzminden. As punishment for his role in the tunnel escape, his wooden leg was confiscated.

After the Armistice, Ernie and his brother sailed for home, but jumped the boat in the United States. They bought a Buick car and toured America and the Canadian Rockies for several weeks.

On his return home, grazier Ernie purchased a property to run sheep, cattle, pigs and horses. In 1922, he married his second cousin, Eileen Fitzsimmons, a world record-holding champion horsewoman. He bought a Sopwith Dove, becoming one of Australia's first private flyers.

Twenty-nine-year-old Ernie's body was found in a train carriage with a self-inflicted gunshot wound to the head in 1924.

Lieutenant Hector Fraser DOUGALL (1896–1960)
No. 54 Squadron RFC

'Fiery Red Dougall' returned home to his family, arriving at St John, New Brunswick, Canada, on 27 January 1919 with the souvenired Holzminden camp flag. Although the painful effects of untreated shrapnel wounds continued to dog him, in 1920 Hector and his flying cohort Frank Ellis became the first aviators to successfully complete a commercial flight into Canada's northland. The 1920s also saw him participating in air shows and barnstorming exhibitions.

Hector surged to the forefront of the Canadian aviation industry and, after moving to Fort William, Ontario, was instrumental in forming the Fort William Aero Club in 1929. He and his business partner acquired the licence for an established radio station in 1931; that gave rise to the Dougall Media empire, which still exists. Hector married twice and produced three children.

In the Second World War, Hector headed Canada's No. 2 Elementary Flying School at Fort William, which trained British and Commonwealth pilots. In 1960, he succumbed to heart disease. The Holzminden camp flag remains in the family's possession to this day.

In 2000, closely following his father's wartime diary, Hector's son, Fraser, went on a pilgrimage to retrace his father's First World War route from France and through Germany. From hours of footage, Fraser produced a twenty-minute DVD tribute, a personal contribution to Canada's National Memory Project for the eleventh day of the eleventh month.

Lieutenant Charles 'Moth' EATON (1895–1979)
No. 206 Squadron RFC

London-born Lance Corporal Charles 'Moth' Eaton transferred to the RFC from the Royal West Surreys in 1917 and was eventually posted to No. 206 Squadron RFC in France. On 29 June 1918, he was captured after crashing into a German trench.

After a series of escape attempts, he was sentenced to six months' solitary confinement in Holzminden. 'The filth, the dirt, the mud, the smell' of the war stayed with him for the rest of his life. Moth was an old-fashioned military man with genteel values and was meticulous with his appearance.

He married Beatrice Rose Elizabeth Godfrey in 1919 and the couple had five children. They migrated to Australia, where Moth joined the Royal Australian Air Force in 1925. He remained at the forefront of aviation, leading a number of dramatic air searches in Central Australia, and in 1939 he established Australia's northern air defences. He is honoured extensively in the Northern Territory, where a lake, a street, a pub and the main road leading to Darwin International Airport are named after him.

Moth distinguished himself during the Second World War and, following an appointment as Australian Consul in Timor in 1946, he was transferred to Indonesia with the United Nations Consular Commission.

He was awarded the OBE, AFC, MID and the Knight Commander of the Order of Oranje Nassau with Swords.

After retiring to the countryside of Victoria, Australia, Moth indulged his lifelong hobby of growing orchids.

Flight Sub-Lieutenant Harold 'Gus' EDWARDS (1892–1952)
Squadron 3 Naval Wing, Royal Navy Air Service

British-born Gus – who began his working life as a trapper boy in the coal mines of Nova Scotia – reached great heights through self-education.

Released from wartime captivity, on his return to England in January 1919, he went before a medical officer who misdiagnosed tuberculosis; in those days, this was a death sentence. After living it up for six weeks and blowing all his cash before the Grim Reaper came to call, Gus received a belated all-clear from the specialist.

He then did what many servicemen did after the First World War ended – he went looking for another war; he found it in Russia. Upon his return to Canada, he applied to the Royal Canadian Air Force (RCAF) and received a commission as flight lieutenant.

At nearly thirty years of age he married Beatrice Coffey, in 1924, and they had two children.

Gus sustained a colourful military career that took him on several home and overseas postings. He rose all the way through the ranks, attaining the position of air marshal in 1942. In February 1943, Gus was invested by the King as a Companion of the Most Honourable Order of the Bath at Buckingham Palace.

In the wake of poor health, Gus retired at the age of fifty-one. In 1952, during a trip to Arizona, he died in his sleep at the age of fifty-nine after a long and painful struggle with illness. His body was flown back to Canada in an RCAF aircraft and laid to rest accompanied by volleys from the firing party, 'The Last Post' and 'Reveille'.

Captain John Owen ENOS (1870–1937)
Master, SS *Cheltonian*
On 8 June 1917, with forty-seven-year-old Welsh-born John as master, the unarmed British cargo steamer SS *Cheltonian* was steaming in ballast between Genoa, Italy, and Oran, Algeria. Suddenly the German submarine *U-72* surfaced alongside, delivering an ultimatum to surrender or be sunk with all hands.

The crew duly surrendered; John and the chief engineer were taken aboard the submarine to disable the line of command aboard the British vessel. The remainder of the crew took to the lifeboats, and when the crew were clear, the *Cheltonian*, built by Bartram & Sons of Sunderland, United Kingdom, was pounded with gunfire and sent to the bottom of the Mediterranean.

The crew took around fifteen hours to row the lifeboats 54 miles (87km) to shore, landing near the French city of Marseilles.

John, a father of two, was sent to Holzminden.

2nd Lieutenant Anthony 'Tony' FIELDING-CLARKE (1899–1974)
No. 100 Squadron RFC

In February 1918, Tony, the son of a doctor, was observer/gunner on a night bombing mission over France with No. 100 Squadron RFC. The aircraft suffered engine failure, and they were forced to land in enemy territory. With his pilot, 2nd Lieutenant O.B. Swart, Tony managed to evade capture for two days but they were finally cornered when the starving pair attempted to thieve food from a German Army hut. The pair were tied together with rifle cords and sent to German Intelligence in St Avold for questioning, and finally transferred through a series of officer POW camps.

In 1930, Tony wed Anglo-Frenchwoman Henriette Hervot Mapleson in Lagos, Nigeria, where he worked for the Nigerian Education Department, and the marriage produced two sons. At the end of the Second World War, Tony was part of the de-Nazification process and was employed to gather evidence of war crimes. Subsequently he divorced Henriette to marry one of the Berlin *Trümmerfrau*;[3] however, his second wife fled the marriage as soon as she was free of postwar Germany.

Tony pursued a deep interest in archaeology, avidly collecting artefacts such as Roman coins and glass, and neolithic spearheads. He was also an accomplished watercolourist. At the end of his working life he was an art teacher in a small private school.

Lieutenant William Henry Dean GARDNER (1883–1959)
Royal Navy, HMS *Warner*

The diminutive navigator of the British Q-Ship *Warner*, sunk by the Germans, went back for Doris, his young lover, now a more respectable twenty years of age. Dean took his new wife back to New Zealand, though some years later they separated and Doris returned to England, leaving their two sons with Dean.

Back in the employ of the Union Steamship Company (USC), Dean worked his way up from Chief Officer to a permanent appointment as a ship's master (captain). However, after a run of three mishaps mid-Second World War, and despite being cleared during the last set of legal proceedings, USC assigned him to a lower class of vessel for a period of time. Dean resigned in disgust in February 1943, and was offered an Australia-based role with the US Army Transport Service.

Upon retirement at the age of sixty-two, Dean ran a small shop in the beachside suburb of Coogee, Sydney. He passed away in 1959, aged seventy-six, and his ashes were scattered over his beloved sea from a USC vessel.

2nd Lieutenant Edgar GARLAND (1896–1973)
No. 66 Squadron RFC

The 'Herculean' flying hero who became trapped in the Holzminden tunnel travelled to the United States, where he took up an appointment as the Deputy Assistant Provost Marshal attached to the British Commission in New York. In mid-1919, Edgar accompanied the Governor-General (the Earl of Liverpool) and the Countess of Liverpool aboard the *Moana* in the capacity of aide-de-camp on the former's tour of Samoa and the Cook Islands.

Edgar settled in the USA, where he became a member of New York's aerial police force. Later he was made vice-president of the Aeronautical Implement and Supplies Company in New York. He travelled the Santa Fe railway route, laying down a transcontinental course of guiding electric lights every 5 miles (8km) and an aerodrome every 50 miles (80km). Although he dabbled in oil distribution for some years, Edgar continued to criss-cross the globe employed as an aerodrome adviser until old age slowed him down.

Lieutenant Christopher Guy GILBERT (1893–1973)
No. 29 Squadron RFC

Guy was one of twelve children born into a wealthy Birmingham steelworks family. At the outbreak of the First World War, eight of the nine Gilbert boys joined up, all qualifying as officers. Two of them were killed during the conflict, while another was seriously injured.

Guy joined the RFC via the 1st/6th Dorsetshire Regiment. One chilly early morning in March 1917, he volunteered for a photo reconnaissance mission. Believing he'd be back for breakfast after the short flight, he threw his flying suit on over his pyjamas, never expecting it was the day he would be shot down as the Red Baron's thirty-first victim. Guy was transferred through a number of POW camps, from which he made repeated unsuccessful escape attempts, and eventually ended up in Holzminden.

In 1924, he married Gay, a performer from the Southsea Theatre. Over the years, the couple ran a series of hotels.

At the age of forty-six, Guy was recalled to duty with the Royal Air Force Volunteer Reserve when the Second World War broke out in 1939. Appointed Officer Commanding Troop Ships, he was to survive several U-boat attacks during the war before officially retiring in 1954 at the age of sixty-one with the rank of wing commander.

Guy developed diabetes in his latter years and died during an asthma attack at the age of eighty. He was honoured at his funeral with the Union Jack draped over his coffin.

Captain Maxwell 'Max' GORE (1894–1981)
59th Battalion Australian Imperial Force

The South Australian bank clerk joined the Citizens Military Forces, which was mobilised when war broke out. At the age of twenty-one, Max became one of three officers in charge of the 11th Reinforcements of the 10th Battalion, embarking for Egypt. He was shot during the Battle of Noreuil, subsequently captured and sent through a series of POW camps to Holzminden. He was on the tunnel escape list, but like many others was prevented from escaping by the collapse.

Ironically, Max learned of his promotion to captain from a fellow prisoner in Holzminden. He was also mentioned in dispatches and awarded the Military Cross.

After the war, Max, a keen gardener and fisherman, found it difficult to settle down; he fathered three children in three marriages. He had many occupations, including owning two second-hand shops, one dealing in antiques.

When the Second World War broke out, Max was living in Western Australia. He served in a range of capacities: training troops in Northam training camp, east of Perth, and guarding the guns at Rottnest Island and the ships on Fremantle Wharf.

Until his retirement at age sixty-five, Max worked as a clerk in a government office. He died of cancer in 1981, facing his death with the courage and fortitude that he had shown during the war. His ashes were scattered, at his request, from his favourite fishing spot in South Fremantle.

2nd Lieutenant Reginald 'Reg' GOUGH (1890–1973)
4th Battalion Oxfordshire & Buckinghamshire Light Infantry

Reg, teacher of the deaf and blind, returned home to his wife, Winnie, and they wasted no time in conceiving a son. Sadly Winnie fell seriously ill – most likely with postnatal depression – and her recovery was painfully slow.

Reg resumed his teaching career at Freeman's School. In 1921, he took up a teaching post at the East Anglian School for Deaf and Partially Sighted Children in Norfolk, where he remained until retirement. In 1924, he was promoted to Deputy Superintendent there. He indulged his passion for river punting, children's interest groups and the scouting movement.

During the Second World War, Reg joined the Observer Corps, whose role it was to man strategic observation posts, searching for any signs of an approaching enemy attack.

In 1942, Reg was promoted to headmaster; in the 1962 New Year's Honours List, he was awarded a British Empire Medal. His last request to his son as he lay in hospital was for a bottle of his favourite sherry.

2nd Lieutenant Louis 'Swaggie' GREIVE (1894–1976)
23rd Battalion Australian Imperial Force

Born in Wagga Wagga, New South Wales, Louis moved around the country with his family, as his bank inspector father's position demanded. A talented swimmer, from time to time he raced against future Australian Olympic champion Frank Beaurepaire and became 220 yard (200m) Victorian champion as a twenty-one-year old, swimming for the Melbourne Swimming Club.

At the age of nineteen, Louis had been in the AIF for less than three months when he sailed with his battalion to Egypt, then on to Gallipoli. A dose of enteric fever (typhoid) saw him evacuated to England, but he returned to his battalion after a short period of recovery. Captured at Flers, France, he was eventually transferred to Holzminden. Nicknamed 'Swaggie' for his Australian roots, Louis was stationed on the far side of the attic eaves as a traffic controller on the night of the tunnel escape, signalling escapees through at timed intervals.

After the war, he returned to Australia on *Orca*, an armed transport, and was discharged from the army in June 1919.

Lieutenant Frederick William 'Will' HARVEY (1888–1957)
5th Gloucester Regiment

Son of a Gloucestershire farmer and horse breeder, Will had embarked upon law studies, but within days of the outbreak of war, he had joined the 1/5 Gloucestershire Regiment of the Territorial Forces. On 17 August 1916 he was captured. Over the next two years he was transferred through seven POW camps, involving himself in several escape attempts, and was sent to Holzminden. He was repatriated through the prisoner exchange program and, after recovering from the Spanish flu epidemic that swept the world, he returned to England in February 1919.

Will went back to the law, qualifying as a solicitor, but his disinterest in material possessions and his passion for defending the underdog ensured that his practice only made a meagre financial return. In 1921, he married Anne Kane, an Irish nurse, and the same year his book recounting his incarceration experiences, *Comrades in Captivity*, was published. Their daughter was born in 1922, followed by a son in 1925.

Dubbed 'the Laureate of Gloucestershire', Will accepted the role of broadcaster for the BBC in Bristol and continued to publish his writing throughout the 1920s. In 1980, he was commemorated with a slate tablet in Gloucester Cathedral. In a BBC poll conducted in 1996, 'Ducks' – composed by Will in Holzminden – was voted one of England's most beloved 100 poems.

Captain Henry Rupert HAWKINS (1893–1972)
No. 22 Squadron RFC

Twenty-two-year-old Rupert interrupted his medical course at Melbourne University in October 1915 to join the RFC, training as a pilot in England and gaining his wings in April 1916. After he was shot down over enemy lines, Rupert and his crew were interrogated in Ströhen about pamphlets found on one of the British aircraft. The four men were sent for court-martial at Hanover on charges of treason. Had they been convicted, they faced the death penalty or ten years hard labour. Although they were found not guilty, a further trial was scheduled for April 1918.

When the trial was postponed, Rupert was sent to Holzminden. Although he was on the escapee list for the July breakout, beriberi had weakened his legs: in reality, escape would have been physically beyond him.

After the war, Rupert returned to Melbourne, where he finished his medical studies and also did a resident year at Royal Melbourne Hospital. In 1922, he returned to Britain to obtain midwifery experience at the Rotunda in Dublin. He married Margery Nicholson in Doncaster, the couple having met through a mutual friend who had sustained him with food parcels as a POW.

Rupert bought a medical practice in Mount Gambier. He spent the latter part of the Second World War in the RAAF as a medical officer. Afterwards, he was quick to grasp the advantages of running a group practice incorporating specialists, and he developed the Hawkins Medical Clinic.

He retired to his Southdown sheep stud and eventually passed away there.

Lieutenant David Edmund Atree HORNE (1875–1937)
Royal Engineers

Born in Hampshire, England, David studied architecture from the age of fifteen. In 1903, he married Louisa Constance Parker while working in the War Office Architects Department in Sheerness, Kent, and together they had four children. Relocating to the picturesque fishing port of Golspie, deep in the Scottish highlands, he began practice as an architect to the Sutherland estate, designing, converting or extending structures within Sutherland County.

David was already forty-two years old at the outbreak of the war. He joined the Royal Engineers and found himself captured and incarcerated in Holzminden. He often took his diary on his walks outside the wire, peppering it with sketches of architecture and streetscapes in neighbouring towns.

At the conclusion of the Second World War, David returned to Golspie and continued to be a driving force in shaping the architecture of the Sutherland district. He was also instrumental in establishing the local fire service, of which he was chief.

Two years after Louisa died, in 1932, David – now aged fifty-seven – married Erica Brooke Broadbent.

2nd Lieutenant Frederick Norman INSOLL (1898–1980)
No. 5 Squadron RFC

Norman, who was born in Camberwell, England, was a member of the Combined Cadet Force at Blundell's School when he was sent to train as a pilot with the RFC at the tender age of seventeen. During a bombing mission with No. 5 Squadron on Boxing Day 1916, he was returning to his base in France when he was intercepted by the enemy near Amiens. He was encouraged to land by a signal from a German pilot, then proceeded to bring his machine down on a tethered cow belonging to the local French villagers. In the ensuing drama, he failed to set fire to his BE2c plane as per regulations.

Following the Armistice, Norman returned home. Although he subsequently lost his arm to gangrene after a car accident, this didn't stop him from joining the Royal Air Force at the outbreak of the Second World War. He was stationed at Duxford, Cambridge, in the intelligence section. His job was to debrief German prisoners in the role of 'good cop' while his partner played 'bad cop'.

At the close of the war, Norman went back to his wife, two daughters and his hobby farm in Pembury, Kent, and lived off his Lloyds investments as a 'gentleman farmer'.

Lieutenant Colin LAURANCE (1891–1958)
Royal Naval Air Service

Early in the new century, Kent-born Colin went to sea in the merchant service. After going ashore in Sydney, Australia, he worked as a steeplejack on the tall buildings then being erected in the city. At the outbreak of the First World War, he joined the Australian Navy and served as a naval infantryman in the campaign to remove the Germans from New Guinea. He then returned to Britain in 1915 and trained as a naval pilot to fly the primitive aircraft of those days.

During an attempt to bomb the dangerous U-boat base in Zeebrugge, Colin was shot down and badly wounded by shrapnel in the side of his head. Nearly unconscious, he was rescued by a submarine returning to base and sent to a German hospital, where the side of his skull was cut away to relieve the pressure on his brain.

Partially recovered, he was sent to Holzminden, but struggling with his head wound, he found the conditions very stressful and made three escape attempts. He was recaptured on each occasion, including the tunnel escape.

On returning to Britain after the Armistice he led a varied life, farming and running small businesses while raising eight children.

Captain Douglas 'Duggie' LYALL GRANT (1888–1968)
London Scottish Regiment

Duggie was born in Putney of Scottish parentage. He started work as a mercantile clerk then in 1911 joined the London Scottish Regiment.

He served in France from 1914 and earned the Military Cross at Messines. On 2 June 1916, he was flying back to France from leave when his pilot, on his first trip to France, got lost and crash-landed behind enemy lines. Captured, he was imprisoned in four different camps, including Holzminden, before being transferred to Holland in April 1918. In contravention of the rules, he had kept a prison diary, which he smuggled out sewn into the waistband of his kilt and hidden in the bag of his bagpipes.

Duggie had married in 1913, but his wife tragically died in 1920 while giving birth to their second child. He married for a second time, to Jane Lennox Higgins in 1922, and had three more children. The family lived in Wimbledon, where he pursued a successful business career, with interests mainly in the Argentine railways. His life was filled with Scottish activities – Colonel of the London Scottish Regiment, Secretary then President of London Scottish Rugby Club and for many years Chairman of Glenalmond Old Pupils.

A few weeks before his eightieth birthday, when returning from the Wimbledon Cricket Club annual dinner, he collapsed on Wimbledon Ridgeway from a fatal heart attack.

Lieutenant Peter LYON (1885–1969)
11th Battalion Australian Imperial Force

Peter was already twenty-nine years of age and married to Ethel May, with two sons, when he enlisted in the AIF in 1915. After being wounded in Gallipoli and shipped to Bristol General Hospital in England for recovery, he rejoined his unit in Marseilles, France, in April 1916.

He was taken prisoner near Dernancourt then passed through the POW camps at Karlsruhe, Crefeld and Ströhen – attempting escape from each of them. At Holzminden, Peter was one of the twenty-nine tunnel escapees but was recaptured after twelve days on the run and remained incarcerated until Armistice.

After his military discharge, Peter began the life of a farmer in the West Australian wheat-belt town of Bruce Rock in 1920. He took on the role of an inspector with the Agricultural Bank, assisting returned servicemen to settle on land under the Soldier Settlement Scheme. Two daughters were born to Lyon and Ethel in the 1920s.

Lieutenant George William MUMFORD (1895–1989)
No. 11 Squadron RFC

George was the son of a Port of London mercantile enquiry agent. He joined the Port of London Authority as a clerk, but his path to the RFC began with the City of London Yeomanry (the Rough Riders), then the Mounted Military Police (London Mounted Brigade, Streetley) and the British Army Service Corps. Flying with No. 11 Squadron RFC in a Bristol F.2b fighter as an observer/gunner with Canadian pilot Lieutenant Neil 'Piffles' Taylor at the joystick, he was shot down over Bullecourt, France. George sustained a large wound in the lower forearm.

After Armistice, George was hospitalised back in England. He was given a war wound pension and was awarded the Victory Medal and British War Medal. He married Irene Congdon and together they had one son. His second marriage – to Joan Isobel Cooper – produced two more sons.

During the Second World War, he became the officer-in-charge of a Home Guard unit near Dorking, Surrey, as part of the line protecting London from invading forces.

George enjoyed a thirty-eight-year career with the Midland Bank; before retiring he was head of the Foreign Exchange Department.

2nd Lieutenant Charles Henry ffrench 'Nobby' NOBBS (1895–1946)
No. 66 Squadron RFC

Born on Norfolk Island, off the Australian coastline, Nobby (also known as Harry) was the grandson of Fletcher Christian Nobbs, a descendant of one of the original HMS *Bounty* mutineers of 1789. One of sixteen children, he was a nineteen-year-old clerk living in Sydney when he enlisted and embarked for the theatres of war in December 1914 with other enlistees of the 6th Australian Light Horse. He was later to exchange the horse's saddle for the cockpit of a No. 66 Squadron RFC fighter plane.

On 20 September 1917, during a bombing mission over Belgium in low visibility, he was brought down by ground fire near Polygon Wood and captured. Holzminden was one of the POW camps in which he was held.

After the war, Nobby returned to Norfolk Island, then moved to Papua New Guinea, where he worked as an aerodrome manager. He went back to the United Kingdom, marrying an Englishwoman, Audrey Copperthwaite, in 1930; the couple had two children.

Thanks to poor health, Nobby was rejected for service when the Second World War broke out. Instead he joined the Local Defence Volunteers, which later became the Home Guard, obtaining the rank of Company Commander of 7th Battalion, North Riding Regiment.

Lieutenant Robert 'Bob' Milner PADDISON (1897–1922)
Duke of Cornwall's Light Infantry

Bob was educated at Blundell's and left with wide-ranging achievements under his belt, including 1st XV, Head of School, president of the Debating Society, editor of *The Blundellian* and winner of the Blundell scholarship to Balliol College. He was also a talented artist.

He was commissioned into the Duke of Cornwall's Light Infantry. Following his capture in April 1917, Bob was held in Karlsruhe, Crefeld and then Holzminden. Like many others, Bob devised a code in his letters home. His mother managed to crack it and sent him escape tools secreted in seemingly innocent items. He escaped via the tunnel, but was one of the nineteen recaptured; he had been on the run for three weeks.

After the war, when Bob took his boots for repair to a cobbler in his home town of Tiverton, Devon, the cobbler discovered, and duly returned, the German currency concealed in the heel.

On 6 August 1922, shortly after starting a career in the publishing industry, Bob drowned while attempting to swim across Loch Lomond. He had been attending a painting expedition.

Lieutenant Leonard John PEARSON (1891–1964)
No. 13 Squadron RFC

One of the six children of Bishop Alfred Pearson of Burnley, Leonard was born in Brighton, England. He gained his flying certificate in 1915 in Montrose, Scotland. After accruing barely eighteen hours' flying training, he was briefed to fly escort on a reconnaissance mission over Vaux in France. When a German Fokker Eindecker attacked, blowing Leonard's Lewis guns off their mountings and two cylinders off the engines, he managed to land safely; his observer, 2nd Lieutenant E.H. Alexander, was wounded. Both were sent to POW camps.

During an escape attempt from a train, Leonard was pursued by Germans and shot twice; he lost the top of his finger and sustained a belly wound. The twenty-seven-year-old was one of the men trapped when the Holzminden tunnel collapse occurred, preventing his escape.

Following the war, Leonard gained his medical diploma in 1930 and in the same year married Marguerite Nixon, the sister of a fellow POW, Lieutenant Leslie Nixon, who had also been caught in the tunnel cave-in.

Captain William 'Willie' Roy PETRIE (1892–1962)
6th Battalion Seaforth Highlanders

Willie was born at Pitairlie, a farm outside Elgin, in Scotland's Morayshire area, and rose to prominence within the farming community. For some years before the war he had been a member of the 6th (Morayshire) Battalion Seaforth Highlanders, and was mobilised at its outbreak. He utilised his superior knowledge of horses to assess and requisition the best and strongest local beasts for the army's transport wagons, a task he found difficult to do as he well knew the hardship that losing good stock would cause the local farmers.

In France in May 1915, Willie's expert marksmanship skills drew the attention of Brigade HQ. His orders were to shoot any pigeons he spotted, in the event they were German carrier pigeons.

Twice Willie was wounded in battle and was finally captured at Arras on 23 April 1917.

During his incarceration, he gave his fellow POWs lectures on farming. Willie was one of the many prisoners prevented from escaping by the collapse of the tunnel.

At Holzminden Willie shared a barracks room with Captain Lyon Hatton and Captain Gerry Crole, which proved fortuitous because after the war he met and married Lyon's sister, Daisy.

In the Second World War, farming was considered a reserved occupation, so he was not required to go to war again.

Lieutenant John 'Jack' SALTER (1892–1969)
11th Battalion Royal Irish Rifles

A native of Skibbereen, County Cork, Ireland, Jack was born on 27 November 1892. As a twenty-three-year-old, he volunteered for the Royal Irish Rifles (RIR) in Belfast and was awarded a commission. In France in 1916, as part of the Somme offensive, he and his comrades of the 11th Battalion RIR were engaged in fierce fighting on the first day of the Battle of Thiepval. Knocked unconscious, he came around to find himself a prisoner behind enemy lines.

Jack was taken firstly to Wurtzburg and later transferred to Holzminden. In an administrative blunder, his family was notified that he had been killed in action; the family grieved for six weeks before they were informed that he was in fact alive and being held in a POW camp.

Because of poor health, he was approved for the POW exchange program and was relocated to Scheveningen, Holland, where he remained for the rest of the war.

After repatriation, Jack returned to his role as a civil servant at the Board of Trade in London. He married Gladys, his sister's best friend, and they took up residence in Epsom and had two children.

Lieutenant Errol Suvo Chunder SEN (1899–1941)
No. 70 Squadron RFC

Born in India to an Indian father and English mother, Errol – whose nickname was 'Buddha' in childhood – relocated at an early age with his mother, brother and sister to England, where he received a British education.

When the war broke out, Errol attempted to enlist but was underage, so he worked for a bank while he waited out the age restriction. He joined the RFC in 1917.

In the early morning of 14 September 1917, he was flying a mission over France with No. 70 Squadron RFC when he was engaged by three enemy Fokkers. They pounded his Sopwith Camel with machine-gun fire, shattering the windscreen and piercing the fuel tank, eventually bringing him down near Menin.

Imprisoned in Holzminden, he was one of the escapees in the tunnel at the time of the collapse.

After the Armistice, the nineteen-year-old Errol returned to England to his family. Later he found employment with the Calcutta police force in India, only to find it a lonely life. Subsequently, Errol and his brother relocated to Rangoon, Burma, where they both found work.

When the Japanese attacked Pearl Harbor, Errol re-enlisted in the British Royal Air Force but he couldn't get out of Burma. He was around forty-two years of age when he attempted to walk out of the country in 1941 and was never heard of again.

Lieutenant Cuthbert Archibald 'Fluffy' SUTCLIFFE (1897–1977)
No. 3 Squadron RFC

The son of British expatriates who lived in the Philippines, Fluffy was educated at boarding schools in England. He began his military training in Oxford in 1916. While stationed in France, he was shot down over Le Cateau. Fluffy and his observer, Lieutenant Tom Humble, were picked up in a staff car by German officer Richard Flashar.

Fluffy did stints in a number of POW camps. Often allocated women's roles in the camp's stage productions, he made an infamous escape attempt from Holzminden by growing his hair long, dressing as a woman and strolling out the front gate on the arm of a fellow officer posing as 'her' German escort.

After repatriation, Fluffy attended Cambridge University, where he studied engineering. He married Doris in the 1920s and they had three children.

During the Second World War, he served in the Home Guard in Surbiton, Surrey.

From the 1930s to the 1960s, Fluffy worked as a senior civil engineer for London's metropolitan area water supply before retiring to a bungalow at East Horsley in the Surrey countryside and tending to his garden.

Lieutenant Randall Henry TOPLISS (1894–1953)
No. 64 Squadron RFC

From an early age, young Randall dreamed of sitting behind the controls of a 'flying machine'. Born into a family of engineers in Christchurch, New Zealand, he left behind the family business, Topliss Bros Engineering, to travel to England to enlist in the RFC. At twenty-three, he found himself a guest of the enemy until the end of the war.

Upon repatriation, Randall returned to England and completed an apprenticeship as an aircraft engineer with the engine manufacturing arm of prestigious company Rolls Royce.

In 1921, Randall married Edith May 'Win' Stimpson. The couple bought Bruce Dale, a farm located at Inchbonnie, on the west coast of New Zealand's South Island, and raised their two sons there. He built his own air strip, named Inchbonnie Aerodrome, which was utilised by a private travel company that flew tourists in to view the spectacular glaciers.

During the Second World War, the airstrip was kept in good working order as an emergency aerodrome and a small office was built for the Home Guard, headed by Randall as captain.

In the years following the war, the aerodrome served as a weather station, a supply drop point for deer cullers employed by the Internal Affairs Department and as an airport for Mount Cook Airline.

After Randall died, at the age of fifty-nine, his wife sold the property with the aerodrome still fully operational.

2nd Lieutenant Francis 'Frank' William VOELCKER (1998–1954)
King's Shropshire Light Infantry

Frank grew up in Kent, England. He wasn't yet nineteen when he volunteered for the King's Shropshire Light Infantry. He saw active duty at the front and was bayoneted through the legs, sustaining severe injuries.

Following a period of recuperation in a German hospital, Frank was kept in a succession of POW camps over the next three and a half years. He made escape attempts on three different occasions, which earned him a transfer to Holzminden.

Artistic from an early age, Frank became adept at satirising the enemy in sketches – something many POWs took to doing during their incarceration.

Back in England after the war, Frank was awarded the Military Cross. He married Nora Hodgson, and two daughters were born to the couple. Nora experienced health problems, and in an effort to aid her recovery the family relocated to New Zealand's North Island. Frank bought 300 acres at Kerikeri in the Bay of Islands and tried his hand at a number of ultimately unsuccessful ventures, including the growing tung oil trees and fruit.

At the outbreak of the Second World War, he enlisted in the New Zealand Army. He was promoted to major and sent to Fiji with the 34th Battalion, which was assigned to defend the small South Pacific island.

In 1945, Frank took up the consecutive positions of governor and United Nations-appointed First Administrator of the tiny South Pacific nation of Western Samoa. On his return to New Zealand in 1948, he received the Cross of the British Empire and later served as a United Nations administrator in Korea.

He passed away at the age of fifty-four after a long battle with bowel cancer.

Lieutenant Edward Darien WARBURTON (1887–1942)
No. 48 Squadron RFC

The middle child of five, Darien was born in Palmerston North, New Zealand, and educated in private boarding schools in London and Switzerland. Following a stint in a solicitor's office and a period of farming, he joined the 4th Waikato Mounted Rifles at the outbreak of the war at the age of twenty-seven. He saw fifteen weeks' action at the Dardanelles before he was shipped out, suffering from acute dysentery.

Darien struggled with a chronic stutter, which barred him from a position of command that would require him to give verbal orders. He was accepted into the RFC and assigned the role of observer/gunner.

Darien was Lieutenant William 'Billy' Leefe Robinson's observer/gunner when, in April 1917, while on a decoy mission, their aeroplane was shot down over France. Darien was moved from camp to camp, including to Holzminden. He involved himself in the tunnel plot but was transferred to Schweidnitz in December 1917, before it was completed.

Following repatriation, Darien returned home to take up farming again and became a master breeder of Romney sheep. He married Barbara Alice Hartgill and together they had three children. His health deteriorated and he passed away at the age of fifty-five.

2nd Lieutenant James 'Jimmy' WHALE (1889–1957)
Worcestershire Regiment

The sixth of seven children born to a blast furnaceman and a nurse, in Dudley, England, Jimmy left school early to aid the family finances. His working life began in the cobbler trade. Money was always tight, so the enterprising Jimmy saved leftover shoe nails to sell for scrap money to pay for his art studies.

He was commissioned into the Worcestershire Regiment in 1916 and a year later, he was captured at the Western Front and incarcerated in Holzminden at the age of twenty-eight.

A talented creative, Jimmy spent a good deal of time at Holzminden sketching cartoons and portraits. He also got a taste for drama after he became heavily involved in the camp theatre productions – as a director, actor, set designer and producer – which ultimately led to his postwar career in theatre and film.

Following the Armistice, Jimmy returned to England and gravitated towards the theatre, initially as an actor and set builder. Directing a number of stage plays eventually led him to a Hollywood career as a film director and producer. He went on to direct horror film *Frankenstein* (1931), which was a huge critical and box office success. Jimmy's Hollywood career flourished for a number of years; he notched up successes – both as a director and a producer – such as *The Invisible Man* (1933) and the musical *Showboat* (1936).

At the age of sixty-seven, the now openly gay Jimmy committed suicide by drowning himself in his Hollywood swimming pool.

In his hometown of Dudley, England, a sculpture in the shape of a film reel commemorates his life and achievements.

Captain Randolph Wilbur WHITE (1894–1928)
No. 20 Squadron RFC

As a twenty-year-old student, Randolph enlisted in the Canadian Expeditionary Force. He joined the 21st Battalion and embarked for the European theatres of war on SS *Metagama*. He spent two weeks in England, which is most likely where he received a tattoo of his regimental crest on both his arms. After training with the machine-gun corps, he was sent to France in September 1915. Struck down by a series of illnesses, he was discharged to duty in 1916 then seconded to the RFC as a flying officer/observer.

While on a mission over France, his aircraft was attacked and spun out of control; the ground impact rendered him unconscious for four days. He was incarcerated in four camps, including Holzminden, and was repatriated in November 1918 and returned to Canada.

Randolph was declared unfit for duty because of continuing health problems: he had developed a nervous condition, poor concentration and sleeplessness as a result of his war experiences and received a medical discharge in 1919.

His marriage to Marguerite Eames was shortlived. Unable to cope with her husband's psychological struggles, she moved to England, where she gave birth to their son, whom Randolph never met.

In 1922 Randolph was awarded the British War Medal and Victory medal, but sadly he never came to terms with his persistent ill health and his broken family life and he turned to alcohol. He lived for only another six years, dying in Chicago at the age of thirty-four of the alcohol-related disease cirrhosis of the liver.

Life After the War, an A to Z

Group Captain Frederick 'Freddie' William WINTERBOTHAM (1897–1990)
No. 29 Squadron RFC

The son of solicitor Frederick Winterbotham and Florence Vernon Graham of Gloucestershire, England, the seventeen-year-old Freddie volunteered for the Royal Gloucestershire Hussars Yeomanry when war was declared. Possessing a natural talent for horsemanship, he soon found himself training men and their mounts for the cavalry. In 1916, he was accepted into the RFC, and while providing air support on an aerial reconnaissance mission, he was shot down over Gheluvelt, Flanders. For much of the remainder of the war he was incarcerated in Holzminden; his family believed him killed in action.

In London in 1921, Freddie married Erica Horniman, the daughter of a tea merchant, and together they had three children. The couple divorced in 1939; Freddie was to marry three more times.

After a quiet career in pedigree stock breeding, in 1929 he was recruited to establish and operate the Air Staff Department of the British Secret Intelligence Service (MI6). In 1938, Freddie and his intelligence colleagues learned of a German encrypting device called Enigma. British cryptologists at Bletchley Park cracked the code, enabling MI6 to intercept top secret and highly sensitive German transmissions to and from Hitler and his staff.

Freddie wrote several books about his work in intelligence. He was made a Commander of the Most Excellent Order of the British Empire in 1943, and was awarded the Legion of Merit in 1945.

SIXTEEN

Friendships Forged

In a camp like this, one came across many men whom one had known in years gone by, in many out of the way places of the world. There were one or two of my old school friends there, and an Australian whom I had met in the Far East, while one of the newcomers from the battle front I had last seen at Cape Helles, in Gallipoli.

Many were the old friendships revived – men who had toiled and struggled together in the wilds of northern Canada, or in the tropical jungles, or fought in the same wars of bygone days – South Africa, in Mexico, or Albania – soldiers of fortune, these, whose tunics bore the ribbons of many forgotten campaigns – hard-bitten men who went from one country to another where there was any trouble brewing. It was intensely interesting to sit of an evening and hear these men talk of their experiences.

Explorers, pearl fishers, skippers of wind-jammers who had spent their lives roaming the seven seas; trappers and gold-diggers, missionaries, men on government service in the heart of Central Africa or in the uttermost corners of the earth.

Sons of millionaires, and ex-convicts, the pampered darlings of London society and beach combers from South Sea islands – what a wonderful collection of tales might have been written of these men had someone of a literary mind jotted down the stories of their lives . . .

– *Lieutenant Charles E.B. Bernard*

Friendships Forged

By the end of January 1919, all military prisoners held in German and Turkish POW camps had been repatriated. Some rejoined their service to continue their military career, others were demobbed and returned home. Some spoke openly of their war experiences, while others refused to revisit the horror.

Ex-POWs received a letter from King George V, which read:

> The Queen joins me in welcoming you on your release from the miseries and hardships, which you have endured with much patience and courage. During these many months of trial, the early rescue of our gallant officers and men from the cruelties of their captivity has been uppermost in our thoughts. We are thankful that this longed for day has finally arrived and that back in the old Country you will be able once more to enjoy the happiness of the home and to see good days among those who anxiously look for your return.

In a grim, dark place, extraordinary lifelong friendships had been forged between men who might otherwise not have met – friendships that in some cases continue to flow down through the families of internees.

In September 1917 at the POW processing centre at Karlsruhe, Norman Birks had met Lieutenant Brian Manning of the Irish Guards, who later became camp adjutant at Holzminden. The two became the greatest of friends, and Brian wrote a poem in Norman's autograph book titled 'Gefangeners' ('Prisoners'), a heartfelt ode to their strong bond of friendship. In it, Brian makes humorous reference to Norman, who at the time of their meeting was dressed in an 'old discarded Russian uniform'; Brian himself had been clothed in a private's uniform, disguising his officer status.

The poem celebrates Brian's view that, despite their mutual confusion upon meeting, the forming of their enduring mateship was almost inevitable.

In part it reads:

> I wonder what you thought when one fine day
> I walked in boldly to your grand abode
> ... Sure pity 'twas that when we two first met
> Our views were mutual and indeed unkind;
> For where a 'Russian soldier' first beset
> My narrow vision and a humbler mind
> In me a 'Private' unannounced you found
> With shabby clothes and unalluring face.
> But Birks, both you and I have come to know
> How things that strike the mind in some strange way
> May often be the seeds that natures sow
> To fructify for them another day ...

A year after the war ended, Brian stepped into the role of best man at Norman's wedding to Liza. By the time Norman had completed his memoirs, over five decades later, his close friend had passed away.

In the early 1920s, Norman had relocated his family from Yorkshire to Surrey. As he was wandering around inspecting his new garden, his next-door neighbour peered over the fence enquiring, 'Is that you, Birks?' In a stunning coincidence, he had bought the house next to fellow ex-Holzminden POW John 'Jack' Salter, formerly of the Royal Irish Rifles. The Birkses and the Salters were to form a lifelong friendship born of those shared circumstances many years before.

★

Friendships Forged

Those doing it tough in bleak German camps would never forget when the hand of friendship was extended to them. Sent straight to a dimly lit punishment cell upon arrival at Holzminden, red-haired Canadian Hector Dougall was over the moon when a familiar, friendly face appeared out of the darkness: good mate Lieutenant Robert 'Bobby' Howell Cowan had made it to the camp ahead of him. Throughout Hector's stay in solitary confinement, Bobby ensured his old mate was adequately fed from his own Red Cross parcels; he also delivered his mail to him, knowing how much letters from home meant.

Hector expressed his deep appreciation in his camp journal:

> . . . the friendship of a real pal is something you don't get every day and after what I have gone through, I will say there has never been a more envious thought in my mind than the history and memory my dearest pal on earth left behind him with his friends and mine in the trenches and the bloody battlegrounds of the Canadians in France.

In typical Hector style, he went on to joke: 'In fact, if Bobby were a girl, I would be forever after him to marry me.'

★

As internees filtered home and introduced their Holzminden comrades to family and friends, sparks often flew. When two captains of the British Army – twenty-six-year-old Willie Petrie of the 6th Seaforth Highlanders and twenty-four-year-old Gerry Crole of No. 43 Squadron RFC – needed to find a third man to share their barrack room, they approached Captain Lyon Hatton of the Royal West Kent Regiment, and the three became firm friends.

Shortly after the war, Lyon, whose family lived in the Midlands, wrote to Willie, who lived in Moray, to advise him that his sister, Margaret 'Daisy' Hatton, was holidaying in Scotland with friends, and suggested they meet up. Willie duly sought out Daisy – so nicknamed for the Marguerite daisy – and caught his first sight of her at the Banff Springs Hotel, relaxing under a potted palm tree. For years Willie liked to tell the story of how he had met his future wife 'under a palm tree': he and Daisy soon became engaged and were married in 1921, now officially linking the ex-Holzminden room-mates by marriage.

By coincidence, the Petries and Hattons added another Holzminden marriage connection many years later. In 1957 Alison Petrie, a daughter of Willie and Daisy Petrie, wed Robin Corbett, whose uncle, Roland Corbett of the RFC, had also been a Holzminden POW. It is possible that room-mates Willie and Lyon had crossed paths with Roland in the camp at some stage. None of the trio would have suspected for a moment that they would, sometime in the future, become related by marriage.

Theirs was not the last of the Holzminden marriage connections. Royal Flying Corps aviators twenty-seven-year-old Lieutenant Leonard Pearson of No. 13 Squadron and twenty-year-old 2nd Lieutenant Leslie Nixon of No. 3 Squadron were two of the would-be escapees who had been trapped in the tunnel when it collapsed. They had developed a close mateship during their imprisonment, and after the war they became brothers-in-law when Leonard married Leslie's sister, Marguerite.

★

Some unlikely friendships were formed. In Holzminden, 2nd Lieutenant Charles Henry ffrench 'Nobby' Nobbs of No. 66 Squadron RFC got on well with fellow internee Michael Claude

Hamilton Bowes-Lyon, the brother of Elizabeth Bowes-Lyon, who later became the Queen Mother. After the war, Nobby was invited to the Bowes-Lyons's ancestral home of Glamis Castle in Scotland. There he met the young Elizabeth, who took to referring to Nobby's birthplace of Norfolk Island as 'Nobby's Island'.

Every so often, the Holzminden links echoed down through the generations – sometimes as a result of an amazing coincidence, as in the case of the Birkses and the Salters finding themselves next-door neighbours. After ex-POW Gerald 'Gerry' Crole died in 1965, his family emigrated to Australia. When grandson Hugh Crole enrolled at the University of Melbourne, he met fellow student Belinda Hawkins, who introduced him to her family. Belinda's father, Stuart, recognised the unusual Crole name and enquired as to whether Hugh was related to Gerry Crole. Consequently it was revealed that Hugh's and Belinda's grandfathers – Gerry Crole and Rupert Hawkins – had been firm friends in the camp a mateship that endured long after their shared Holzminden experience, as evidenced by the letters and photo in Stuart's possession.

Jim Bennett, Stanley Purves and Jock Tullis – three of the successful escapees – remained friends for many decades, long after they had families of their own. Jim and Jock lived within thirty minutes of one another, and the families would get together on occasion at one or other's home. Mrs Laurie Vaughan, Jim's daughter, remembers the childhood excitement of the tall trees at the Tullis home, from which a series of ropes were strung; as a youngster she loved to swoop from tree to tree.

Even after Stanley moved to Bangkok then Australia, the three men maintained their correspondence and a warm friendship. Stanley returned to England on several occasions to attend POW reunions and to catch up with his old mates.

Unlike many POWs, who harboured an understandable loathing of their prison experience, Osbert Guy Stanhope Crawford – who had assessed and advised the tunnellers on the soil and strata composition of the tunnel – looked back on his time in Holzminden with some fondness. Having no family to speak of, the prominent archaeologist discovered a sense of community and belonging among the POWs of Holzminden, later revealing:

> I have never had the same sense of one-ness with my fellows in any other surroundings.

Nearly a decade after the war had ended, sixty-one ex-POWs from Holzminden gathered at the Hotel Cecil in London in December 1927 for a reunion of the old gang, with Charles Rathborne – now Group Captain Rathborne – at the helm.

In 1932, the reunion concept was formalised in typical military fashion. The idea had grown into the Holzminden Dining Club, complete with Captain R.W. Ainsworth as president and two honorary secretaries, Brian Manning and Vernon Coombs. A year later, membership had opened to include all POWs, not just those from Holzminden, and the club had been renamed the Officer Prisoners of War Dining Club.

On the twentieth anniversary of the tunnel escape – 23 July 1938 – a group of ex-POWs came to Ye Olde Cheshire Cheese in Fleet Street armed with camp memorabilia, including the compasses used to guide them out of Germany, the camp football and digging tools. Out of the twenty-five who attended, eighteen were officer escapees and the rest were former orderlies who had assisted with the escape.

An absentee with a crack sense of humour sent a telegram

that brought the house down: 'Greetings STOP I know damn all about you and your dinner STOP Charles Niemeyer STOP'

The reunions were to continue until the ex-prisoners grew too old to attend or had passed away.

Holzminden Camp: A Century Since

Today, the barracks precinct is utilised as a Bundeswehr (Federal Defence Force) establishment and is now called Medem-Kaserne (Medem Barracks). With a long military engineering history, it is currently the home of the PzPiBtl 1 (1st Armoured Engineers Battalion). For decades, PzPiBtl 1 service personnel have been involved in deployments to trouble spots around the world, including Somalia, Kosovo, Bosnia and Afghanistan, and have been at the front line of natural disasters on home soil.

The barbed wire, patrolling sentries, rebellious POWs and tyrannical Kommandant are all long gone. The property located at Bodenstrasse 9-11 no longer sits isolated and ghostly white in the middle of farmers' crop fields but over time has been enclosed by the encroaching streets of Holzminden.

An army vehicle parking lot now sits over the tunnel site and no trace remains of the field of rye and beans that provided the escapees with cover on that dark, rainy night. The spot under the stairs in the basement of Kaserne B where the tunnel began is still there and may be viewed one weekend each year, when Kaserne-Medem opens its doors to the public.

Descendants' pilgrimages to the site have been made over the years. Despite the modernisation of the barracks, one can still stand in the doorway of what used to be the orderlies' entrance of Kaserne B and get a sense of the achievement of digging a tunnel roughly half the length of the average football field through layers of rock and solid earth, using little more than kitchen cutlery and determination.

They have all passed from our lives now, these courageous men of Holzminden who shared adversity and adventure. But they reach out to us through their photographs, artwork, poetry and diaries, and they live on in our memories.

And in our hearts.

About the Author

An Australian screenwriter based in Brisbane, Queensland, Australia, Jacqueline succumbed to the siren's call of storytelling as a child when she began scribbling poems and short stories and sent them to patient family members. When asked what she wanted to be when she grew up, the answer would vary depending on the book she was reading at the time – a nurse, a vet, a magician, a prima ballerina and, the shining jewel in the bunch, a horseback stunt rider.

By the time Jacqueline had learned to tie her own shoelaces, she was mesmerised by the experience of visual storytelling on the big screen. Years later, this led to the abandonment of a luminous career under fluoro office lights for the pursuit of screenwriting.

Going to the movies is still one of her favourite things to do, and – like everyone else on the planet – she's written a few film scripts. However, if it turns out she's kidding herself, she hasn't given up on her childhood dream of flipping around on the back of a galloping horse, waving to an adoring crowd. Or maybe she might pursue that prima ballerina idea, if she can find ballet slippers big enough.

Jacqueline battles a condition called *cacoethes scribendi*, which, roughly translated from Latin, means *an insatiable urge to write*. This is Jacqueline's first book.

www.jacquelinecook.com

Acknowledgements

The author wishes to extend her heartfelt thanks to the families and estate keepers of profiled Holzminden POWs and Miss Mary Elizabeth Chomley, all of whom generously opened their treasure chests of memorabilia and memories.

At the risk of unintentionally omitting any individuals who provided information behind the scenes but with whom I did not have direct contact, I have opted to list the names of the men below and extend my gratitude to all family members concerned:

George Augustus AVEY; Leonard James BENNETT; Charles Edward Burton BERNARD; Algernon BIRD; Norman Arthur BIRKS; William Swanson Read BLOOMFIELD; Arthur Stanley BOURINOT; Ian CAMERON; Peter Clifford CAMPBELL-MARTIN; John Richard CASH; Mary Elizabeth Maud CHOMLEY; Andrew Mearns CLOUSTON; Vernon Courtenay COOMBS; Roland CORBETT; Osbert Guy Stanhope CRAWFORD; Gerard Bruce CROLE; Ernest Osmond CUDMORE; Hector Fraser DOUGALL; Charles 'Moth' EATON; Harold 'Gus' EDWARDS; Anthony FIELDING CLARKE; William Henry Dean GARDNER; Edgar Henry GARLAND; Christopher Guy GILBERT; Maxwell GORE; Reginald George Henry GOUGH; Douglas LYALL GRANT; Louis 'Swaggie' GREIVE; Frederick William HARVEY; Henry Rupert HAWKINS; David Edmund Atree HORNE;

Sidney Stewart HUME; Frederick Norman INSOLL; Caspar KENNARD; Colin LAURANCE; Peter William LYON; Harold William MEDLICOTT; George William MUMFORD; Leslie Gordon NIXON; Charles Henry Ffrench NOBBS; Robert Milner PADDISON; Leonard John PEARSON; William Roy PETRIE; Stanley Stuart Beattie PURVES; Charles Edward Henry RATHBORNE; William LEEFE ROBINSON; John SALTER; Harold R. SURTEES; Cuthbert Archibald 'Fluffy' SUTCLIFFE; Randall Henry TOPLISS; John 'Jock' TULLIS; Francis William VOELCKER; Edward Darien WARBURTON; Randolph Wilbur WHITE; Lester Janson WILLIAMS; Frederick William WINTERBOTHAM.

All biographical information, diary excerpts and photographs from personal collections relating to the above have been reproduced with the kind permission of descendants' families and relevant copyright holders.

With further thanks to:

Jenelle McCarrick in Australia and Sue Baker Wilson in New Zealand for their long hours of dedicated research; further research kudos to John Wilson, Hilton Doidge, Marina Borland, Elizabeth Fisher, Steve Fuller, Irma Dieffenbacher and Frank McGonigal; Sara Morton-Stone and her colleagues at the Australian Red Cross for reviewing and approving all content relating to the Australian Red Cross; Aaron Pegram, Senior Historian at the Australian War Memorial, who ensured historical accuracy; Verena von der Heiden for her painstaking German–English translations; Michael Melching and Horst Rummel for locating information and research at the German end of things; John Grech, who so generously shared his research and images of No. 66 Squadron RFC members (www.66squadron.co.uk); Terrence Antoniak (www.terrenceantoniak.com), graphic

Acknowledgements

designer and voiceover artist, for his visual and auditory contributions to our project website; and Rose Lindsay, our loyal website designer, who set up both our English- and German-language sites and lived to tell the tale (www.adminondemand.com.au).

And finally, a hearty thank you to the many and varied organisations who kindly agreed to post messages and articles on their websites on the project's behalf.

Image Credits

The author and publisher are grateful for permission to reproduce images of the following individuals:

Lt George Avey – courtesy Joy Graeff; Lt Leonard Bennett – courtesy Fleet Air Arm Museum, UK; Lt Charles Bernard – courtesy Christopher Bernard; Lt Algernon Bird – courtesy Peter Bird; Lt Norman Birks – courtesy Oliver Harris; 2nd Lt Cecil Blain – courtesy Royal Aero Club, UK; Capt. William Bloomfield – courtesy Tom Bloomfield; Lt Arthur Bourinot – courtesy Library and Archives, Canada; Lt Ian Cameron – courtesy Ian Raven; Pte John Cash – courtesy Australian War Museum, ID P02983.001; Miss Mary Chomley – courtesy Chomley family; Lt Vernon Coombs – courtesy Royal Aero Club, UK; Capt. Gerard Crole – courtesy Andrew Corbett; 2nd Lt Ernest Cudmore – courtesy Royal Aero Club, UK; Lt Hector Dougall – courtesy Fraser Dougall and Brenda Dougall Merriman; Lt Charles Eaton – courtesy Charles Eaton; Flt Sub-Lt Harold Edwards – courtesy Suzanne Edwards; 2nd Lt Anthony Fielding-Clarke – courtesy Hat Jodelka; 2nd Lt Edgar Garland – courtesy Alexander Turnbull Library, Wellington, New Zealand (SP Andrew Collection) ID: 1/1-013963-G; Capt. Maxwell Gore – courtesy Maxine Taylor; 2nd Lt Reginald Gough – courtesy Michael Gough; Capt. David Gray – courtesy Royal Aero Club, UK; 2nd Lt Louis

Greive – courtesy Martyn Greive; Lt Frederick Harvey – courtesy Doug McLean Publishing; Capt. Henry Hawkins – courtesy John Hawkins; Lt David Horne – courtesy Leslie Moore; 2nd Lt Frederick Insoll – courtesy John Fisher; Lt Colin Laurance – courtesy Tony Laurance; Capt. Edward Leggatt – courtesy Royal Aero Club, UK; Lt Peter Lyon – courtesy Mal Lyon; Lt George Mumford – courtesy Alan Mumford; 2nd Lt Charles Nobbs – courtesy John Grech; Lt Leonard Pearson – courtesy Ian Pearson; Capt. William Petrie – courtesy William Corbett; Lt Stanley Purves – courtesy Alec Purves; Lt Col Charles Rathborne – courtesy Royal Aero Club, UK; Lt John Salter – courtesy Maureen Morris; Lt Cuthbert Sutcliffe – courtesy Nick Sutcliffe; Lt Randall Topliss – courtesy Royal Aero Club, UK; 2nd Lt John Tullis – courtesy Royal Aero Club, UK.

Notes

1: Welcome to 'Hellminden'

1. Another camp, housing Russian, French, Polish and Belgian civilians, was located on the outskirts of Holzminden and was run separately from the officers' camp.
2. Spikenard was a plant used in the essential oil that anointed Jesus's feet.

3: Survival

1. Other ranks (ORs) are soldiers who rank below officers.
2. Orderlies were called batmen in the field.
3. The hospital was dismantled at the end of the war.
4. Dromkeen passed from the Chomley family and was later opened as a children's picture book art museum until the collection was moved to the State Library of Victoria in 2013.
5. Swat was eventually absorbed into Pakistan in the twentieth century.
6. www.nationalarchives.gov.uk/pathways/firstworldwar/document_packs/women.htm
7. A person who performs a specific duty.
8. Ten shillings – the price of each parcel fluctuated with food prices.

4: Air, Sea and Land

1. Edgar trained with M.C. MacGregor of Ohaupo, J.M. Warnock of Nelson and M. Matthews of Rangiriri.
2. Fifty years after Edgar's feats of derring-do, when he was seventy-three, the Wellington *Evening Post* wrote an article describing his escapades as straight out of an episode of the satirical WWII-based television series *Hogan's Heroes*.
3. New Zealanders of European descent.
4. Indigenous New Zealanders.
5. Slang for 'avoiders'.

6   After fifty hours at sea, the survivors were picked up by a British submarine and delivered to Galway, on the west coast of Ireland.

5: Home and Hearth

1   In October 1915, the MMGS merged with the Machine Gun Corps.
2   The bullet-ridden mascot took pride of place on the mantelpiece back home after the war.
3   John Frew became a doctor after the war.

6: Art and Entertainment

1   Captain Frederick Moysey, British Army (Suffolk Regiment).

7: Barbed Wire Disease

1   The Armistice between the Entente powers and Turkey was signed at Moudros on 30 October 1918.
2   Lieutenant James Whalley Boumphrey was later captured and imprisoned at Holzminden.
3   The region was still part of the Prussian empire in 1918, but reverted back to Polish territory after the Second World War. Schweidnitz is now known by its Polish name, Świdnica.
4   Breslau is now known by its Polish name, Wroclaw.
5   Legal private weapon ownership was prevalent at the time; the government cracked down after the war.
6   Shephard, Ben, *A War of Nerves: Soldiers and Psychiatrists, 1914–1994*, Pimlico Books, London, 2002.
7   Ibid.

8: Crime and Punishment

1   Puttees were bandage-like strips of cloths wound from the ankle to the knee for added protection and support.
2   2nd Lieutenant Robert 'Bob' Howell Cowan of No. 65 Squadron.
3   The 'Colonel Bogey March', written by Lieutenant F.J. Ricketts in 1914, is a jaunty British tune often used to satirise the enemy from the First World War onwards.
4   During the Second World War, Stephenson was to become the British spymaster known as 'Intrepid'.

9: Unbreakable Spirit

1   From a report by Captain T.W.M. Morgan.
2   From the Medlicott family history (www.medlicott.eu).
3   HMCS *Niobe* had been a Diadem-class cruiser in the late 1800s until she was transferred to the Canadian Navy in 1910.

10: The Tunnel

1 'Munshi' means teacher of languages.
2 Lieutenant Colquhoun later rose to the rank of brigadier general, serving in the Second World War.
3 Trieste was part of the Austro-Hungarian Empire before it was annexed to Italy in 1920.
4 'Crammer' schools are designed to fast-track students through a specific subject or subjects.

12: The Big Stunt

1 The term 'swaggie' is short for swagman, an Australian and New Zealand reference to an itinerant worker from the era.

14: Back in Enemy Hands

1 The Holzminden flag remains in the possession of Hector's family to this day.

15: Life After the War, an A to Z

1 www.shell.com.hk/en/aboutshell/who-we-are/history/country.html
2 A fraternal organisation originating in Ireland to promote Biblical Protestantism.
3 A 'rubble woman' who helped clean up and reconstruct bombed cities after the war.

Bibliography

Diary, Letter and Memoir Excerpts
From the private collections of Charles Edward Burton BERNARD; Norman Arthur BIRKS; John Richard CASH; Mary Elizabeth Maud CHOMLEY; Roland CORBETT; Hector Fraser DOUGALL; Edgar Henry GARLAND; Maxwell GORE; Reginald George Henry GOUGH; David Edmund Atree HORNE; Robert Milner PADDISON; Charles Edward Henry RATHBORNE; John 'Jock' TULLIS and Edward Darien WARBURTON.

Books
Bills, Leslie William, *A Medal for Life: The Biography of Captain William Leefe Robinson, VC*, Spellmount Ltd, Kent, 1990.

Durnford, Hugh, *The Tunnellers of Holzminden*, Cambridge University Press, Cambridge, 1921.

Edwards, Suzanne, *Gus: From Trapper Boy to Air Marshal*, General Store Publishing House, Ontario, Canada, 2007.

Franks, Norman, Giblin, Hal and McCrery, Nigel, *Under the Guns of the Red Baron*, Grub Street, London, 1998.

Hanson, Neil, *Escape from Germany*, Transworld Publishers (Random House), London, 2011.

Harvey, FW, *Comrades in Captivity*, Douglas McLean Publishing, Gloucestershire, 2010.

Hume, Roland Cunningham, *History of Two Families: The Origins of the Hume Family in Argentina*, self-published, 1973.

Moynihan, Michael, *Black Bread and Barbed Wire*, Pen & Sword Books Ltd, Barnsley, 1978.

Rimell, Raymond Laurence, *The Airship VC*, Aston Publications Ltd, Buckinghamshire, 1989.

Schmitt, Margaret, *John Cash: A Prisoner of War – An Extraordinary Man*, self-published, 2007.

Seeliger, Matthias, *Garnisionsstadt Holzminden: Die Geschichte der Kaserne seit 1913*, Verlag Jörg Mitzkat, 2001 (Holzmindener Schriften).

Shephard, Ben, *A War of Nerves: Soldiers and Psychiatrists, 1914–1994*, Jonathan Cape, London, 2000.

Winchester, Barry, *Beyond the Tumult*, Allison & Busby, London, 1971.

Newspaper Articles and Periodicals

Baird, Harvey, 'Psychoses in Officers in the 1914–1918 War', 1941. Excerpts reprinted with the permission of the *British Journal of Psychiatry*.

Taylor, Stewart, 'Surrogate Son', *Over the Front* (magazine), Volume 24, No. 2, 2009.

Documentation

Medical records of Lieutenant Sidney Stewart Hume, courtesy of John Grech, Clickerty-Click, 66 Squadron, UK.

Bibliography

Websites

Australian War Memorial
www.awm.gov.au

National Library of Australia
www.trove.nla.gov.au

New Zealand Defence Force Base Records, Archives New Zealand
www.archives.govt.nz/

New Zealand History Online
www.nzhistory.net.nz

Papers Past, National Library of New Zealand
www.paperspast.natlib.govt.nz/cgi-bin/paperspast

INDEX OF NAMES

A
Ainsworth, Captain R.W. 282
Aldridge, Private John 118–19
Aldridge, Matilda 119–20
Allouche, Capitaine 165–66
Andrew, Stanley Polkinghorne
    61–62
Armstrong, Captain A. 103
Avey, Lieutenant George Augustus
    'Gus' 238

B
Baird, Captain Harvey 116–17
Barnard, Brigadier General J.H.
    42
Bartlett, Lieutenant Clarence 226
Bennett, Lieutenant Leonard James
    'Jim' 179, 209–10, 212, 232,
    281
Bernard, Lieutenant Charles Edward
    Burton 18–21, 25, 51–52, 148,
    150, 152, 239, 276
Biddlecombe, Commander Thomas
    Wyburn 73
Birch, Lieutenant Douglas Clarkson
    179, 217
Bird, Padre Major 226
Bird, Lieutenant Algernon 'Algie'
    29, 239–40
Birks, Mercy Anne (Wood) 85–86,
    91, 92–93, 95

Birks, Lieutenant Norman Arthur
    30, 85–97, 218, 240–41,
    277–78
Birks, Walter 86, 94
Blain, 2nd Lieutenant Cecil William
    165–66, 173–74, 188, 193,
    210–12, 232
Bloomfield, Captain William
    Swanson Read 241–42
Boumphrey, 2nd Lieutenant J.W. 110
Bourinot, Lieutenant Arthur Stanley
    22, 242
Bousfield, Lieutenant John Keith
    179, 215, 233
Bowes-Lyon, Michael Claude
    Hamilton 280–81
Boyd, Major Owen 110
Brean, Lieutenant Timothy 190
Briggs, Captain Clement 85
Burrill, Lieutenant Thomas Frank
    179, 217
Butler, Lieutenant Walter 174, 192,
    194, 195, 217

C
Caldwell, Keith 60
Cameron, Lieutenant Ian Donald
    29, 182, 242–43
Campbell-Martin, Lieutenant Pierre
    (Peter) Clifford 'Cliff' 179,
    209–10, 212, 233–34

Cash, Albert 13
Cash, Arthur 11
Cash, Cecilia 'Cissy' (née Lobb) 11, 13, 84–85
Cash, Ernie 13
Cash, Private John 'Dick' 11–16, 34, 36, 84, 185–87, 243–44
Cash, Myrtle 13
Cash, Wally 13
Cavell, Edith 45
Chidson, Major M.R. 153–54
Chomley, Arthur Wolfe 41, 44–45
Chomley, Aubrey 44–45
Chomley, Charles Henry 43
Chomley, Eileen 44–45
Chomley, Hussey Malone 41
Chomley, Juliana Charlotte (née Hogg) 41, 42
Chomley, Mary Elizabeth Maud 39–48, 54–58, 98–99, 244
Chomley, Violet Ida 42–43
Clouston, Lieutenant Andrew 174, 217
Coghlan, J.L. 158
Collinson, Private Ernest 195
Colquhoun, Lieutenant William Gourlay 'Shorty' 166
Cooke, 2nd Lieutenant Ernest 226
Coombs, Lieutenant Vernon Courtenay 245–46, 282
Corbett, Captain Roland 21, 24–25, 32, 50, 280
Couston, Lieutenant Alec 48, 147
Cowan, Lieutenant Robert 'Bobby' Howell 29–30, 133, 136, 279
Crawford, 2nd Lieutenant Osbert Guy Stanhope 185, 245–46, 282
Crole, Captain Gerard 'Gerry' Bruce 246–47, 279, 281

Cudmore, 2nd Lieutenant Ernest 'Ernie' Osmond 247–48

D

Davidson, John 93
de Crespigny, Major 85
Delysia, Alice 140–41
Dieckmann, Kapitänleutnant Victor 73–75
Dougall, Lieutenant Hector Fraser 125–36, 218, 220, 223, 225–27, 248–49, 279
Dougall, Jessie Isabella (née McFadyen) 126
Dougall, Mabel 126, 130, 132
Dougall, William C. 126
Doyle (English POW) 129
Durnford, Hugh George Edmund 17–19, 187, 191, 195, 199
Dykes, Private Norman 35

E

Eaton, Lieutenant Charles 'Moth' 249–50
Edwards, Benjamin 154, 156
Edwards, Flight Sub-Lieutenant Harold 'Gus' 154–59, 250–51
Edwards, Kate Louisa (née Warburton) 140
Edwards, William 'Will' 154
Elder, Captain W.L. 159
Ellis, Lieutenant 166
Enos, Captain John Owen 251

F

Ferrier, Detective Inspector John 119
Festner, Vizefeldwebel Sebastian 141
Fielding-clarke, 2nd Lieutenant Anthony 'Tony' 252
Fokker, Anthony 29
Forty, Louisa (née Soame) 78

Index of Names

Frew, Lieutenant John G.H. 90–91, 94–95
Fryer, George 118–19
Fullarton (officer) 125

G
Gallus, Colonel 222
Gardiner, Captain George Guyatt 'Guy' 57
Gardner, Lieutenant William Henry Dean 'Dean' 68–75, 83, 252–53
Garland, 2nd Lieutenant Edgar Henry 60–68, 83, 199–201, 253–54
Garland, Frank Le Manquais 62, 66
Garland, Laura (née Gibson) 62
Gibbs, Philip 122
Gilbert, Lieutenant Christopher Guy 254–55
Gore, Captain Maxwell 'Max' 51, 100, 125, 136, 138, 151–52, 190, 194, 255
Gough, Amy (née Hinton) 76
Gough, George Edghill 76, 78
Gough, 2nd Lieutenant Reginald George Henry 'Reg' 31, 49–53, 76–83, 105, 136–37, 146–47, 219, 256
Gray, Captain David Benjamin 'Munshi' 163–66, 173–74, 188, 191, 193, 210–12, 234
Greive, Lieutenant Louis 'Swaggie' 197, 256–57

H
Habrecht, Colonel 24
Haig, Major 176
Hall, Harry 54
Harvey, Lieutenant Frederick William 'Will' 101–3, 257–58
Hatton, Captain Lyon 52, 279

Hawkins, Captain Henry Rupert 258–59, 281
Helder, Lieutenant 163–64
Horne, Lieutenant David Edmund Atree 23, 31–32, 221, 223–27, 259–60
Hume, Agnes Lilian 'Lily' 108, 117, 121
Hume, Alexander Scott 'Sandy' 107–8, 120
Hume, Marie Henriette Adelaide (née Mundt) 107, 117
Hume, 2nd Lieutenant Roland Cunningham 107–8, 110, 111–15
Hume, Lieutenant Sidney Stewart 106–21
Hume, Violet Theodora 108, 120

I
Illingworth, 2nd Lieutenant Fred 179, 217
Insoll, 2nd Lieutenant Frederick Norman 30, 260

J
Jarrett, Corporal 118
Johnson, Bernard 93–94
Johnson, Elizabeth 'Liza' 87–88, 91–92

K
Kasten, Feldwebel 149
Kennard, Captain Caspar 165–66, 173–74, 188, 193, 210–12, 234–35
Kohlhagen, Herr Dr 91

L
Langren, Captain William Henry 174, 217

Latta, Captain J.D. 110
Laurance, Lieutenant Colin 33, 147–48, 174, 217, 261
Leggatt, Captain Edward Wilmer 179, 198, 212–15, 235–36
Liebert, Otto 203, 218
Luscombe, Lieutenant Bernard P. 179, 217
Lyall Grant, Captain Douglas 'Duggie' 35, 261–62
Lyon, Lieutenant Peter William 179, 217, 262–63

M
MacLeod, Lieutenant Neil 175, 217
McPhail, 2nd Lieutenant Angus 103–4
Manning, Lieutenant Brian 94, 277–78, 282
Mardock, Lieutenant Frederick 174, 217
Meadows, Mabel 77–78, 79
Medlicott, Lieutenant Harold 151–54
Menckhoff, Vizefeldwebel Carl 90
Morris, Lieutenant Arthur 175, 216–17
Morrogh, Major John 179, 217
Moynihan, Michael 34–35
Moysey, Captain Frederick 'Mossy' 102
Mumford, Lieutenant George William 51, 263–64

N
Niemeyer, Heinrich 25
Niemeyer, Captain Karl 24–28, 83, 96–97, 138, 143, 150–52, 159, 166, 171–72, 201–2, 204–8, 217–19, 221–22
Nightingale, Florence 39–40

Nixon, Lieutenant Leslie 280
Nobbs, 2nd Lieutenant Charles Henry ffrench 'Nobby' 264, 280–81

O
Oliver, Major Norman 116

P
Paddison, Lieutenant Robert 'Bob' Milner 149, 174, 193, 216–17, 265
Pankhurst, Emmeline 46
Parish, Sister Connie 57
Pearson, Lieutenant Leonard John 265–66, 280
Petrie, Captain William 'Willie' Roy 266–67, 279
Purves, Lieutenant Stanley Stuart Beattie Bruce 178, 197, 212–15, 236, 281

R
Rathborne, Lieutenant Colonel Charles Edward Henry 158, 176–80, 188, 193–94, 196, 204–8, 216, 237, 282
Roberts, Lieutenant R.M. 110
Robertson, 2nd Lieutenant A. 110
Robertson, Lieutenant Clifford 175, 217
Robinson, Captain William 'Billy' Leefe 139–45, 221
Rogers, Colonel 122

S
Salter, Lieutenant John 'Jack' 267, 278
Schramm, Wilhelm 140
Sen, Lieutenant Errol Suvo Chunder 268

Sharpe, Captain Frank 179, 217
Shipwright (POW) 217
Shirley, 2nd Lieutenant A.V. 110
Sims, Chief Petty Officer 74
'the Skipper' (POW) 134
Smith, Captain Philip Norbert 179, 217
Stephenson, Captain William Samuel Clouston 143
Sugden-Wilson, Lieutenant William Hodgson 100
Sutcliffe, Lieutenant Cuthbert Archibald 'Fluffy' 190, 269

T
Teague, Violet 43
Tollmache, Captain Eric 100
Topliss, Lieutenant Randall Henry 270
Tullis, 2nd Lieutenant John 'Jock' 179, 180, 181, 183, 188–89, 197–98, 212–15, 237–38, 281

V
Voelcker, 2nd Lieutenant Francis 'Frank' William 271–72

von Hanisch, General 26, 29–30, 32
von Richthofen, Manfred Albrecht Freiherr 28–29

W
Wainwright, Lieutenant David 174, 217
Walter, Captain Joseph 151–54
Warburton, Lieutenant Edward Darien 141–43, 144–45, 272
Westwood, Winifred 77–79
Whale, 2nd Lieutenant James 'Jimmy' 100–101, 273
White, Captain Randolph Wilbur 274
Williams, Doris Elizabeth 70–71
Williams, Lieutenant Sedley Gerald 'Willo' 129–32
Winterbotham, Group Captain Frederick 'Freddie' William 275

Y
Yuile, Lieutenant F.J. 74